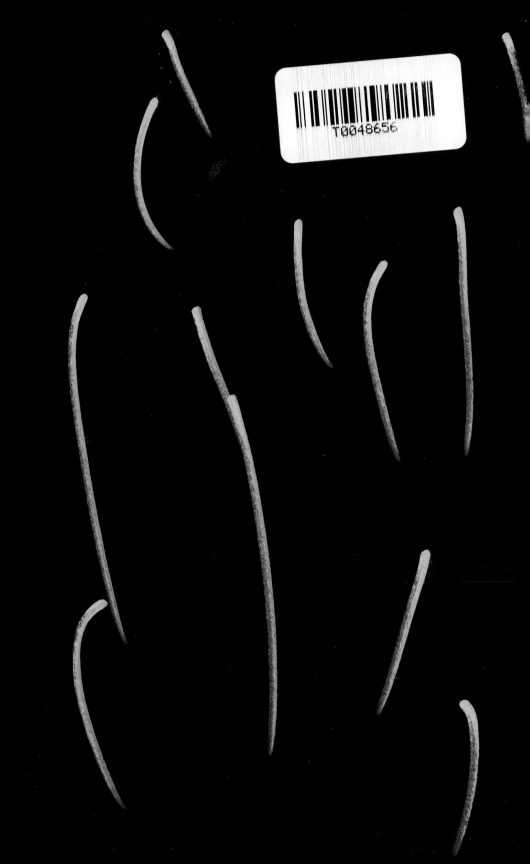

EICHMANN'S JEWS

In memory of Franzi Löw-Danneberg and Willy Stern

EICHMANN'S JEWS

THE JEWISH ADMINISTRATION OF HOLOCAUST VIENNA, 1938–1945
DORON RABINOVICI

Translated by Nick Somers

polity

First published in German as *Instanzen der Ohnmacht. Wien 1938–1945. Der Weg zum Judenrat* © Jüdischer Verlag Frankfurt am Main 2000

This English edition © Polity Press, 2011

Polity Press
65 Bridge Street
Cambridge CB2 1UR, UK

Polity Press
350 Main Street
Malden, MA 02148, USA

The translation of this work was funded by Geisteswissenschaften International – Translation Funding for Humanities and Social Sciences from Germany, a joint initiative of the Fritz Thyssen Foundation, the German Federal Foreign Office, the collecting society VG WORT and the Börsenverein des Deutschen Buchhandels (German Publishers & Booksellers Association).

The publisher gratefully acknowledges the support of the Jacob Burns Institute for Advanced Legal Studies of the Benjamin N. Cardozo School of Law.

ISBN-13: 978-0-7456-4682-4

A catalogue record for this book is available from the British Library.

Typeset in 10.5 on 12 pt Sabon
by Toppan Best-set Premedia Limited
Printed and bound in Great Britain by MPG Books Group Limited, Bodmin, Cornwall

The publisher has used its best endeavours to ensure that the URLs for external websites referred to in this book are correct and active at the time of going to press. However, the publisher has no responsibility for the websites and can make no guarantee that a site will remain live or that the content is or will remain appropriate.

Every effort has been made to trace all copyright holders, but if any have been inadvertently overlooked the publisher will be pleased to include any necessary credits in any subsequent reprint or edition.

For further information on Polity, visit our website: www.politybooks.com

CONTENTS

CONTENTS

PREFACE

The subject of this book has haunted me for years. Discussion of the Jewish councils touches the post-1945 Jewish identity and more than anything else shows how the Nazi extermination policy even managed to rob the victims of their dignity. I have never been able to make light of this and have therefore attempted to make an academic study of the material, although realizing at the same time that words alone are inadequate to do justice to the subject.

In the Jewish youth organization I belonged to in Vienna, called Hashomer Hatzair, we sometimes carried out mock trials. The issue in dispute was fixed and there were guidelines for each of the protagonists but we usually improvised as we went along. One of us was the judge, another the defendant; there was a defence lawyer and a plaintiff, speeches and pleas and witnesses to be cross-examined. I recall one case – I must have been eleven years old – that particularly marked me. One of us, barely older than seventeen, was on trial as head of the Jewish community. 'Partisans' testified against him and other 'survivors' spoke in his favour: in other words, a reconstruction by a group of young people in Austria in the mid-1970s of the unofficial Jewish courts that were set up after 1945 in various countries, particularly in the displaced person camps. Some of our parents might well have taken part in proceedings of this type. We spectators were the jury and had to reach a decision. Without knowing much about it, we quickly found the defendant guilty. After the Holocaust, young Jews sought a new identity, and could only see themselves as members of the resistance. It was impossible to imagine what it had been like as a member of the Jewish councils.

This book, by contrast, attempts to understand the situation of Jewish functionaries under the Nazis. By looking at the point of view of the victims, we can see how unfathomable and absurd everything that was done to them must have appeared. Their despair and their powerlessness reflect the extent and nature of the crime. A critical study can possibly shed light on aspects that the victims were unable to see or to comprehend at the time and might also draw attention to some of our own weaknesses and blind spots.

Considerable research has been carried out on Jewish councils in other parts of Europe, but the Jewish administrative bodies in the German Reich have long been extensively ignored. In Germany and Austria, a study of the Jewish community leaders and the involvement of Jews with the Nazi regime that organized their expulsion and extermination has been just too sensitive an issue.

Consideration of the situation in Vienna is, however, of vital importance. To understand how the Jewish councils came about, it is essential to consider the developments in Austria. It was here that department II-112 of the Security Service under Adolf Eichmann developed the model for the Nazi Jewish policy. The Vienna model was then copied in other cities like Berlin, Prague or Paris. Eichmann set up the first Central Office for Jewish Emigration in Vienna as the Nazi authority responsible for organizing the mass expulsion and later the deportation to extermination camps. The Jewish organizations were completely at the mercy of the regime. The Jewish administration was restructured in its entirety. The Vienna Jewish Community authorities (Kultusgemeinde) under Nazi rule can be regarded as a prototype for the future Jewish councils.

I am grateful to a large number of people and institutions for their indispensable aid in researching this subject. This book could not have been written without the support of the staff of the following archives, listed here alphabetically: Archive of the Republic of Austria, Vienna; Archive of the Landgericht, Vienna; Central Archives for the History of the Jewish People, Jerusalem; Central Zionist Archives, Jerusalem; Documentation Archive of Austrian Resistance, Vienna; Documentation Centre of the Association of Jewish Victims of the Nazi Regime, Vienna; Yad Vashem, Jerusalem. I should like to thank them for helping me with my research. Hadassah Assouline, director of the Central Archives for the History of the Jewish People, not only gave me access to the Kultusgemeinde archive in her institute but also referred me to the private archive there of Benjamin Murmelstein. Elisabeth Klamper from the Documentation Archive of Austrian Resistance helped me to locate documents.

Dolfi Brunner, Walter Fantl, Marcel Faust, Gerda Feldsberg, Paul Gross, Franz Hahn, Mares Prochnik, Herbert Schrott and Martin Vogel, along with Willy Stern and Franzi Löw-Danneberg, who have both died in the meantime, allowed me to interview them for hours and gave me the benefit of their recollections.

I should also like to thank Evelyn Adunka, Leonhard Ehrlich, Pierre Genée, Herbert Rosenkranz and Hans Schafranek for discussing problems with me, referring me to source material, recommending literature or providing me with copies of unpublished documents and interviews. I am grateful to Jacques Adler, Brigitte Bailer-Galanda, John Bunzl, Abraham Hodik, Yaacow Lozowick, Dan Michman, Jonny Moser, Wolfgang Neugebauer, Bertrand Perz, Dinah Porat, Herbert Rosenkranz and Simon Wiesenthal for their ideas and suggestions.

Gabriele Anderl, Florian Freund and Hans Safrian offered technical help and friendly support. Günther Kaindlsdorfer and Tessa Szyszkowitz took the time to proofread parts of my work. I am also grateful to many friends for their patience, questions and suggestions. I would like to express my profound gratitude to the translator of this abridged version of the text, Nick Somers, for his enthusiasm and commitment. I am particularly grateful for all the help and advice I have received from Peter Goodrich.

I thank Nadine Meyer, my editor at the Jüdischer Verlag, for her collaboration and her attentive and critical editing of my manuscript.

I owe a particular debt of thanks to Karl Stuhlpfarrer, my academic mentor at the University of Vienna. He encouraged me for years and spurred me on with advice, criticism and praise.

I am extremely grateful to my parents, Shoshana and David Rabinovici, for their sincere support.

LIST OF ABBREVIATIONS

A/W   Archive of the Vienna Kultusgemeinde in the CAHJP

CAHJP   Central Archives for the History of the Jewish People

CZA   Central Zionist Archives

DÖW   Documentation Archive of Austrian Resistance

IKG   Kultusgemeinde (Jewish Community authorities)

P   Private archive of Benjamin Murmelstein in the CAHJP

YIVO   Yidisher Visenshaftlicher Institut

YvS   Yad Vashem

— 1 —

PROLOGUE

When I was teaching in Cleveland, a young Jewish political scientist, engaged to a German woman, said to my face, without flinching: 'I know what you survivors had to do to stay alive.' I didn't know what we had had to do, but I knew what he wanted to say. He wanted to say: 'You walked over dead bodies.' Should I have answered: 'But I was only twelve'? Or said, 'But I am a good girl, always have been'? Both answers implicate the others, my fellow prisoners. Or I could have said, 'Where do you get off talking like that?' and gotten angry. I said nothing, went home to my children, and was depressed. For in reality the cause of survival was almost pure chance.

Ruth Klüger,
Landscapes of Memory: A Holocaust Girlhood Remembered[1]

Survivor guilt

The mass murder of millions of Jews was a collective crime. Although it was organized centrally, the work was split up and carried out by different authorities. Not just the police and the judiciary, but also the railways and banks, universities and industry offered their services to help isolate and rob the Jews, expel and exterminate them. What happened in the concentration camps and behind the front was officially kept secret, but here, too, quite a few people were involved in the misdeeds, and many were aware of some of the things that were going on. Only a few might have had an idea of the full magnitude of the crimes, but practically everybody knew that it was something not to be talked about.

A study of the files reveals the zeal, speed and thoroughness with which the anti-Jewish measures, decrees and laws were passed in

Vienna in 1938 – a far cry from the proverbial sluggishness of Viennese bureaucracy. The crime was a social phenomenon: its progress was acclaimed in the newspapers and the plundering, beatings and pogrom that took place in November 1938, the deaths, arson and rape, were hailed triumphantly.

The mass murder would not have been possible without the indulgence and tacit consent of the population. One aspect of the misdeed was that the victims were deprived of any support. They were betrayed and at the mercy of everybody, completely defenceless in the face of the crimes committed. Before the physical annihilation, the victims were destroyed socially and psychologically.

On 15 October 1945, the head of the Vienna State Police filed charges with the public prosecutor's office against Wilhelm Reisz. During the Nazi era, Reisz had been subordinate to SS-Scharführer [squad leader] Herbert Gerbing. He was involved in the *Aushebung*, as it was called, of the Jews (literally 'lifting out') – finding out where Jews listed for deportation lived, noting their names and helping them to pack the few things they were allowed to take with them. Reisz's actions, remarked the Austrian head of the State Police, were 'particularly reprehensible' because he 'brought misfortune on his compatriots in order to gain advantage for himself'.[2]

Why was Reisz exceptional? Was he 'particularly reprehensible' because otherwise Austrians did not bring misfortune on their compatriots in order to gain advantage for themselves? Not at all: the National Socialist Jewish policy in Austria was not imposed from without, by the Old German Reich against the will of the people. Austrian anti-Semites went to work with great fervour in 1938, proceeding with a fanatical sense of duty that was as yet unimaginable in Berlin. Was Wilhelm Reisz then unexceptional in a country that after 1945 styled itself merely as Hitler's 'first victim'? No, he was an exception: Reisz was a Jew – and he survived. He 'brought misfortune', as the Vienna State Police put it, 'on his compatriots', Jews persecuted by the Nazis.

Wilhelm Reisz had been appointed by the Kultusgemeinde [Jewish Community authorities – IKG] in 1939 after he had demonstrated his ability to obtain passports even in difficult cases. When, after 1941, Jews were no longer being expelled but deported and killed, the SS demanded Jewish marshals [Ordner] from the IKG to assist the SS men in their round-ups. Josef Löwenherz, the head of the IKG, attempted initially to obstruct this request, but the SS threatened to use members of the Hitler Youth to collect Jews from their homes and take them to the assembly points. Then the Nazi authorities appointed a Jewish Gestapo informer to recruit a squad of thugs. At this point, Löwenherz agreed to designate trusted Jewish employees, who would answer directly to the SS men.[3] Each member of the SS was to be accompanied by a Jewish Gruppenführer [group leader] and a troop of assistants [*Ausheber* – literally 'lifters']. Those who refused were likely to be immediately deported.

Wilhelm Reisz was Gruppenführer of the Jewish marshals under SS-Scharführer Gerbing. He had not volunteered for this task but was not in any position to refuse it. As a victim of the Nazi persecution of the Jews he was forced to cooperate, drawing attention to himself through his excessive zeal as a means of making himself indispensable and of surviving in this way. Testimony relating to Reisz was mixed. Some said under oath that they had him to thank for their lives. He had worked initially in the emigration department of the Kultusgemeinde and helped Jews to flee from the Nazis. As a Gruppenführer, he also intervened in individual cases to prevent expulsion. For most of the victims, however, he was known as the 'meshuggene Reisz', roughly treating the people he rounded up and singling out to the SS-Scharführer the ones who were to be deported. For the round-up operations, Gerbing sent his subordinate Reisz in advance. Gerbing himself remained in a car in front of the building, or sat comfortably in an armchair and dozed off while Jews were being ferreted out and their homes cleared. Once he had a dentist explain his medical equipment to him while Reisz was getting on with the 'official business'. Jewish witnesses described Gerbing as a 'would-be medical student' with refined manners, 'not as rough and vigorous as the other Scharführer, most of whom were butchers', said one witness at Reisz's trial before the Austrian People's Court.[4] The judgement reflected this estimation.

Witnesses in other trials, by contrast, present a Herbert Gerbing who was not particularly notable for his good manners. One witness of a round-up recalled at the trial of Anton Brunner: 'When we left the house, I saw Gerbing battering a certain Dr Gross with brass knuckles until the man's eye dangled from its socket and his nose was broken.'[5]

And yet Gerbing gave many victims to understand that he had nothing to do with the round-ups. While some of his colleagues enjoyed tormenting the Jews themselves, Gerbing appears to have taken particular pleasure in letting Reisz do the work for him. Sometimes, if they were not working satisfactorily, the *Ausheber*, including Reisz, were beaten. The Jewish Gruppenführer had to hope for his own sake that he would find enough victims. His own life depended on it. Sometimes, if the quota was not filled, if people listed for deportation could not be found, the Jewish helpers were transported in their place. The court said on this matter: 'The accused took on work in this way that was not in fact part of his duties.'[6]

Wilhelm Reisz also volunteered for a journey to Berlin. Three Austrian Jews had been ordered to show how the round-ups in Vienna were being carried out. On his return, he expressed his surprise to other Jews that the non-Jewish population of Berlin resisted the round-ups. One witness stated that even in Theresienstadt, Berlin Jews had complained about the Viennese methods, mentioning Reisz explicitly.[7]

The Austrian People's Court found Reisz guilty and sentenced him to fifteen years' imprisonment, including three months' hard labour. Fifteen years for a Jew who had previously been under a death sentence and had escaped the mass extermination only because as a Gruppenführer he had made himself indispensable to Gerbing.

Johann Rixinger, the Gestapo clerk responsible for Jewish affairs in Vienna, who had had enormous decision-making powers during the deportations and was implicated in the organization of the mass murder, was sentenced to ten years' imprisonment. He served only six and a half years.[8] The Gestapo treasurer Bernhard Wittke was sentenced to three years.[9] The notoriously brutal SS man Ernst Girzik, holder of the Blood Order, was sentenced to fifteen years' imprisonment like Reisz – albeit without having lived constantly in fear of death in the same way Reisz, as a Jew, had done. He was granted amnesty by the Austrian Federal President in December 1953.[10]

The Jewish Gruppenführer Wilhelm Reisz thus received five years more than Johann Rixinger. Unlike Reisz, Gestapo officials could claim that they had been obliged to obey orders. It might be pointed out in this regard, however, that police officers or soldiers in the Third Reich were able to refuse to participate in crimes against civilians and in shootings and mass killings. No one was prosecuted because he did not feel capable of taking part in genocide. All that it meant was that he would be transferred and not get promotion. Reisz's 'zeal', by contrast, was held against him: 'The accused did more than was required of him. The People's Court does not condemn him for having been a marshal. He was under coercion. The testimony indicates, however, that he worked with a certain amount of "zeal", which he must now be held accountable for.'[11]

The court was not interested in the fact that, as a Jew in Vienna, Reisz was in constant danger. It took no account of the fact that he had to work with particular 'zeal' for the SS-Scharführer so as to avoid being deported to a death camp. Gerbing exploited the Jew Reisz first for the round-ups from 1941 to 1943 and then again in court after 1945. Like many of his SS colleagues from the Vienna headquarters, he disappeared and was never found and called to account for his deeds.[12]

On the day after sentence was passed, Reisz hanged himself in his cell.[13] For seven years, he had suffered under Nazi persecution and survived extermination. And now he committed suicide. Unlike many Nazi criminals, who committed suicide to escape capture, trial or conviction, Reisz did not kill himself until after the judgement had been passed. He had not expected to be convicted and saw himself not as a perpetrator but as a victim of the Nazi regime. The very things that had helped him to survive were held against him in the trial. Was he overcome by guilt? Or was it simply despair that those who had committed the crimes and their accessories, who had involved him in their acts, had now got off more lightly than he had?

The severity of the sentence is surprising, particularly in comparison with the judgements otherwise passed down by the Austrian judiciary after 1945. Of the 136,000 people who appeared until 1956 in Austria before the People's Courts, as they were called, for Nazi crimes, 108,000 proceedings were discontinued or suspended. Of the remaining 28,000, just under half ended in conviction. In many instances, however, it was not a case of crimes committed against others, but rather of technical offences [*Formaldelikte*], such as illegal membership of the Nazi Party between 1934 and 1938.[14]

Although Reisz was the only Jew to be convicted by the Austrian People's Court, proceedings were instigated against other Viennese Jews in Austria and other countries after 1945. In February 1949, Oscar Reich was tried before a military tribunal in Paris.[15] Born in Vienna in 1914, Reich had been a well-known football player there and had been able to escape to France in 1938 after being signed by the Association sportive de Cannes. When war broke out, he was interned for a lengthy period in various camps in Vichy France before being imprisoned by the Gestapo in early October 1943 in the camp at Drancy. There he was recruited by the SS to the internal camp police and was engaged in round-ups outside the camp, avoiding deportation to Auschwitz in this way. On trial with Reich was the SS man Josef Weiszl, who had helped to organize deportations to Auschwitz from Drancy and was far senior in rank to Reich. In Vienna, Weiszl had been a colleague of SS-Scharführer Herbert Gerbing and had been particularly enthusiastic in his persecution of

Jews: 'He was the most horrible *Ausheber* and always performed "merit tasks demonstrating his industriousness". Not only did he drag designated Jews from their dwellings; he also grabbed anyone he encountered on the way or who lived in the same house where he was to perform a seizure.'[16]

Weiszl also rounded up people who according to the Nazi laws were exempt from extermination, such as the Jewish partners in mixed marriages. He was notorious in Drancy for his brutality, and witnesses described physical punishment, beatings with his rifle butt, whipping and torture. On hearing of her impending deportation, one woman slit her arteries. Weiszl refused her medical attention and forced her into the wagon, where she died on the journey to Auschwitz.[17]

The military tribunal in Paris allowed the SS man Josef Weiszl mitigating circumstances. It sentenced him to life imprisonment, commuted in 1952 to twenty years' penal servitude. He was released in 1955. By contrast, Oscar Reich, who could not claim merely to have been following orders, was sentenced to death by the same tribunal and executed by a French police firing squad at Fort de Montrouge on 5 July 1949.[18]

Josef Weiszl returned to Vienna in December 1955 where, as he said himself, he was received by the State of Austria as a late returnee [*Spätheimkehrer*] and was allocated welfare benefits as such. Although the tribunal in Paris had convicted him only for crimes committed in France, Vienna's 'most terrible *Ausheber*' was not called to task by the Austrian public prosecutor's office. In May 1956, the judiciary decided not to pursue Weiszl any further because he had already been convicted abroad.[19]

This book is not meant to be an apology for the Jewish *Ausheber*. The examples of post-Fascist jurisprudence described here are not intended to demonstrate that Jewish defendants were all innocent, but rather to show the imbalance in the judgements. That the perpetrators committed criminal acts is a self-evident truism. Jewish victims who did not fit in with the prototype 'victim' of Nazi extermination, however, were seen as particularly reprehensible and disgraceful. They were accused of collaborating with the totalitarian criminals. The responsibility for this relationship was sought not with the perpetrator but with the victims, as if they had had a particular interest in this deadly constellation.

Wilhelm Reisz and Oscar Reich were under constant threat of death during the Nazi regime. Primo Levi, a survivor, writes of this situation:

The condition of the offended does not exclude culpability, which is often objectively serious, but I know of no human tribunal to which one could delegate the judgement. If it were up to me, if I were forced to judge, I would light-heartedly absolve all those whose concurrence in the guilt was minimal and for whom coercion was of the highest degree.[20]

Why did the judges fail to reach the same conclusion as Primo Levi? Why did so many of the critics take no account of the defendants' predicament? The constant fear of death and the will to survive were frequently ignored in the judgements of Jewish SS accomplices.

There is also the claim that Jewish community officials wanted 'merely' to save themselves and their families. The myth that Jewish community officials acted, whether consciously or unconsciously, only out of their own selfish interests is nothing other than a form of defamation, while in reality the idea of social responsibility could well have been at the root of their decision to collaborate. In other words, the leaders of the community were prompted not by a desire to survive themselves but rather, at least initially, by the hope of being able to negotiate with the SS and to rescue Jews by enabling them to emigrate. Later on, they endeavoured to stay the complete annihilation of the community; and ultimately they sought to alleviate the suffering.

Jewish *Ausheber* like Wilhelm Reisz or Oscar Reich were accused of having done more than was necessary merely to survive; they are said to have identified with the perpetrators and to have taken part with relish in the crimes. In other words, their status as victims was denied. They were stylized as 'would-be Nazis'[21] who had acted voluntarily rather than under the threat of death.

There has been much discussion about the identification of a victim with the perpetrator. The phenomenon is known in psychoanalytical literature,[22] but this identification of a victim with his or her tormenter is based on the indisputable and immutable difference between the persecutor and the persecuted, between the tormenter and the victim. A Jew could be an accomplice within the Nazi regime, but he remained a Jew and as such was fair game. Whereas the perpetrator found enjoyment in killing others, the victim sought first and foremost to escape his or her fate. The identity of the Jewish victim was that of a person with a wretched and doomed existence. No Jewish Gruppenführer could escape this identity and become a member of the master race. Even those who attempted to emulate the Nazi brutality remained Jews who did not act voluntarily but were involved in the crime under coercion and in extreme adversity.

7

Wilhelm Reisz, whose deepest emotional impulses are completely unknown to us, was not a 'would-be Nazi'. He was not a Gruppenführer because he wanted to be a Nazi or perpetrator; he was obliged against his will to serve the Nazis because he was a victim.

Identification with the tormenter is a typical victim reaction. It confirms the victim's identity and status. This psychological explanation also carries the risk of posthumous denunciation, however. No peculiar ulterior motives are needed for a person, in fear for his life, to help clear Jewish homes and round up victims for deportation. The threat of death is sufficient.

The psychological questions raised in this chapter refer not to the behaviour of Jewish people during the Nazi regime but to the sentencing after 1945 of survivors accused of collaboration. It does not discuss whether victims could also be perpetrators, but rather the disgraceful circumstance whereby victims were sentenced more severely after 1945 than their tormenters and thus remained victims. The tactic employed by the Nazis worked only too well. The Jewish community itself was called upon to announce the discriminating laws, to ensure the exclusion and branding, to handle the people being deported until the last moment and to manage the 'collection points'. The Kultusgemeinde was required to register the Jews and to keep records so as to permit emigration initially and then, as was discovered too late, to facilitate extermination. The Jewish community became an instrument of the Nazis, an 'agent of its own destruction'.[23]

The Jewish victims, persecuted or abandoned by the non-Jewish population, were deceived twice over. They obeyed the Nazi regulations announced by the Kultusgemeinde, directing their indignation at their own representatives. It was not the SS or the Gestapo but the Jewish officials who promulgated the Nazi decrees. It was not the members of the Gestapo Jewish department but the head of the Jewish community who was to remain imprinted in the survivors' memory, not the SS-Scharführer but the Jewish marshals. In this way, the victims' trust in their own leaders was abused and broken as a means of preventing any protest against the crimes.

This Nazi tactic of deception worked and continued to work after the German Reich had been defeated. Even after 1945, victims were mistaken for perpetrators or deliberately replaced them.

Criticism was heaped upon the Jewish administrative leaders after 1945, and even those who had not cooperated at all during the deportations but had on the contrary illicitly attempted to assist those in hiding were accused of having collaborated with the Gestapo.

In the Soviet-occupied zone of Germany, former Communists and Social Democrats who had survived the Nazi regime – in some cases in concentration camps – were interned again after 1945 because their very survival was seen as suspicious. Communist comrades who could demonstrate that they had belonged to Nazi Party organizations were left alone. They had obviously come to an arrangement; they could not therefore have been informers, traitors or kapos and would soon – before many who had been interned in camps because of their beliefs – be welcomed into the Socialist Unity Party of the German Democratic Republic.[24]

The Soviets were not the only ones who were harsh on their own people. Collaborators in France were often punished more severely than German perpetrators in the French-occupied zone. Treason from within appeared to incite greater inner fear than misdeeds committed by the enemy. And again, anyone who had survived the extermination was suspicious for that reason alone.

Survivor guilt is a psychoanalytical term. It refers not to authentic guilt but rather to an irrational feeling of guilt by survivors.[25] The mourning for the dead forces the survivors to ask why they managed to survive, and this evokes a feeling of guilt. No survivor can be as innocent as a dead victim, murdered defencelessly in a gas chamber. Individual shortcomings pale into insignificance in the face of the monstrous immensity of the crime, and the dead are automatically seen as 'good'. Primo Levi, himself a survivor, was convinced: 'The worst survived, that is, the fittest; the best all died.'[26]

The survivors' guilt was also influenced by the generally negative tone of public discourse after 1945. Survivors reacted in different ways to the public mood. Unlike Primo Levi, Ruth Klüger, for example, wrote:

> So we survivors are either the best or the worst. And yet . . . the truth is concrete, meaning specific. The role that prison life plays in the life of an ex-prisoner cannot be deduced from a shaky psychological rule, for it is different for each one of us, depending on what went before, on what came afterwards, and on what happened to each during his or her time in the camps. . . . It was a unique experience for each of them.[27]

In those countries that had until recently proclaimed that the Jews were responsible for everything, it became particularly important that no aspersions be cast on the victims. In the anti-Fascist mood that now prevailed, those who had been connected in any way to the killing could not be seen as victims, but were simply counted among the perpetrators so as not to spoil the idealized image of the victim. As a witness at the trial of Wilhelm Reisz stated: 'I feel obliged to testify because I cannot accept that because of the asocial behaviour of a few Jewish elements, all other respectable Jewish Austrians are disqualified.'[28]

The behaviour of those Jewish officials and assistants whose relations with the perpetrators were held against them was often not studied on an individual basis but simply condemned universally. There has been lively discussion as to how their actions should be judged, but what any individual did and his reasons for doing so are all too frequently ignored. Thus the truth is studied without any account being taken of the underlying reality. If we are not to fall into the trap of making general and exaggerated accusations, we must look more closely at the psychological mechanisms in action after 1945 with regard to the survivors.

Under the Nazis, the victims were forbidden to live. After the liberation, they had to justify their survival. Paradoxically, the anti-Semitic logic that the only good Jew is a dead one has itself survived the Third Reich.

Breaching taboos

'That's too much to take; you'll have to leave that out,' said jurist and political scientist Franz Leopold Neumann about a chapter in the MA dissertation by his student, Vienna émigré Raul Hilberg,[29] author of the standard work on the extermination of European Jewry.[30] He was referring to the chapter in Hilberg's paper about the attitude of the Jewish communities to the Nazi extermination policy. Neumann, author of the first major structural analysis of the Nazi regime,[31] refused to permit this chapter to be included, finding it too terrible to discuss the powerlessness and hopeless situation of Jewish victims forced against their will to become agents of their own destruction.

The attitude of Jewish functionaries is still a taboo subject today, although not an unbroken one. It has already been addressed in various ways, not infrequently with a reference to the general reluctance to broach the subject. Those who study the matter tend to encounter general interest, occasionally reserve and suspicion, but usually welcome curiosity. When mention is made of the subject, practically everyone will point out its sensitivity. Some question the ideological necessity to study or write about this uncomfortable issue and warn of the possibility of approval from the wrong people. There are also those who carefully avoid the subject for personal reasons.

For many people, however, breaking taboos has a certain attraction. The sensitivity of the subject evokes the possibility of discovering exotic secrets or something obscene. The imagination of some was fired by the thought of victims becoming perpetrators, the vague idea that the victims might have participated and taken secret pleasure in the crimes committed against them. Peter Wyden, for example, explained why he wrote the book *Stella*. It tells the story of Stella Kübler, who was tortured, threatened and cajoled by the Gestapo into finding hidden Jews, or 'U-boats', as they were called. She became a 'catcher' (*Greifer*), the most feared and notorious in Berlin. Wyden described his interest in his former fellow pupil as follows: 'And why, why was she willing to agree to this Faustian pact with Hitler? I had always wanted to find an explanation for the secret of this beauty, whom I had once worshipped. [. . .] I had to find out. I had to know about about Stella and these incestuous murders, my war's last taboo.'[32]

The Jewish functionaries are part of this 'last taboo'. In the Jewish identity after the Shoah, they were often symbols of unresisting Jews who were unable to assert themselves or put up a defence, the antithesis of the heroic partisan struggle and a sovereign Israel.

The study of the attitudes of Jewish victims under the destructive regime is always in danger of turning into a complacently moralizing reproach, shifting the blame for the crimes to the victims. This book is not about taboos or criticism but rather about the motives behind the accusations, reproaches and denunciations. In ideological disputes, Jewish organizations are sometimes accused of having collaborated in the crime. Zionism was said to have cooperated with the Nazis because it helped to organize the emigration to Palestine, because – confronted by the alternative of life or death – it negotiated with the Nazis on the transfer of capital to Palestine. The whole world, although not placed under the same pressure for survival as the Jews, was unable to maintain a boycott, but the Zionist leadership was expected to have done so.

It would be so convenient in the minds of anti-Semites if the Jews could be held responsible for their own extermination. I would like to give an example of this kind of distortion. For different reasons, the Nazis and Zionists attempted between 1933 and 1939 to get as many Jews as possible out of Germany – the Nazis with the aim of expelling them, the Zionists in an attempt to save them. The two sides were not equal partners. The Zionist organizations were obliged to cooperate with the Nazi rulers in the interests of Jewish survival. Francis Nicosia discusses the problems connected with this policy in his book *The Third Reich and the Palestinian Question*. He refuses to make hasty judgements, contenting himself with a description of what went on.[33]

One thing that Nicosia had not envisaged was that a German publishing company specializing in extreme right-wing literature would bring out an unauthorized translation of the book. It appeared in German under the title *Hitler und der Zionismus*.[34] Druffel-Verlag ignored the letter of protest by the author and wrote in the jacket text: 'This book clearly shows that the German Reich government, in particular the SS, consistently supported the Jewish element in Palestine, encouraged emigration and provided practical development aid in various areas.'

'The Führer gave the Jews a state' is the subtext. The historian Julius H. Schoeps asked in connection with this jacket text: 'Do the publishers mean to say that the Jews should be grateful to the Reich government and in particular the SS for what they did? Or are they saying that it wasn't like that at all and that historians who have studied the Jewish policy in the past give a completely false picture of what actually happened?'[35]

Revisionism is the order of the day in the German translation.[36] It basically suggests that the victims were not better than the perpetrators and for this reason the perpetrators cannot have been that bad.

The accusation that the Jews collaborated was, of course, used by the former perpetrators in court. In his defence, for example, Franz Murer in 1963 made reference to the participation of Jewish func-tionaries in the extermination process. The 'butcher from Vilnius', as he was called by the victims, was deputy regional commissar (*Gebietskommissar*) of the ghetto. Charged with seventeen murders, he denied everything, saying that it was too much to expect him to remember all the details twenty years later. He also recalled that the Jewish administration in the ghetto also had the authority to dole out punishment: 'The actions of the Jewish police, who were equipped with rubber truncheons issued by the civil authority – the regional commissar – has nothing to do with me.[37] The perpetrators attempted to accuse the victims of their own murder.

Alain Finkielkraut wrote in his book *The Imaginary Jew:*

It's unbearable, this arrogant summoning of ghetto dwellers and camp prisoners to answer before an abstract tribunal, a scandal. Yet for all our disgust, the indictment still requires a response. Jews who forty years ago suffered through Hitler now need lawyers for defence. Today and for the foreseeable future, we are reduced to justifying the victims for a massacre carried out against them.[38]

All too often, the criticism among Jews of the survival strategies of the Jewish communities has been in danger of degenerating into a surrogate ideological war at the expense of the dead. Not infrequently, they have been reduced to objects of academic study. The victims have been glorified as martyrs and their suffering as a passion leading to redemption and the creation of the State of Israel.

The death of millions was all the more terrible because, as Bruno Bettelheim notes, it was completely senseless, even if it might have had some purpose for the murderers.[39] The people killed by the Nazis did not die as martyrs. Martyrs die for a conviction they believe in. The victims of the Nazis were killed, however, simply because they were Jews or were defined as such by the Nazi regime. Whether babies or converts, they were all killed professionally and bureaucratically. To give the mass murder a belated higher meaning is simply to whitewash it.

Criticism of the failed survival strategy of the Jews comes from a historically secure position. The discussion should not be disallowed, but it must take account of the historical circumstances. Before 1938, no one could imagine what would happen. Even the future murderers did not know in 1933 or 1939 that millions of Jews would be murdered within the next few years.

The historical taboo preventing any discussion of ignominious behaviour by the victims was based on an idealized and dehumanizing idea of the victims. They could be portrayed only as completely innocent. They were denied a real existence that would admit a paradoxical biography and ambivalent character. But it is just as fatal to break the taboo dictated by this same dehumanizing conception and to criticize the victims for not complying with our idealized projections. Breaking a taboo is not the same as getting rid of it.

A taboo and the breaking of a taboo, both of which present the victims as icons, as saints or demigods, are the reverse side of all of those accusations that the Nazis levelled against the Jews. All of the irrational, unconscious aggression hidden by the taboo is released when the taboo is broken.

No mass murder without victims

The mass murder of millions of Jews under the Nazis was not the work of a dehumanized machine obeying the orders of an all-powerful demon. On the contrary, the crime has a name and an address, as Bertolt Brecht said. Many of the criminals retained their rank, name and social status even after 1945. The perpetrators have no right to anonymity and they cannot be exonerated from personal responsibility.

Whereas no discretion should be allowed to the murderers in the historical narrative, the suffering of the victims should not be sensationalized. At the same time, however, the victims should not be denied their place in history and their right to exist as individuals.

The history of the murder is not just the history of the murderers. The victims also had various ways of acting and reacting. Without considering the victims, it is not possible to understand the crimes committed against them.

The Nazi strategy was clear: all sympathy for the wretched and defenceless Jews by their non-Jewish neighbours was to be eliminated. The public deprivation of rights shattered the self-esteem of the Jews and made them more amenable to further persecution. The upright and independent attitude had first to be destroyed so as to permit the 'processions of human beings going like dummies to their death'.[40]

The crime says nothing about the essence of the Jews but everything about the character of the murderers. The persecution and murder has nothing to do with a Jewish destiny or the behaviour of the victims but took place because of the actions of the perpetrators. Even if the crime is not explained by the essence of the victims, however, the crime itself remains inconceivable if the victims are not taken into account. It is only by considering their desperation and the hopelessness of their situation that the extent and nature of the crime can be recognized.

Vienna was the first place in which the 'solution of the Jewish question', as it was called, was attempted. It was here that it was tried out. The Jewish people could not have been prepared for what happened. They were still citizens of the Reich but already outlaws. They could still escape legally with a passport and at the same time they were already threatened with deportation. They were defenceless against the anti-Semitic bloodlust of former neighbours and colleagues because they were not, as the anti-Semites insinuated, separate and conspiratorial, an isolated community living apart from the rest of the population, but a heterogeneous group. Nazism made them into the number one public enemy but, unlike the Jews in the countries occupied later, they were still citizens of this anti-Semitic state.

What strategy was available to the Jews in their isolation? What did the Jewish movements decide to do? How did the Kultusgemeinde or the Jews of Vienna react to the experience of Jewish communities in the Germany of the Third Reich? How did they prepare for the threatened power takeover by the Nazis? What tasks did the Jewish institutions set themselves after March 1938? Was their policy before the annexation consistent with their reaction to the Nazi rule? Who were the functionaries? What did they have in common and how were they different? Had they already been active within the Jewish community before the Nazis came to power or were they put in place by the Nazi authorities? Which community leaders were an obstacle to the Nazi leadership and which appeared compliant? Did the Viennese Jews ever attempt to rebel against the Nazi Jewish policy? What were the tasks of the Jewish administration during the Nazi era? What type of contact existed between the community leaders and the Nazi authorities? How much did the Jewish functionaries know about the mass murder? When did they find out about the extermination? What did they have to do, how did they cooperate when the assembly points were set up and mass transports to the concentration camps began? How did the attitude of the Jewish functionaries change when the external conditions began to alter? Was there disagreement within the community leadership about the attitude to the Nazis and what were the differences about? How was the attitude of the individual Jewish functionaries regarded after 1945?

In order to consider the reaction of the Jewish community leaders in Vienna to the Nazi persecution and extermination policy, there is no need to relate the entire history of Austrian Jews from 1938 to 1945 but rather merely to discuss the relevant events. Every person and every situation needs to be dealt with separately. This calls for historical consideration of a subject that has barely been studied in the past.

In 1966, Hugo Gold published his *Geschichte der Juden in Wien*, in which he discusses the extermination.[41] In the same year, Jonny Moser wrote about it in *Die Judenverfolgung 1938–1945*.[42] These were followed in 1978 by the highly informative work by the Jerusalem-based historian Herbert Rosenkranz *Verfolgung und Selbstbehauptung*.[43] Various aspects of the Nazi persecution of Austrian Jews have also been dealt with in academic papers.[44]

15

This book discusses the functionaries and employees of the Vienna Jewish community authorities and their offices. They always worked, whether they cooperated or attempted to sidestep official decrees, under direct Nazi control. It shows that they were completely at the mercy of the perpetrators and that they got caught up in the crime. They were members of an institution whose divisions and departments never had independent power. Within the Nazi criminal regime they were nothing but authorities without power.

The question of authorities without power is not only of historical importance. The totalitarian crime forces its victims to sacrifice themselves and incorporates them in the machinery of destruction.[45] Michel Foucault said: 'Power functions. Power is exercised through networks and individuals do not simply circulate in these networks; they are in a position both to submit to and exercise this power. They are never the inert or consenting targets of power; they are always its relays. In other words, power passes through individuals. It is not applied to them.'[46]

Although, if not quite because, the principle of power, as Foucault describes it, permeates the entire system, a clear distinction must always be made between perpetrators and victims, between the power of authority, in particular a tyranny, and the powerless.

— 2 —

THE VIENNA KULTUSGEMEINDE
BEFORE 1938

Securing evidence – at the scene of the crime

In the late nineteenth century, anti-Semitism in Vienna assumed a political dimension and for the first time elections were won on an anti-Semitic political platform. During the Monarchy and the First Republic, anti-Semitism was not just a tacitly agreed general mood but the overt credo of the bourgeois parties. The Christian Socialist and German National parties vied with each other in their anti-Semitism, and even the Social Democrats used anti-Jewish caricatures in their propaganda.[1]

Karl Lueger, who was mayor of Vienna from 1897 to 1910, ignited the first mass anti-Semitic movement in the capital. He used anti-Semitism systematically to attract support. His successful concept became a model for Hitler's populism. It was here in Austria that Hitler developed his view of the world. He admired the racist German nationalism of Georg Ritter von Schönerer's pan-German movement and venerated Karl Lueger's charisma as an anti-Semitic populist and leader of the masses.

Vienna had the largest Jewish population of any city in the German-speaking world. In the bureaucratic and dynastic centre of the Catholic Habsburg monarchy, 'the Jew' was usually a negative symbol of modernism and social change. By anti-Semites, Jews were seen as profiteers of emancipation, protected by the court. In Vienna, the capital of the multiethnic state, the Jews lived at the hub of nationalist movements and calls for assimilation. They became the target of all regressive sentiments.

Vienna at the beginning of the twentieth century was a city of ideological contradictions. It was the administrative centre of the

17

Monarchy, where Catholic taboos, social snobbery and anti-Semitic traditions were opposed by artistic and scientific innovators. Many of the Jewish personalities of the time, who were to become famous throughout the world, were for a long time repudiated by the Viennese.

A large section of the Jewish population came from the eastern parts of the Monarchy. Of the 175,000 Jews living in Vienna in 1910, only one fifth had been born there.[2] The 1934 census counted 191,481 Austrian Jews, 2.8 per cent of the population. On 11 March 1938, there were only 185,028, in spite of the stream of refugees from the German Reich. The Jewish community of Vienna in 1934 had 176,034 members, 9.4 per cent of the population; in March the figure had shrunk to 169,978. Some of the Jewish population had left Austria; others had moved to the provinces.[3]

There were thirty-four Jewish communities in various towns and cities in Austria before 1938. In Vienna, apart from the Vienna Israelite Community (IKG), there was also a partially autonomous Turkish Sephardic community. It had been incorporated in the IKG in 1909 as the Turkish Israelite Community. The IKG was the only unified community in the large cities of Europe. It is no coincidence that it called itself 'Israelite' rather than 'Jewish', and even today people talk of the 'Mosaic faith' and the 'Israelite community'. The Vienna IKG statutes of 1890 stated that every 'Israelite' living in Vienna was required irrespective of nationality to be a member of the community. In this way the various classes and groups were united within the IKG.

The Vienna Jewish community before 1938 had around 440 associations. Of these, seventy-nine were prayer house or temple associations. This figure does not include prayer rooms that were not registered with the community. The Jewish administration was responsible for 23 synagogues. Eight associations alone belonged to the orthodox Agudath Israel. The community also had two schools, a secondary school, a trade school for girls, a library, five kindergartens, four orphanages, two girls' homes, one student residence and one day care centre. There were 24 Jewish school associations to deal with questions of education and training. Health care was provided by a hospital, a paediatric clinic, an institute for the blind and an old people's home. There was also a hospice and children's holiday home owned by the community outside Vienna.[4]

Apart from many volunteers, the Kultusgemeinde had over 600 salaried staff. They worked in various departments responsible for religious affairs, cemeteries, hospital care, old age care, finance, technical issues, statistics and taxes. Over 60,000 people were registered as receiving welfare support.[5] There were 119 welfare associations looking after poor and needy Jews.[6]

The Kultusgemeinde also had a Historical Commission, which published a series on the history of the Jews in Vienna and Austria. The Jewish students had 22 fraternities, including duelling fraternities. One of these organizations called itself the Association of Palestinian Students.

The Zionist Association for Austria had 18 sections. The Zionist associations had 12,000 members and there were 82 separate Zionist groups. All questions regarding Aliyah or immigration to Palestine were dealt with by the Palestine Office, which was in contact with the Jewish Agency, the body that represented Jewish interests during the British Mandate.

The liberal Union of Austrian Jews had some 3,000 members, and the many clubs – ranging from scientific and cultural associations and sports clubs to the Association of Jewish Animal Lovers and the Austrian Association of Israelite Butchers and Meat Traders – bear witness to the diversity of Jewish life in Vienna.[7]

Jewish strategies to counter anti-Semitism

For decades, the Union of Austrian Jews was the most powerful faction in the Viennese Kultusgemeinde and was able to maintain its supremacy until 1932. In the first post-war elections in 1920, it obtained twenty of the thirty-six seats. The balance soon shifted, however, forcing the various parties into changing coalitions. In 1924, the Union combined with the bourgeois General Zionists and the orthodox Adath Israel to form a voting block without the newly founded Social Democrat party, the religious socialist Zionists of the Misrachi and the orthodox Beth El. In 1928, the coalition changed again. The Union and Adath Israel, the political representatives of the anti-Zionist orthodoxy within the Jewish community, amassed eighteen of the thirty-six seats.[8] Both of these Jewish factions distanced themselves from any Zionist or Jewish national identity.

The Union described itself as a 'non-Jewish national party' and proudly claimed to represent 'not Austrian Jews but Jewish Austrians'.[9] It was not that it did not espouse Jewish positions, nor was it a supporter of assimilation, but it believed in the Austrian state and strove for constitutional equality and emancipation within society. It sought to counter anti-Semitism by legal means or through interventions and complaints to politicians. In other words, it relied on the state institutions to deal with discrimination and resentment. It also sought affiliation outside the community with other liberal forces in the fight against anti-Semitism. It called on its clientele to vote for liberal parties in the national elections. Its confidence in Austrian liberalism proved to be misplaced.

At the national level, many Jews gradually began to support the Social Democrats while turning to the Zionist movements within the community. Following the failure of its emancipatory utopia in an anti-Semitic society, the fortunes of the Union went into decline and in 1932 it lost its supremacy in the Jewish community.

The issues had changed. While the Union and Adath Israel had formed a bourgeois patriotic Austrian voting bloc in 1928, four years later these two parties were joined by the non-Zionist Social Democrats in a non-Jewish national alliance. This shows how nationalism was becoming increasingly important at the expense of social issues. In 1928, the Social Democrats had had both Zionist and non-Zionist members. In 1929, these two factions parted company.

The Zionist Socialists managed in 1932 to win almost as many votes as the Social Democrat list, consisting of Zionists and non-Zionists, had achieved together in 1928. The vast majority of Socialist Jews within the Jewish community voted Zionist. All of the Zionist parties gained seats to take control of the Kultusgemeinde.

The Union's members came in part from established Viennese families, mostly from the 'west', i.e., Austria, Hungary or Czechoslovakia, whereas many of the Zionists were 'Ostjuden' from Galicia and other places. In fact, many years earlier the Zionists had already established their predominance among the Jews arriving in Vienna from eastern Europe. The Union also increasingly lost the support of orthodox Jews.

The Zionists proposed a completely different way of dealing with anti-Semitism and discrimination. In 1920, Robert Stricker, a Zionist member of parliament and one of the movement's leading personalities, had submitted a motion for recognition of Jewish nationality. Although his proposal still allowed Jews to choose between German or Jewish nationality, it caused a storm of protest among the Unionists, who feared that it would be seen as a form of separatism and could reinforce anti-Semitism. Indeed, independently of the Zionist motion, the anti-Semitic politician Leopold Kunschak called for a law discriminating against Jews as an alien minority.[10] There was no need for Zionist demands to fuel the anti-Semitic imagination. On the contrary, the Zionist movement reacted to the anti-Semitic reality in Austria.

Zionism in Austria and Germany was above all a search for a Jewish identity.[11] The leading Zionists were convinced that the only possible reaction to a 'Jewish question' was a confident Jewish answer. The anti-Semites would not be swayed by goodwill or loyalty to the country. The Zionists wanted to confront the enemies of Judaism on an equal footing. In a world of national states, a Jewish state was only logical. This homeland was sought in Palestine, but in fact more for the harried families in the east of Europe than for themselves. For a long time, Viennese Zionists were in no hurry to emigrate to Palestine and many of them identified just as much with Austria as they did with a Jewish state. The idea of a powerful Jewish national workers' movement that was not Zionist found a following only among eastern European Jews.[12]

The Union did not reject the idea of Jews settling in Palestine and it also hoped for the 'reconstruction of Eretz Israel', but its Jewish identity was different: it defined itself as being 'non-Jewish-national'. A conflict that took place in 1934–5 highlights the difference between the Zionist and non-Zionist camps within the Kultusgemeinde. A government decree called for a distinction between Jewish and non-Jewish pupils and for the establishment of collective Jewish classes in some Viennese state schools. A protest submitted on 19 September 1935 by the Kultusgemeinde had next to no political impact. The restructuring did not in fact take place, but the confessional segregation already existing in schools was maintained, prompting the Zionist leadership in the community to change its tactics. They decided not to demand the restoration of normal joint lessons but the establishment of independent Jewish schools. In this endeavour they had greater success, and a Jewish primary school was opened in the same year.

In a 1992 interview, Raul Hilberg recalls his own schooldays:

> You should not forget that it was very difficult for the Jewish population even before the Annexation. There was a rumour, for example, that Jewish pupils would have to sit at separate desks. My parents therefore put me in a Jewish secondary school; my mother said that if I had to sit at a Jewish desk it would be better if it was in a Jewish school. I was nine years old at the time.[13]

The orthodox Adath Israel welcomed the government decree as a preliminary to a purely confessional Jewish school.[14] It saw itself as Jewish in terms of religion and Austrian in terms of nationality. The popular conception of the Jewish religion was not, it felt, in line with the modern conception of the state. It used religious values in its attempt to combat the anti-Semitism of the Christian Socialists. The Union, by contrast, insisted on a joint Austrian school, fearing not just discrimination by the state but also the fostering of Jewish national character by an independent educational establishment.[15]

Beyond the internal political quarrels, however, there were some Jews, Zionist and non-Zionist alike, who were not content to combat the threat of anti-Semitism with words alone. The Association of Former Jewish Front Soldiers, whose members always insisted on their loyalty to the fatherland, organized militant units to protect themselves against Nazi attacks. It was founded in 1932 and just a year later had 8,000 members. The Hakoah sports club wanted to show that Jews could also be successful in sport. Several Jewish organizations in Austria attempted to counter the suggestion that Jews were cowardly or incapable of 'giving satisfaction'.

All attempts to counter anti-Semitism by force had to be abandoned when the Nazis came to power in Austria. In spite of anti-Semitic fantasies to the contrary, the Jewish community was not an autonomous foreign body within the Austrian population but remained a semi-integrated and already assimilated heterogeneous minority.

Shortly before the Anschluss, the entry of German troops into Austria in March 1938, a group of young people had been organizing firing practices in a quarry in Sievering, remaining dispersed so as not to attract the attention of the Vaterländische Front (Patriotic Front). Immediately after the Nazis came to power, Jewish people were chased through the streets not only by groups of hooligans but also by an anti-Semitic mob and militant Nazi Party groups. Willy Stern, one of the youths who had taken part in the firing practice, made sure to get rid of his weapon as quickly as possible by dismantling it and throwing it in the Danube. Within hours the Jewish military unit had ceased to exist.[16]

The corporate state – in the shadow of the Third Reich

The Vienna Kultusgemeinde had to deal with Nazism and its ramifications even before the Anschluss in 1938. After the Nazis came to power in Germany, the Jewish community was faced with the consequences of Nazi government policy. The suppression of the Jews in Germany had a direct impact on the IKG in Vienna. Refugees from the German Reich streamed to Austria and had to be supported. Moreover, the anti-Jewish discrimination in Germany exacerbated the anti-Semitic witch-hunts and exclusion from jobs in Austria.

The Nazi power takeover appeared to confirm and strengthen the Zionist position. Shortly after 1933, Jewish community organizations in the German Reich still tried to affirm their loyalty to Germany. The publications at the time showed up their efforts to avoid exclusion. In 1933, the president of the association of synagogues in Hanover, for example, exhorted the 'honourable members of the congregation': 'as good Germans to fly the black, white and red Reich flag on the German workers' holiday on 1 May.'[17]

With the introduction of the Nuremberg Laws in 1935 all hope of a German-Jewish future disappeared. The stream of Jewish refugees from the German Reich forced the Vienna Kultusgemeinde to make arrangement to provide for the new arrivals. The refugee welfare department under Leo Landau was responsible for this task. Unmarried refugees received 100 schillings a month from the Kultusgemeinde and married refugees 125 schillings. They were also entitled to a free lunch and if necessary a place to sleep. Arrangements were made with two or three cafés to allow the refugees to sit and read newspapers. The community also set up its own tea rooms.[18]

When the Austro-Fascist government was in power in 1933–4, a regulation of 16 February 1934 excluded Socialists from the board of the IKG. Four Zionist and non-Zionist Social Democrat groups were banned. The Zionist workers' movements were allowed to continue provided that they worked solely to promote emigration to Palestine. Many young people from Jewish families who had rejected Judaism for ideological or other reasons participated in 1934 in the uprising of the Austrian workers against Austro-Fascism. Others took part from 1936 onwards in the struggle by the democratically elected Spanish Popular Front government against Franco.[19]

Austro-Fascism took its style from other authoritarian and Fascist states. The various Jewish factions submitted to the Austro-Fascist government as the lesser of two evils, compared with Nazi Germany. Many Jews saw the Austrian corporate state as the only remaining defence against Hitler. Although it protected the Jews from Hitler, its own anti-Semitic discrimination was so extreme that the government of the United States of America intervened, and Nahum Goldmann remonstrated with Mussolini about the situation of the Jews in Austria on 13 November 1934. Jews were excluded from government positions, banks and insurance companies. The policy of the anti-Semitic minister of education and Christian Socialist party head

Emerich Czermak prevented Jewish intellectuals from gaining access to research and academia. At the same time, however, the government appointed Desider Friedmann, president of the Kultusgemeinde, to the State Council.

In July 1936, the authoritarian system under Kurt Schuschnigg concluded an agreement with the German Reich. The Austrian government undertook to suppress all anti-Nazi propaganda, to grant amnesty to Nazis in prison, to include the 'national' minister Edmund Glaise-Horstenau in the government, thereby stepping up its discrimination against the Jews. In early 1936, the Zionist movement in Palestine became concerned about the anti-Jewish incidents and the discrimination in Austria through newspaper reports. In the face of the Nazi threat and the Austro-Fascist situation, the Jewish factions and organizations found that their possibilities for responding were dwindling.

The Jewish institutions supported the idea of Palestine as a refuge and, in spite of the anti-Jewish measures, they put their entire faith in the Austrian corporate government. They pursued a policy of patriotic goodwill in an effort to protect themselves from the Nazi crimes in Germany and the popular anti-Semitism at home.

The Jewish organizations protested when Jewish refugees from Germany and Poland attempted to enter other countries illegally. On 15 November 1937, shortly before the Nazis came to power in Austria, community delegates from all over Europe met for a conference in Vienna to decide what to do about the many refugees from Germany and Poland. A central card index was set up in Paris with individual details of the refugees. This allowed assistance to be provided on a personal basis in providing the costs for travel. The conference attempted to raise funds for humanitarian aid and to put a stop to 'uncontrolled emigration'.

The organization sought 'controlled' emigration. No refugee should leave the country of origin without the agreement of the welfare committee in the destination country except in the case of official expulsion. Those who fled 'without coercive reasons', as it was called, should be 'sent back to Germany if this could be done without risk' at the expense of the central aid organization.[20] The Jewish organizations thought that illegal emigration would make countries less willing to take in the refugees and would thus close the borders to legal and illegal immigration alike. A few months later, the members of the Jewish community could no longer be in any doubt of the risk for Jewish men and women in the German Reich. Flight, be it legal or illegal, was now the only hope.

On 19 February 1938, following a meeting of the Austrian Federal Chancellor Schuschnigg with Hitler in Berchtesgaden, a few weeks before the Anschluss, Oskar Grünbaum, president of the Zionist Association for Austria in Vienna, wrote a letter to the executive board in London. He appeared to be at pains not to damage Austria's image in the world.

> The government believes that it can deal with the situation if there is no panic or boycott. [. . .] I therefore cordially urge you to point out in your circles that all of the newspaper articles about discrimination against Jews since the agreement in Berchtesgaden are untrue and that the dissemination of false news about Austria would only make the government's situation more difficult.[21]

At the same time, Grünbaum reported that the Zionist Association for Austria had recruited 500 members in the last few months alone: 'Since the new situation has been in place, the meetings have been overrun and the room has had to be closed by the police because of crowding.'[22]

During the Austro-Fascist period, the Jewish community had already learned to cooperate with an authoritarian state as a means of protecting its interests. Austria had long ceased to be a democratic society. When the Nazis came to power, they discovered a Jewish institution that was already well practised in submitting to state authority. The Jews did not make any preparations of their own for the takeover by the Nazis. To avoid misunderstanding, it should be pointed out that the Jews could not have resisted the German army and the Austrian anti-Semites on their own, but they took no precautions whatsoever because the Kultusgemeinde believed in the constancy of the Austrian government. There were no information networks, no contingency plans, no emergency action committee, no secret meeting places, no evacuation measures for specific institutions or persons, no flight preparations, no transfer of financial or cultural resources or documents.

The leaders of the Jewish community supported Schuschnigg against Hitler. When the Austrian government announced a referendum on the continuation of Austria as an independent state as a means of countering the pressure from Berlin, the Kultusgemeinde made a huge donation. It placed all of its hopes in the continued existence of the Austrian state and attempted to safeguard its existence through patriotic compliance and loyalty.

— 3 —

PERSECUTION

Wer redt mit die Händ und wer hatscht mit die Fieß?
Der Jud!
Wer macht a Geseires und mauschelt so sieß?
Der Jud!
Er ist überall auf der Erde zuhaus
Und ist so verbreitet wie Wanze und Laus.
Der Jud – der Jud, der Jud!

Viennese children's song 1938,
to the tune of 'Es klappert die Mühle am rauschenden Bach'[1]

The German invasion and the Austrian response

The German troops marching into Austria on 12 March 1938 were met by cheering crowds. Never again was the invading army to be greeted with such unflagging enthusiasm as it crossed a border.

The Nazis did not have to fear general opposition to their Jewish policy in Austria. On the contrary, the authorities could count on a mass of profiteers and sympathizers; at the same time, they underestimated the zeal with which their policies would be pursued.

The Jews of Vienna were not victims of a policy coming from without. The excessive response and the plundering, which were quite different to what had happened in Germany, contributed to the distinctive ambience in Nazi Vienna. Moreover, they had already started before the German troops crossed the border. On 4 February 1938, five weeks before the Anschluss, juveniles had tossed a smoke bomb into the temple on Hetzgasse. Now, on 11 March, the night before the Anschluss, the Austrian Nazis were able to get to work properly.[2]

The victims received support only from isolated individuals. It is therefore all the more important to recall these exceptions and not to remain silent about their often heroic interventions.

The Anschluss of Austria cannot be compared with the occupation of other countries by the German army. The incorporation of the Saar and Rhineland followed a completely different pattern, and most of the other occupied countries were enemies whose non-Jewish population was usually oppressed for not being German. Moreover, the situation in the Saar and Rhineland was merely assimilated to that of the Reich. In Austria, by contrast, the anti-Jewish persecution reached a new level.

The Gestapo in Vienna was entrusted with implementing the Jewish policy. The *New York Times* wrote on 23 March 1938: 'It is becoming clear that whereas in Germany the first Nazi victims were the Left political parties – Socialists and Communists – in Vienna it is the Jews who are to bear the brunt of the Nazis' revolutionary fire.'[3]

After an initial intensive spate of arrests, the hounding of political opponents soon tailed off. On 4 September 1938, SS-Gruppenführer Reinhard Heydrich, head of the Security Police, said that there were still 1,142 prisoners in protective custody in Austria. On 1 April 1938, the first transport left for the concentration camp in Dachau; of the 151 deportees, 60 were Jews.[4]

The Jewish international organizations were informed about the developments. Zionist officials travelled to Vienna and Berlin to find out about the situation. In the first weeks after the Anschluss, the Viennese public watched on enthusiastically as Jews were forced to clean the crutch cross symbols of the corporate state and Schussnigg slogans from the streets using brushes and caustic lye. Where there were no crosses, the SA daubed new ones so as to entertain the public for months afterwards.[5] Torah scrolls in synagogues were burnt. Orthodox Jews were dragged through the streets and their beards shaved off to the delight of onlookers. The victims were fair game for anyone wishing to give vent to their passionate hatred, envy or personal dissatisfaction or bad mood. The Viennese anti-Semites were able to indulge in this witch-hunt with jeering cynicism.

The delight in inventing new humiliations for the victims appeared insatiable. The uncontrolled terror of Viennese anti-Semitism, which had already started the night before the German army entered Austria, was not in keeping with the pseudo-legal and official veneer that the new authorities wished to give their Jewish policy. The victims were at the mercy of their persecutors' bestiality. They could not determine whether the people who burst into their homes and confiscated their

27

property were ordinary burglars or people legitimized by the Nazis. Anyone daring to complain to the police was likely to be deported to a concentration camp.

The Zionist emissary Leo Lauterbach wrote a report on 29 April 1938 to the Executive of the Zionist Congress describing the feeling of fear and hopelessness prevailing in the community. He said that he would prefer not to mention all of the names of the Jewish people he had spoken to. It was not the Aryanization, the searches of houses, apartments and business, the mass arrests and deportations to concentration camps that provoked the greatest desperation among the victims as much as the public humiliation and sadistic violence of their previously well-disposed neighbours. Lauterbach was aghast to realize that some of his Jewish acquaintances were no longer willing to leave their homes or come to his hotel. When he visited Jewish homes, he encountered people shaking and stuttering with fear. In summary he wrote: 'It revealed to them that they were living not only in a fool's paradise, but in a veritable hell.'[6] The Jews of Vienna had been made to realize suddenly that the Vienna that they had regarded as their home was in fact a trap.

The public did not need to be persuaded by the government or party to espouse the anti-Semitic policy. On the contrary, the Nazi authorities had to appeal to the people to moderate their enthusiasm. As early as 14 March 1938, the new rulers banned excesses undertaken on individual initiative and the uncoordinated confiscation of property.[7]

Expropriation through the deprivation of rights

The Nuremberg Laws were not immediately applied to the 'Ostmark', as Austria was now called, but their de facto enforcement coincided with the Anschluss. The new rulers passed a whole series of anti-Jewish laws and decrees as a way of legalizing the anti-Semitic discrimination and exclusion. The robbing of the Jews went hand in hand with their marginalization and downgrading.

The systematic deprivation of rights was initiated with the decree by Ostmark governor (Reichsstatthalter) Arthur Seyss-Inquart on 15 March 1938 demanding that all public officials take an oath to Hitler. Those who refused to do so were immediately removed from office. According to the records, no one in the Vienna city authorities refused to take the oath. Jews were forbidden to take an oath to Hitler and were thus automatically removed from office.

On the same day, the *Kleine Volkszeitung* reported an order by the Minister of Justice that all Jewish or half-Jewish judges and lawyers were to be dismissed from office. Jews and all those who were defined as such were no longer allowed to be lawyers or notaries. The cover of files in the commercial court in which the defendants were Jews was marked with red ink and the case a priori decided against them.[8]

It was difficult for the Jews of Vienna to keep track of all of the laws, proclamations, regulations, decrees or orders that were heaped upon them every day. In a list compiled by the Kultusgemeinde in 1938 alone, there were around one hundred new provisions.[9]

In April, Jews were banned from studying at the university and students were removed from courses. Many of them had already stopped going to classes after the Anschluss for fear of being attacked.[10] Jewish journalists, musicians, actors and lawyers were banned from working. By the end of March, all Jewish lecturers and professors had been dismissed from the University of Vienna.[11] Viktor Christian, dean of the Philosophy Faculty, wrote a letter to all lecturers calling on them to provide evidence of their 'racial affiliation'. The definition of a Jew was based on the Nuremberg Laws, regardless of religious affiliation, Halakha or rabbinical commandments. The Nuremberg Laws and the Law for the Protection of Blood and Honour defined the persons to whom the discriminatory regulations were to apply. The provisions were complicated and the ambiguities also taxed the authorities for a considerable time.[12]

Marriage or extramarital relationships between Jews and non-Jews were forbidden. Aryan women under forty-five years of age were prohibited from working for Jews. From July 1938, the identity cards of Jews were stamped with a 'J'. New passport regulations were decreed on 5 October 1938 and the passports of German Jews had to be specially marked and stamped with a 'J'. This law resulted in the tightening of immigration regulations in some countries and even the temporary suspension of visas for the United Kingdom. The regulations compelled Jews from other countries and stateless Jews to leave the Reich territory without undue delay. In the time allowed, it was impossible for them to obtain the necessary emigration and immigration papers. In this way, they made themselves liable for prosecution from the outset.

Doctors who had not been struck off the register were only allowed to treat Jewish patients. Businessmen were no longer allowed to manage their companies. In this way, Jewish families were impoverished and torn out of their social context. Jews were also forbidden from owning weapons or wearing their military uniforms.[13]

In the summer of 1938, the regulation came into force in Austria whereby every Jew had to take on the additional name 'Israel' for men and 'Sara' for women unless they already had what the Nazis regarded as one of the 'Semitic' names on a list drawn up by the Ministry of the Interior.[14]

The discrimination had three main purposes. First, the public humiliations and incessant acts of violence destroyed the self-esteem of the Jews and made them more pliable. The flood of laws also made it more difficult for the victims to analyse their situation. In fact, it was not so much a situation as an enduring disaster. All thoughts, so went the perpetrators' strategy, should be focused on the latest attack on the victims' existence, giving no time to consider the developments as a whole.

Second, the last remnants of sympathy and solidarity by non-Jewish citizens for the ostracized, dismissed and impoverished Jews had to be eradicated. The marginalized and oppressed Jews began more and more to resemble the anti-Semitic stereotype of the wretched ghetto Jew.

Finally, they were clearly recognizable as victims. It was now settled who could feel safe from anti-Semitic oppression because the rules for possession of an Aryan identity card were defined and the fear of 'German nationals' that they might also be persecuted were allayed.

The hunt for booty

The organized plundering started in Austria on the night of 11–12 March 1938 in accordance with lists prepared in advance. In the night of 13–14 March and the following days, the SS, SA, police and gendarmerie forced their way into hundreds of Jewish homes in order to steal all conceivable items of value. The booty was removed indirectly to Hotel Metropol, the Gestapo headquarters.[15]

In the first few weeks, the 'Aryanizers' grabbed Jewish businesses, department stores and small shops. Some non-Jewish shop owners in Vienna hung signs saying 'Aryan business'. Jewish shop owners were forced to paint the Star of David on their window displays. Nazi sentries stood in front of shops with signs saying 'Don't buy from Jews'. Non-Jews who persisted in going to Jewish shops were likely to have to pass through a jeering cordon. Some non-Jewish women who had entered a Jewish shop had a swastika shaved on their heads or branded on their bodies. To amuse onlookers, a sign was hung on the victim saying: 'This Aryan swine only shops with Jews'.[16]

The initial mass plundering of Jewish property took place without state control. A distinctive feature in Austria was the system of 'temporary administrators' (*kommissarischer Verwalter*). According to Hans Fischböck, the Austrian Minister of Economic Affairs and Labour at the time, there were some 25,000 unofficial administrators in Austria.[17] On 13 April 1938, the Law on the Appointment of *Kommisarische Verwalter* and Supervisors authorized the governor to appoint *kommisarische Verwalter* for Jewish businesses. They were to arrange the Aryanization – effectively the expropriation – by 10 October.[18]

The Viennese anti-Semites appeared too zealous for the Nazi rulers and the *Völkischer Beobachter* of 26 April 1938 called the Austrian people to order:

> Please note that Germany is a state ruled by laws. This means that in our Reich nothing occurs without a legal basis. No one has the right to make his own private contribution to the solution of the Jewish question by acting on his own initiative. There can be no pogroms, not even by Mrs Hinterhuber against Mrs Sara Kohn on the first floor next to the water pipe! [. . .] There is no need for impatience: the paperwork is tedious and sometimes boring, but we have five years of experience in the Reich to convince ourselves that if it is done in a quiet and orderly manner it will ultimately lead to success.

The plundering was finally nationalized in May 1938 with the creation of the Property Control Office (*Vermögensverkehrsstelle*) in the former Austrian Ministry of Trade.[19]

The Aryanization was not carried out secretly. On the contrary, business takeovers were proudly announced and advertised. Businesses that continued to exist were boycotted.

The negative social policy of the Nazis created more dwellings for the non-Jewish population of Vienna than the housing policy of Red Vienna had ever managed.[20] The Kultusgemeinde was obliged to keep a file card index of the vacated dwellings.[21] With this form of persecution, this very special redistribution, the Nazi Party satisfied the greed of its clientele.

The Jews had to fill out forms giving details of their financial circumstances.[22] In this way it could be determined how much they had to give up. Anyone owning more than 5,000 Reichmarks (RM) had to pay 20 per cent in levies. In 1939, Jews were allowed to possess next to no objects of value.

The expropriation of the Jews took place in stages. Through dismissals and employment bans many Jews lost their incomes; at the same time it was made sure that there were no Jews working in public authorities, the army or in business, as these sectors were to participate in the anti-Jewish persecution. The Aryanization was aimed at Jewish businesses. From 18 November 1938, it was also possible for 'antisocial and subversive assets' to be confiscated. They were subject to special levies and 'atonement taxes' (*Sühneabgaben*). The victims were put on forced labour details; their possessions could be confiscated without further explanation and their bank accounts frozen.

The procedure in the Ostmark became a model for the Altreich. In the 'discussion of the Jewish question' on 12 November 1938 in Berlin, Göring was highly enthusiastic about the Austrian method of Aryanization of the German economy.[23]

The extent of the expropriation of the Jews can be seen from a report of 14 August 1939 by Walter Rafelsberger, head of the Vermögensverkehrsstelle, to Heinrich Himmler, Reichsführer-SS and Head of the German Police:

> I should like to take this opportunity to recall that the Vermögensverkehrsstelle effectively completed the task of eradicating Jews from the economy of the Ostmark in a period of just under 1½ years. In particular, Jewish shops and businesses have completely disappeared. Of the 33,000 or so Jewish businesses in Vienna at the time of the Anschluss, around 7,000 were dissolved . . . in the throes of the change-over. Of the remaining 26,000, around 5,000 were Aryanized and the remaining 21,000 duly liquidated.[24]

The expropriation of the Jews was completed in Austria more thoroughly and quickly than in the Altreich. In May 1939, 30 per cent of the self-employed Jewish businesses still existed in Berlin after six years, compared with just 6 per cent in Vienna after a single year.[25]

— 4 —

STRUGGLE FOR SURVIVAL AND ESCAPE

Not at all. We were overwhelmed.

Franzi Löw-Danneberg, former
Jewish Community welfare worker, when asked how the community
had prepared for a potential seizure of power by the Nazis[1]

The decapitation of the Jewish Community

On 13 March, one day after Nazi troops entered Austria, 150 Jewish bankers and businessmen were arrested by the SS and SA. The offices of the Zionist Association for Austria, the Zionist National Funds Keren Kayemet and Keren Hayessod, the Palestine Office and the editorial offices of the Zionist *Stimme* were vandalized and closed down. The intruders seized any money they found. The lodges of Bnai B'rith, the international Jewish fraternity, were dissolved. On the same evening, armed troops in SA uniform and civilian plunderers roamed the streets, looting Jewish synagogue offices and taking action without authority against Jewish functionaries.[2]

On 16 March, the Nazi authorities entered the offices of the Kultusgemeinde for the first time. They checked the accounts and liquidation office and requisitioned calculators and typewriters; the inventory became a plundering foray.[3] On 18 March 1938, Reich Commissioner Josef Bürckel ordered the suspension until the plebiscite of 10 April of activities by all Austrian associations except those 'performing tasks essential for the state and fulfilling social obligations for their members'.[4] The new regime decided that the tasks of the Jewish Community were not essential. On the same day the Kultusgemeinde offices were occupied in a lightning raid.[5]

SD officer Adolf Eichmann, who had arrived in Vienna from Berlin on 16 March, also took part in this raid. He was put in charge of

Department II–112 in SS-Oberabschnitt Austria (later SS-Oberabschnitt Danube) after his predecessor had returned to Berlin on 11 April.[6] Department II–112 of the SS Sicherheitsdienst (SD) began to coordinate the anti-Semitic policy in Austria. In the Old Reich, the SD Jewish Department had merely supported the Gestapo in its anti-Jewish actions. In Austria, the members of SD Department II–112 under Adolf Eichmann managed to appropriate this agenda for themselves. It had drafted ideas on the Jewish policy in Berlin and advised the Gestapo on how to proceed. Now the occupation of Austria offered the local SD command the possibility of acting in its own right, parallel to and in competition with the Gestapo.[7]

The Jews of Vienna were forced to pay RM 500,000 as an 'equivalent to the intended Jewish contribution to the Schuschnigg referendum fund'.[8] The receipts for this contribution provided the Gestapo with the desired excuse to arrest the leaders of the Jewish community present at the time. President Desider Friedmann, vice-presidents Josef Ticho and Robert Stricker, former Zionist National Council member, director Josef Löwenherz and many religious leaders, including municipal councillor Jakob Ehrlich, be they members of the ruling Zionist party or the opposition Union, were taken into custody.[9]

In her book *Eichmann in Jerusalem*, Hannah Arendt writes that Adolf Eichmann had to liberate representatives of the Jewish community from prisons and concentration camps immediately after his arrival in Vienna.[10] Arendt probably bases this assertion on Eichmann's false statements to his Israeli interrogating officer.[11] In fact, Eichmann was in Vienna before the arrests. In his book *Eichmann's Men*, Hans Safrian points out that the SD Jewish Department II–112 Sonderkommando under Herbert Hagen, who was Eichmann's superior, had a list of Jews from Berlin who were to be arrested.[12] All institutions were shut down.[13]

The Jewish community was at the mercy of the persecutors without being able to respond. For this reason the remaining Jewish functionaries attempted to maintain the organization on a temporary basis and to have the IKG reopened. Emil Engel, head of the welfare department, and Rosa Rachel Schwarz, in charge of juvenile welfare, managed while the IKG was occupied by the Gestapo to salvage the money for the Schuschnigg election fund.[14] After the Kultusgemeinde offices had been closed, Emil Engel, Rosa Schwarz and Leo Landau attempted to help needy Jews unofficially with these funds. Various members of the community alongside Emil Engel and Rosa Schwarz met – 'by chance' – first in a small restaurant, then in Café Franz Josefs-Kai, Café Rappaport and the Jewish Rothschild Hospital. First they had breakfast together, then they discussed 'acquaintances', people without means who were to receive assistance.[15]

Immediately after the Nazis came to power in Austria, members of the community endeavoured to set up a Jewish self-help service, which now offered the only salvation for many people who had lost all of their assets.[16] The American Joint Distribution Committee and Norman Bentwich from the Council for German Jews supported the Jews of Vienna with subsidies.[17]

Emil Engel and Rosa Schwarz attempted to keep up and supply Jewish homes, an almost hopeless task as many children's homes had been evacuated and taken over by Nazi Party associations.[18] The Rothschild Hospital and the old people's home (*Versorgungshaus für alte Menschen*) were able to continue their work. In Leopoldstadt, eight free kitchens were set up with financial aid from overseas. Poor relief had to be extended to all those who after the Nazis came to power no longer had accommodation or income. Now there were 8,000 people instead of 800 previously who had to be fed. Free meals were distributed eight times a day. The SA and BDM (League of German Girls) took delight in disrupting the distribution. They upturned the tureens on the street and stole food.[19]

In the second half of March, Adolf Eichmann summoned the leaders of the various Jewish organizations to the ransacked Palestine Office. Eighty functionaries from all institutions and factions were to meet at Marc-Aurel-Strasse 5 at 9 a.m. on a Friday morning, probably 25 March.[20] Yehuda Brott, formerly Weissbrod, one of the survivors, recalls: 'Eichmann sat at a desk in the large room in the Palestine Office. The room was completely empty; I remember Eichmann sitting there at the end of the room, like when people were summoned by Mussolini. There were no chairs and everyone had to give their reports standing up. I gave my report and was dismissed.'[21]

Other Jewish survivors also described the terror that Eichmann inspired: 'And then came Eichmann, like a young god; he was very good-looking, tall, dark, radiant in those days. The pictures of him today [meaning the trial in Israel in 1961; D. R.] bear no resemblance to how he used to be.'[22]

In Vienna, he did not convey the image as he did in the trial in Jerusalem of the subordinate and banal official described by Hannah Arendt and in the film *Ein Spezialist*. Eyewitnesses in 1938–9 speak of his anti-Semitic and imperious demeanour. He refused 'for ideological reasons' to shake hands with Jewish representatives or even Zionist emissaries.[23] He berated, threatened and taunted the Jews.[24]

While he had still been a subordinate figure in Berlin in 1937, he took the initiative in Vienna to manage the terror and the persecution.[25] He enjoyed his new work. He no longer had to sort index cards or write reports on Zionist associations as he had done just a couple of years earlier in Berlin. He now had executive powers; people could be jailed or deported to concentration camps at his command.

> His work consisted mainly of putting pressure on the intimidated officials of the Kultusgemeinde. Now he could make others work for him and supervise the officials he had appointed to draw up and execute proposals and plans. All he had to do was to choose, accept, or reject. The thirty-two-year-old Eichmann, who had accomplished nothing in his earlier profession, now was empowered to order about people who only recently had been esteemed, honoured members of Austrian society, far superior to him in training and professional experience. Now he could, as he phrased it with obvious pride, "light fires under them".[26]

In spite of the fear that Eichmann inspired, the representatives of Jewish organizations understood from the meeting that Eichmann was interested in the continued operation of the Kultusgemeinde, albeit with a completely different structure. Unlike the wild manhunt on the streets of Vienna, the Nazi authorities had a calculated plan. To those who attended the meeting, it appeared that the Nazis were interested not in murder and manslaughter or pogroms but 'merely' in the systematic expulsion of the Jews. The functionaries hoped that their organizations would continue to exist because they had been given until the following Monday to submit written reports and to make proposals for the future.[27] Most Jews had lost their livelihood through the ban on working and Aryanization, the witch-hunts and terror. It was almost impossible to provide the necessary relief or assistance in fleeing, however, because the Kultusgemeinde offices were closed. Jewish functionaries therefore tried to have the Jewish organizations reinstated.

Emil Engel had made contact with the Gestapo with a view to organizing welfare. He was forced to raise the 'equivalent' mentioned earlier for the proposed Jewish contribution to Schuschnigg's referendum fund. Engel wrote a letter to the members of the Jewish community asking them to raise RM 550,000.[28] In response to this appeal, the Jews raised RM 250,000 in ten days.[29]

Several individual Jews attempted to contact the Austrian Nazis to elaborate a plan for Jewish emigration. Efforts were to be stepped up to encourage emigration and 10 to 15 per cent of the assets withheld from the emigrants were to be put into an emigration fund. In this way, wealthier Jews would be able to finance the flight of those without means. An aid office was set up and Frank van Gheel Gildemeester appointed its director. Gildemeester had helped illegal Nazis during the period of Austro-Fascism. Because of these prior activities, he was known to the new authorities. Hans Fischböck, Minister of Economic Affairs and Labour, agreed to the proposal. In April 1938, the Gildemeester Organization for Assistance to Emigrants started work.

For the victims of the Nazi policy, of course, emigration meant nothing more than expulsion or flight – in other words, saving their skins. At the end of March 1938, the SD-Judenreferat II–112 drafted a 'proposal for the structure of the Jewish policy in Austria' in which the 'reorganization of the existing Jewish organizations', i.e., the elimination of all assimilationist tendencies in favour of Zionist ones, was discussed. In this letter, the future policy regarding the Jews in the German Reich was also formulated: 'removal from society . . . with a view to encouraging emigration'. On 29 March, the letter was sent to SS-Gruppenführer Reinhard Heydrich, head of the Security Police, and approved by him.[30] Eichmann ordered Alois Rothenberg, former nationalist member of the Jewish council and head of the Palestine Office, to reorganize the office and to elaborate a plan for an umbrella association for all Zionist organizations, together with the historian and Jewish community functionary Adolf Böhm.[31]

On 20 April 1938, in order to help the completely powerless Jewish community in Vienna, the Reich Agency of Jews in Germany (*Reichsvertretung der Juden in Deutschland*) drafted a plan 'for the organization of Jewish welfare work in Austria'. It proposed departments to deal with emigration to Palestine, emigration to other countries, political aspects of emigration, welfare and economic aid and the transfer of property and assets to Palestine and other countries.[32]

Leo Lauterbach travelled with Sir Wyndham Deedes, who was to negotiate with the Nazi authorities regarding Jewish emigration on behalf of the Council for German Jewry in Britain. In the conclusion of his report on the Vienna community to the Zionist leadership in London, Lauterbach appealed to the Zionist Executive to make contact with the organizations in Vienna and to send emissaries there. Efforts should be made to bring about the immediate reopening of the Palestine Office and to prepare and support the emigration of Austrian Jews to Palestine.[33] 'In Austria the circumstances under which emigration from Germany was still possible were regarded as fantastic,' claimed Charles J. Kapralik in his memoirs. In the Old Reich money, furniture, household goods, works of art and valuable objects could be taken from Germany. All of that was inconceivable in Austria.[34] Lauterbach came to the following conclusion in his report:

> There has been no public announcement of a clear policy with regard to the Jewish problem in Austria, nor have we been informed of one in the few interviews we have managed to obtain. The impression is inescapable, however, that this policy is significantly different from the one pursued in Germany and that its aim could be the complete extermination of Austrian Jewry.[35]

The dissolution of the IKG made it easier for Eichmann to select his Jewish subordinates. The chaos was to be put to productive use by the perpetrators. In the weeks of the administrative interregnum, the IKG leadership, which was merely to function as an implementing body for the Nazi authorities, crystallized. The Jewish community made every effort to reinstate the IKG, even if it was under the control of the Nazis, as the only means of organizing welfare and flight.

The attempt to escape or 'Get rid of the Yids and keep their money here!'[36]

From 12 March 1938, hundreds and thousands of Jews queued day and night before the international consulates in Vienna to obtain the papers needed to escape, in spite of the dangers lurking on the streets. Uniformed men attacked the defenceless Jews, chased and harassed them. The queues became confused and many, particularly the weak and sick, lost their place they had spent the night keeping.[37]

In his fragmentary novel *Mainacht in Wien*, Leo Perutz describes the situation at the time. The novelist managed to leave Vienna legally on 10 July 1938.

> At first the attempt to obtain permission from the police to leave the country offered about the same prospects for success as winning the jackpot in the lottery. [. . .] Later this chaos was replaced by a rigid system. Permission to emigrate was granted to those who were 'politically unobjectionable' and had obtained the authorization of the tax authorities.

The tax authorities were not a single office that granted or refused permission, but a complex structure consisting of different offices,

38

usually far apart from one another and each dealing with a different type of tax, of which there were many. Proof was needed that the sales tax and pension tax had been paid on time, that there was no outstanding inheritance tax, emergency tax or dog licence payments, that the rates, rent and overheads were paid up and that no other fees or levies had been overlooked.[38] As the emigrants were obliged to sell their possessions at giveaway prices, it was possible that they no longer had enough to pay the taxes and levies on their former assets.[39]

By 1 April 1938, no less than 6,000 visa applications had been submitted for Australia alone. Illegal emigration to other countries increased. Many Jews attempted to escape either with the aid of smugglers or on their own. The Nazi authorities did not want the Jews to leave before they had got hold of all their assets, however. The police authorities were ordered by SS-Reichsführer Werner Best, head of the German police, to prevent Jews from emigrating illegally.[40]

— 5 —

THE VIENNA JEWISH COMMUNITY
UNDER NAZI CONTROL

At all events, you can be sure that I have got them on the go. They are now working very hard. I have demanded from the Kultusgemeinde and the Zionist Association an emigration list of 20,000 Jews without means for the period 1 April 1938 to 1 May 1939, which they have promised to provide. [. . .] Tomorrow I will check up on the offices of the Kultusgemeinde and the Zionist Association. I do this at least once a week. I have got them completely under my control here. They do not dare to make a move without consulting with me first. This also makes it easier for me to keep control over them.

Adolf Eichmann on 8 May 1938
in a letter to Herbert Hagen,
his superior in Berlin[1]

The reorganization of the Kultusgemeinde

The Vienna Kultusgemeinde was to become the prototype for a Jewish administration under Nazi control and a precursor of the later Jewish councils.[2]

Eichmann ordered Josef Löwenherz, who had been arrested, to work out a concept to enable 20,000 Jews without means to emigrate from Austria that year. On 20 April 1938, he had him released from prison.[3]

The Jewish functionaries began to entertain hopes. On 22 April, Josef Löwenherz and Alois Rothenberg were summoned to appear before the Gestapo, together with some other functionaries. Rothenberg was given five days to elaborate a concept for a central Zionist association and to offer a list of potential committee members.[4] Unlike Rothenberg, Josef Löwenherz was not explicitly forbidden from including people who were being held in prison. Both Löwenherz and

Rothenberg were prohibited from including 'organized assimilationists',[5] i.e., members of the Union of Austrian Jews.[6] On 27 April, Löwenherz gave Eichmann a 30-page draft. Rothenberg presented a 40-page report. On 28 April, Eichmann told the Jewish representatives Rothenberg and Löwenherz that the Kultusgemeinde offices would reopen on 2 May. He rejected Löwenherz's recommendations, saying that individuals who were in prison were not acceptable.[7] A new list presented by Löwenherz also appears to have been refused and further modified.[8]

Löwenherz was put under pressure by Eichmann from the outset. At their first meeting, he had cuffed him.[9] Löwenherz had been the administrative director before. Eichmann first pressured Adolf Böhm to become president of the community and the Palestine Office, but Böhm, an industrialist and historian and recognized Zionist authority, was too old and sick to take on this responsibility. In April 1941, he died of a nervous disorder which had befallen him in 1938 after meeting Eichmann.[10]

As administrative director and lawyer, Löwenherz was familiar with bureaucratic and organizational procedures and also guaranteed institutional continuity. In 1936, he had given up the honorary position of vice-president of the IKG in favour of the paid position of administrative director. He was subsequently praised by other Jewish functionaries for his courage in confronting the Gestapo.[11] Eichmann could well have been irritated by the dignified appearance of the Viennese Jewish administrative director. He appeared at all events to enjoy humiliating Löwenherz, an academic twenty years his senior. For example, he offered the representative of the Jewish community in Graz a chair but made Löwenherz stand for hours.[12] The slap that he had given Löwenherz 'in a moment of uncontrolled temper', as he described it in the 1960s, troubled him for decades, and he expressed greater regret for it to the Israeli interrogating officer than the murders for which he shared responsibility. He testified that he had later apologized to Löwenherz 'in uniform and before my men'.[13] This admission in Jerusalem sounds as if Eichmann had enjoyed both scenes equally and there is no doubt that the apology was a further act of humiliation or at least an opportunity for further mockery, since Löwenherz, a victim whose life depended on Eichmann, was being forced to forgive the executioner for something that was unforgivable.

The Nazi authorities reopened the Kultusgemeinde office so that the Jewish administration could expedite the persecution and announce and communicate the countless discriminating laws to the

Jews. In a letter of 8 May 1938, Eichmann described the situation to Herbert Hagen, his superior in Berlin: 'All Jewish organizations in Austria have been ordered to submit weekly reports, which are to be handed to the relevant official in II-112.'[14]

The Kultusgemeinde was reorganized by Eichmann on the 'Führer principle'. It was no longer an elected body representing the community but the implementing instrument of the state authority. Löwenherz assumed all rights and obligations that had previously been exercised by various committees. He alone was answerable to the authorities for the institution. This made it easier for the Nazi authorities as only one person had responsibility for the fulfilment of all tasks. He could be held liable and subject to arrest for any insubordination. The committee was intended only to provide support for Löwenherz.[15] It had eight members, six of whom had belonged to the board of the Kultusgemeinde hitherto.[16]

After September 1938, only two members of this board remained in position: Leo Landau and Josef Löwenherz.[17] Many Jewish functionaries, including religious ones, had tried to leave the country as quickly as possible. The Jews of Vienna joked bitterly that they had 'gone ahead of their community'.[18] Even the rabbi Benjamin Murmelstein applied after April 1938 for a religious or academic position in various cities outside the German Reich but was unsuccessful.[19] Murmelstein, who was soon to hold a leading position in the community, later said that he had not left Vienna because he wanted to remain with the community and like a soldier did not want to desert his post.[20]

Many functionaries indeed insisted on remaining, although they had exit visas or the chance to leave, because they did not want to leave the community in the lurch. This fact should be stressed: the functionaries and honorary members of the Kultusgemeinde knew the dangers better than anyone and most of them also had the opportunity to leave. Some went abroad or to Palestine to negotiate with aid organizations and returned to Vienna because they felt responsibility for their community. The responsibilities of the Kultusgemeinde had become much greater. Those without means had to be taken care of and the children who were no longer allowed to attend school had to be looked after.

After the restoration of the IKG, an emigration department consisting of several sections was put under the control of the welfare centre. Separate emigration advice sections were established for doctors, lawyers, artists, engineers and businessmen. A section looked after correspondence and another was responsible for records. There was an emigration processing section and a liaison office with the Hias emigration organization. A management board coordinated all of these sections.[21] On the board, which was answerable directly to Josef Löwenherz, there was a need for managers with bureaucratic and organizational skills. As the months went by, they became increasingly important, as did those who worked as welfare assistants while the Jewish administrative apparatus had been closed.

An advice section was set up to deal with currency issues, together with the Palestine Office. The former bank manager Charles J. Kapralik was selected for this position. Kapralik had wanted to emigrate. He was already in the French consulate to collect a visa for himself and his wife when he was requested to head the finance section. He and his wife agreed although they both knew 'that dealing with currency issues meant putting one's head in the lion's jaw and that alleged breaches of currency regulations were the favourite pretext under the Nazi regime for putting people in prison.'[22]

Another section within the Kultusgemeinde trained emigrants for professions in demand in foreign countries.

A law was promulgated on 1 April 1938 by which Jewish communities in the Altreich lost their status as public corporations; they became associations. In Austria, however, although the IKG was completely restructured, it did not undergo any legal transformation and it was not renamed. This was due to differences in the law. In Austria, organizations did not have to be entered into a register of associations, which meant that they were not completely under state supervision. As an association under private law, the Kultusgemeinde also had to pay taxes. As the emigration and expulsion from the Ostmark, as Austria was now called, was financed by the international and Austrian Jewish organizations themselves, however, tax payments would merely have reduced the amount of money available for Jewish emigration. This was not in the interests of the Nazi authorities. In a letter to Gauleiter Josef Bürckel, Reich Commissioner for the Reunification of Austria with the German Reich, Eichmann said that the Jewish community received considerable foreign exchange from abroad that could be used to finance emigration. The denial of its rights as a corporation would cut off this source of funding.[23]

Apart from the Kultusgemeinde, there were two independent umbrella organizations devoted solely to emigration to Palestine: the Palestine Office and the Dachverband des Zionistischen Landesverbandes für Deutschösterreich (umbrella organization of the

43

Zionist Association for German Austria). The Zionist Association included the Makkabi sports club, Misrachi religious Zionist organization, the Zionist Youth Association, the Keren Hayessod and Keren Kayemeth Zionist national funds and the Wizo women's charity organization. In the place of Oskar Grünbaum, the former president of the Association who was now in prison, the young and inexperienced but committed Eduard Pachtmann was entrusted with its leadership.[24]

Alois Rothenberg was put in charge of the Palestine Office, which reopened on 3 May. Within the Palestine Office was also Hechalutz, the umbrella organization of the left-wing Zionist youth associations whose members aspired to be farming pioneers in kibbutzim. In addition, there was the Youth Aliyah, which also prepared young people for a pioneer's life in Palestine, and the anti-Zionist religious group Agudas Yisroel led by Julius Steinfeld, which helped orthodox Jews from Burgenland to emigrate to Palestine. The Association of Jewish War Victims, which was not part of the Kultusgemeinde, was also housed in the Palestine Office.

The Gestapo instructed Rothenberg that his function was merely to act as an intermediary between the authorities and the Zionist organizations. He was described in a report by the Zionist functionary Georg Landauer as 'a well-meaning, hardworking Zionist but weak and very sick, completely exhausted and sometimes even intimidated by his dealings with the Gestapo'.[25] The officials of the Zionist youth movements were more confident in their dealings with the Nazis, not least because they were not as directly exposed as Rothenberg.

All cooperation between the Berlin and Vienna Jewish communities was forbidden.[26] Heinrich Stahl, chairman of the Jewish Community of Berlin, visited Vienna in the second half of May. After his arrival at the IKG offices, however, Eichmann appeared with Otto Kuchmann, Gestapo senior secretary. Eichmann ordered Stahl to leave immediately and allowed Löwenherz only written contact with the Jewish communities in Germany, which was to be restricted to essential matters. He told Löwenherz that if he needed advice, he should consult Eichmann and that he should not forget that emigration was the most important thing for all Jews.[27] The Austrian Jews should not go by the experiences of German Jews. The Nazi authorities sought a more brutal Jewish policy in Vienna as a means of expediting emigration. Moreover, the Sonderkommando in the SD Jewish Department did not want to see its supremacy in Vienna undermined by Berlin.

The reopening of the Kultusgemeinde offices did not bring about any decrease in the persecution. On the contrary, Georg Landauer wrote a letter from Trieste on 7 May 1938 in which he described what he had seen and experienced in Vienna a few days previously: 'If the current policy by the German government towards Austrian Jews is an indication of its final intentions, this large and valuable community is likely to be destroyed in a very short time, i.e. the aim announced by General Göring to clear all the Jews out of Vienna within four years would be achieved in a few months.'[28]

The situation in Austria also aggravated the conditions in the Altreich. Between 25 and 27 May 1938, some 2,000 people were arrested in Austria by order of the Gestapo and taken in four transports to Dachau. Altogether, 5,000 Jews were deported to Dachau between 2 May and 20 June 1938.[29] In July, Martin Rosenblüth sent this confidential message to Jerusalem: 'Twelve Jewish urns have come in the last two weeks from the labour camps – one near Weimar – set up by the German government specially for Jews. The inmates are treated like slaves with whippings and half rations for the Jews.'[30]

The IKG Vienna was required to keep quiet about these incidents. Furthermore, so as not to jeopardize the welfare and emigration of the victims, they were obliged to publicly defend the Nazi policy. While the Nazis were 'preparing the end' for the Viennese Jewry, Josef Löwenherz was forced by the SS to sign the following text on behalf of the IKG to be sent to the World Jewish Congress:

> The Vienna Jewish Community authorities point out that the statement by the Geneva office of the World Jewish Congress about the treatment of Jews in Austria is incorrect. The Jewish organizations have not all been disbanded and have merely had a temporary ban on their activities as a result of the changed political circumstances.
>
> There are no plans in future either to disband all Jewish organizations.

The authorities were 'merely at pains to put an end to the organizational fragmentation without reason of the Jewry so as to help the organizations to work systematically on a Zionist basis that can only be of benefit to the Jews in Austria. We are of the opinion that we should accept a situation that has evolved naturally.'[31]

Jewish self-help and welfare

The closure of all Jewish associations on 18 March 1938 also meant that all welfare organizations ceased to exist. Unlike the Kultusgemeinde offices, most of them were not reopened. The new regime decreed that welfare should also be organized centrally by the Kultusgemeinde. On 19 July 1938, Eichmann informed the Kultusgemeinde that the library and archive were to be moved officially to Berlin.

While the Nazi government provided RM 600,000–700,000 for Jewish welfare in the Altreich, the Jewish organizations in Austria had to cover their expenses themselves, even though they had also been preyed upon by the state and by private individuals from the very beginning. On 31 May 1938, Löwenherz attempted to negotiate with liquidation commissar Anton Brunner, who was responsible for the disbanding of prohibited associations in Austria. He tried to persuade the Nazi official to unblock the confiscated accounts of the suspended Jewish associations and foundations so that they could be used by Jewish bodies. Brunner allowed a limited amount of funds to be used for emigration. He decreed that RM 15 to 20 would be allowed per person. The funds of welfare organizations could be used to finance free meals.

On 17 August 1938, Löwenherz and Rothenberg visited Eichmann to report on the eviction of Jews from their homes. They also told of the difficulties in finding hospital beds and places in nursing homes for the old and sick. They requested that Jewish doctors be allowed to work.[32]

After the Kultusgemeinde had reopened, it received numerous donations, but the average amount was just RM 10. Whereas RM 906,000 had been donated by members of the community in the first three months of the year, in the last nine months only RM 594,000 was received.[33] Even those welfare organizations that had not been banned therefore had difficulty in operating. While revenues dwindled, the work of the Jewish institutions grew enormously.

Franzi Löw worked in the Kultusgemeinde juvenile welfare department. She took over the legal guardianship of around 200 illegitimate Jewish children after the Vienna municipal authorities had renounced it. Löw also became the legal guardian of around twenty mentally handicapped juveniles living in a non-Jewish institute. The Jewish administration had a home for infants as well, but the welfare authorities did not receive any milk for the babies. Two bakers in the 18th district declared their willingness to provide Löw illegally with two 10-litre bottles of milk and 20 kg of bread per day. She had to travel every day at 5 a.m. to the 18th district and then carry the milk and bread to the 2nd district before starting work. In doing so, she risked her life. The Gestapo could not be allowed to find out where she had obtained it.[34]

Löw also provided food and linen to Jewish prisoners who had been arrested after the Anschluss. Later, she sent packages to those who had been deported to concentration camps.[35]

By the end of 1938, between 16,000 and 18,000 people were being fed in free kitchens every day.[36] In December 1939, 50,000 of the 55,000 Jews remaining in Vienna were reliant on free meals and support. Whereas these welfare services were almost impossible to finance, several health insurance companies refused to deal directly with the Jewish hospital.[37] Non-Jewish hospitals refused to admit Jewish patients. The Jewish Rothschild Hospital was overcrowded. Doctors and staff of the hospital fled abroad. Several members of staff committed suicide. Most Jews who wanted to go abroad had to have a medical examination in order to obtain permission to emigrate. They also visited the hospital, which was completely overrun and overburdened.[38]

On 17 March 1939, only 3.8 per cent of the Jewish population was still employed.[39] In order for the emigrants to find work in the destination countries, the Kultusgemeinde had to organize professional retraining for the members of the community. The right profession became a matter of life and death. Some 20,000 people had attended training seminars by the end of 1939.[40]

One area of vocational training focused specifically on young people. In mid May 1938, Jewish children were prohibited from attending public education institutions. They were grouped together in schools in which the percentage of Jewish pupils had already been high before the Nazis came to power.[41] In crowded classes, frequently with 70–80 children or juveniles in a single room, the pupils were taught by teachers who often regarded their new position as a drop in standing.[42] The Kultusgemeinde wanted to ensure that only Jewish teachers taught in Jewish schools so as to find work again for the unemployed teachers and also to protect the children from anti-Semitic teachers.[43] In all schools and courses, juveniles were instructed for Aliyah, emigration to Palestine.

Meanwhile, the situation of those who remained in Vienna went from bad to worse. In general, it was easier for men to escape from the Third Reich because they had less difficulty finding work abroad. They frequently believed that they would be in a better position from abroad to finance the subsequent emigration of their families. In most cases they were unsuccessful. Many women remained behind without their husbands and had to look after the children and grandparents alone.

The Kultusgemeinde was required to help all those who could not manage on their own. Rosa Schwarz, head of the juvenile welfare service, recalls that 'a fourteen-year-old girl came to me requesting accommodation in a home for her sister and herself. "We don't need it for long. We only want to go to the burial and sit shiva [ritual mourning; D.R.] for our father when the urn comes." '[44] The girl had intercepted a telegram addressed to her mother, who suffered from a nervous disease, and hidden it from her. The father was one of those deported to a concentration camp following the November pogrom in 1938.

'Emigration' – mass expulsion

All efforts focused on escaping abroad. The first urns were arriving from Dachau; unannounced house searches and groundless arrests caused panic within the Jewish community. The IKG was responsible, together with the Palestine Office and the Zionist associations, for organizing the departure of Jews. Löwenherz and Rothenberg had been required to promise Eichmann that emigration would be arranged for 20,000 Jews without means between 1 May 1938 and 1 May 1939. The term 'emigration' hid the fact, however, that the Jews did not leave the Third Reich voluntarily. On the other hand, the words 'expulsion' and 'escape' also hid the fact that victims did not necessarily seek refuge in Palestine against their will.

The Palestine Office maintained contact from 1938 onwards with Yishuv, the Jewish population of Palestine, and distributed certificates and immigration visas. Hechalutz, the umbrella organization of all Zionist pioneer organizations focusing on 'halutz', the colonization of Palestine, within the Palestine Office, was responsible for the 12,000 members of the Zionist youth organizations. Apart from Hechalutz, the Youth Aliyah, which prepared young people for agricultural work and life in the kibbutzim, was also located in the Palestine Office. In spite of the efforts of the Jewish organizations, the possibilities of escaping were meagre. Immigration to Palestine was limited and was offered above all to young people. There was some argument, however, as to how the certificates should be distributed. Each group attempted to have its ideological supporters included in the Zionist undertakings as the 'true' pioneers who would build up the country.

Sharp words were exchanged between the Palestine Office and Hechalutz. Rothenberg, as head of the Palestine Office, spoke for the interests of more established and bourgeois representatives of the Zionist movement, the old-timers, known in Hebrew as 'vatikim', whereas Willi Ritter from Hechalutz represented the youth movements. Rothenberg was forced to pass on the orders from the SS. The functionaries of the youth movements had more freedom, however, as unlike Rothenberg they were not directly answerable to the Gestapo. They were also supported by Zionist emissaries, or *shlichim*, who advised them and established contacts with the head office in Palestine.

The British kept Jewish immigration to a minimum. As very few people were allowed to go to Palestine, the Zionist organizations had to select those who would be most useful to the Jewish settlements there. All of the Zionist groups in Vienna were in agreement, however, that it was important for as many Jews as possible to escape from Nazi Vienna. The Palestine Office had to follow the instructions of the Jewish Agency, which was caught between the Nazi expulsion policy and the British quota system. It passed on this pressure to the emigrants. The suitability and health of young people had to be vetted before they were allowed to travel to Germany to train for agricultural work. The Palestine Office in Vienna protested when a child was prevented from emigrating because he was underweight. In Vienna the decision must have seemed like a mockery. In the prevailing circumstances, there was no possibility of putting on weight; the boy would never be able to get to Palestine. Dr Noack, senior physician of the Youth Aliyah in Jerusalem, wrote:

> The children themselves will be the ones to suffer from a charitable or 'soft-hearted' selection that does not meet the minimum requirements. It is not true that our selection to date has been strict. . . . While fully appreciating the precarious situation of the Jewish children in Vienna . . . it is not advisable to 'rescue' needy children by sending them to an environment for which they are not suited.[45]

Eichmann was not interested in the difficult conditions in Palestine. He knew merely that older Zionists were willing to pay more money to get away. He saw this as a way of financing the expulsion of hundreds more Jews. Why should he prefer Jews without means if he could expel older and richer emigrants whose assets would remain in the Third Reich?

Ten certificates per month could be issued for emigration to Palestine to 'capitalists'. A 'capitalist' had to have at least 1,000 pounds. The Nazi authorities allowed emigrants to take 1,000 pounds with them to Palestine but not to any other country. The selection of ten persons or families allowed to emigrate under these conditions was made by the Palestine Office and the Jewish Agency in Jerusalem.[46] These certificates were sold for many times their face value. Many Jews complained about this procedure. They accused the Kultusgemeinde, although it was the Palestine Office that was responsible for choosing ten families from among the applicants.

Most emigrants wanted to go to the USA and ever-lengthening queues formed in front of the consulates of the USA, Australia, Great Britain and the countries of South America.[47] Within three weeks after the reopening of the IKG, some 40,000 people had registered for emigration.[48] In June 1938, Löwenherz and Rothenberg were given permission to travel to London to negotiate with the international Jewish organizations. 'Make sure that you get money,' Eichmann told them.[49]

The American Joint Distribution Committee and the Central British Fund were willing to provide 50,000 dollars a month for emigration on the condition, however, that the foreign exchange did not end up in the Reichsbank but was made available solely to the Kultusgemeinde. Eichmann was satisfied with this arrangement and, in spite of the difficult foreign exchange situation experienced by the Third Reich, the Reichsbank and state exchange control office gave their approval. The currency was transferred to a special account at the Länderbank, to which the Kultusgemeinde had access only with the agreement of the emigration section at the exchange control office in Vienna. Moreover, a foreign exchange section was to be established in the Kultusgemeinde offices.[50] The Kultusgemeinde was permitted to sell the Joint funds for Reichmarks and determine the exchange rate. Wealthier Jews had to pay double or treble the rate for foreign exchange while the less wealthy could purchase them at the official rate. Those without means were given foreign currency and tickets free of charge. In this way, wealthier Jews financed the departure of the less wealthy.

The Jewish organizations had to pay for the departure while complying with the conditions set by the Nazi authorities. The emigrants were effectively stripped of their assets before they could leave the country. The emigrants had to endure time-consuming and difficult administrative procedures. Just in order to obtain tax clearance (Steuerunbedenklichkeitsbestätigung), they needed documents from four different offices that were only open at certain times and were always overcrowded. As emigrants had to pay a Reichsfluchtsteuer, the tax for escaping the Reich, of up to 30 per cent of their assets, a

Sühneabgabe (atonement tax) of up to 20 per cent and a contribution to the 'emigration fund' of 5 per cent, it often happened that they were unable to pay the levies because they had already been forced to sell their assets at giveaway prices although they were assessed for tax purposes in accordance with their real value.[51]

As the deadline for leaving approached, precious time was lost going from one office to another, and most of the officials also demanded bribe money. Victims frequently came to grief as they ran this gauntlet of humiliation. As the tax clearance was only valid for three months, the document had often expired before the emigrant had obtained the desired visa.[52]

Some Nazi lawyers, like Erich Rajakowitsch, who later coordinated the mass deportations from the Netherlands to the death camps, specialized in dealing with these chicaneries, profiting from the suffering of the Jews by charging a fee from those who could still afford it. Less wealthy Jews had no way out of this bureaucratic jungle; the SS pulled them out of the queues in front of the offices and they were unable to obtain emigration papers. The Nazis had to decide whether they wanted to torment the Jews or get rid of them. There were some, so it would appear, who could not resist terrorizing the objects of their hate. Others, notably the members of the Vienna Sonderkommando of SD Department II-112 under Adolf Eichmann, worked towards the rapid and ruthless expulsion and emigration. This tendency prevailed.[53]

In contrast to the Altreich, where SD Department II-112 merely advised the Gestapo on its Jewish policy, it took the initiative in Vienna. Eichmann exceeded the authority previously granted to him and was able to oust the Gestapo.[54] In the 1960s, he told the interrogating officer in Jerusalem that Löwenherz had appeared before him one day and said: 'Hauptsturmführer – or was I an Obersturmführer at the time? – this can't go on. And they suggested that I should somehow centralize the work.'[55]

In truth, it is highly unlikely that Löwenherz would have spoken to Eichmann in such a forthright manner. No doubt the Jewish functionaries were interested in simplifying the emigration process, but the initiative for a reorganization of 'Jewish emigration' will have come from the SD Sonderkommando under Adolf Eichmann. The idea of setting up a Central Office for Jewish Emigration had already been voiced in the SD in 1937 but had been abandoned thereafter as Department II–112 did not have the power base that it was to establish in Vienna, where it would have the possibility of controlling the Kultusgemeinde precisely through the setting up of a Central Office.

Moreover, this office enabled Eichmann to develop a personal power base. He was aware of the financing system behind the Gildemeester aid, which used some of the assets appropriated from rich emigrants to enable Jews without means to flee. He wanted to establish a central office that operated on the same principle.[56] Löwenherz was ordered by Eichmann to make a proposal for the establishment of such a central office. In his 'proposal for an action programme by a future Central Office for the Emigration of the Jews of Austria', Löwenherz envisaged an office that would provide advice and make arrangements for emigration.[57] He could not have imagined the consequences of his idea and could not have known that they would have precisely the opposite results to those he had envisaged.

The establishment of the Central Office for Jewish Emigration headed nominally by SS-Standartenführer Franz Stahlecker, but de facto by Adolf Eichmann himself, made it possible to step up the terrorization of the Jews. The Central Office became the main instrument of control over the Kultusgemeinde alongside the Gestapo and the coordinator of the Nazi Jewish policy in Austria. It was able to force Jews to leave and to blackmail them into leaving all of their assets in order to save their lives. They were obliged to give up everything they owned in order to escape, in order to allow themselves to be expelled. This model was later used in Berlin and Prague and then copied in other countries.

The Central Office operated on a conveyor belt system; people were systematically processed. They left the office divested of their property but with an emigration visa and a fixed date for leaving the country. If they did not leave the Third Reich within ten days, they were likely to be arrested and deported to a concentration camp.

The Kultusgemeinde had also been obliged to arrange for payment of a Jewish levy since November 1938 and to provide asset lists with estimates of objects of value for which a 100 per cent additional tax was payable. The capital had to be deposited in a bank with power of procuration. Certificates had to be obtained from the customs authorities and the police showing that all taxes had been paid. The dog licence had to be paid three months in advance and was payable even if the emigrant did not have a dog.

SS men paraded in front of the Central Office with whips and often laid in viciously to the people waiting there. Inside the Central Office, applicants went from one counter to another, paying what was demanded by the various departments and bodies until they had nothing left.[58]

Within the party, Nazi lawyers who had previously profited from the general chaos agitated against the Central Office but they were unable to prevail. The terror and the success of the expulsion were so great that Nazi officials in the Ostmark were able to boast at a conference on 12 November 1938 that they had expelled 50,000 Jews. At the time 'only' 19,000 had left the Altreich.[59]

At an international conference convened in Evian in July 1938 to discuss the refugee issue, most governments refused to help the persecuted Jews. Australia even announced that it had no 'racist problems' and was not interested in importing them.[60] Evian was a declaration of bankruptcy by the western world that did little apart from adopting a few resolutions and establishing an Intergovernmental Committee on Political Refugees.[61]

Illegal escape

The Kultusgemeinde organized legal emigration. It feared that illegal escape would discredit the entire 'emigration' and that other countries would impose even stricter limits on legal immigration. However, appeals and threats did nothing to stop illegal escape but at most made it necessary to find different routes. In their desperation, the victims had no other choice.

Uncontrolled illegal migration was only one way of attempting to get away without a visa. Of particular interest in this regard was the organized illegal migration to Palestine. The British, who had promised in the 1917 Balfour Declaration to set up a Jewish homeland in Palestine, imposed a strict quota system so as to restrict Jewish immigration. On the day of the Anschluss, when the pogroms erupted in Vienna, only sixteen certificates for Palestine were available to the entire Jewish community of Austria.[62] Active young Zionists, both left- and right-wing, had been organizing illegal immigration to Palestine since 1934. The extreme nationalist and revisionist Zionist wing had been particularly aggressive in this regard.

The certificates for Aliyah, immigration to Palestine, had to be distributed among the various youth movements. The proportion of certificates that an organization received depended on its participation in Hachshara and the number of activists receiving instruction in Hachshara camps. As the revisionist youth association Betar hardly sent any young persons for agricultural training in Hachshara, it received only a very small percentage of immigration documents.[63]

All attempts by the Palestine Office in Vienna to reach a compromise between the executive in Jerusalem and the Austrian revisionists failed.[64]

The problem had already existed before the Anschluss but it now became worse because, in contrast to Berlin where the Gestapo favoured the revisionist leader Georg Kareski, Eichmann prohibited the Vienna Betar as a group from joining the Hechalutz. In this situation representatives of the Zionist right and their supporters, such as Willy Perl, Hermann Flesch and Paul Haller, organized their own transports to Palestine. To do so, they had to illegally bypass the immigration restrictions imposed by the British Mandate. The project was given the Hebrew name 'Af-Al-Pi', meaning 'despite all'.

The IKG, Jewish aid organizations and even the majority of the Zionist leadership in Jerusalem disapproved of illegal migration at the time as it feared that it would jeopardize legal migration. The IKG published warnings against Af-Al-Pi. The Jewish organizations suspected that the British government would simply deduct the illegal immigrants from the official quota. Erich Rajakowitsch and Rudolf Lange, head of Department II b of the Vienna Gestapo, supported illegal migration in Vienna. The revisionist activists also managed to obtain unofficial aid from the Kultusgemeinde.[65]

After 1938, parts of the Zionist workers' movement started organizing illegal transports. Haganah, the Jewish underground army in Palestine, and Hisadrut, the Jewish trade union organization, founded Mossad le-Aliyah Bet (Institution for Immigration B). The Mossad emissary Moshe Averbuch-Agami and leaders of the local youth groups, like Ehud Avriel-Überall and Teddy Kollek, were among the main organizers in Vienna. For all of the transports, Mossad and the revisionists required the support of the Gestapo and the Central Office. Without the Gestapo, the illegal emigrants could not have changed their money into foreign currency so as to pay for the ships, nor would they have been able to obtain emigration papers or transit visas.[66]

On 9 June 1938, the first revisionist transport left Nazi Vienna. The juveniles assembled an hour before departure at the Südbahnhof. They had just taken leave of their families and knew that they would probably never see their parents again. Uniformed and civilian officials observed the assembly. They removed the film from a camera that a journalist had with him as they did not wish the media to report on this unusual form of cooperation. Rudolf Lange, Adolf Eichmann and Erich Rajakowitsch were at the station. In the heart of Nazi Vienna and before the eyes of the Gestapo and the SS, Willy

Perl mustered the Jewish youths and gave orders in Hebrew. Then he gave an official speech. He recalls:

> For a moment there was total silence after my speech.
> Then a thin sound was heard. A girl started singing *Hatikvah* ("The Hope"), the Jewish national anthem. In seconds the sound swelled into a truculent, then triumphant loud chorus. As they stood, now at attention, they raised their blue-and-white pennants and sang of the never-ending hope of rebuilding Jerusalem and the Jewish state. I could not keep quiet. Flanked by three Nazis, come what may, I joined in.[67]

The Zionist endeavours not only assured survival but also helped restore the victims' spirits and liberated them from the ignominy of persecution. They wanted to leave Europe not in humiliation but with pride, as pioneers of a Jewish state.

The illegal immigration had proved successful but, under diplomatic pressure from the British government, the transit countries Italy, Yugoslavia and Greece changed their policy. They refused to issue visas to the Zionist refugees if they did not have a valid immigration visa for Palestine. The British threatened ship-owners that they would seize their ships and prosecute their crews if they carried illegal immigrants. The United Kingdom also violated international maritime law and intercepted ships in international waters. Escape through Italy appeared to be impossible. In spite of all political obstacles, the transports were able to continue after autumn 1938 on the Danube, which was regarded as an international waterway, and the ships were able to reach Palestine via Romanian and Bulgarian ports. An illegal escape route had been found. When war broke out in September 1939, the possibilities for organizing illegal transports of this sort dwindled. The cost of passage rocketed. The Zionist organizers were at the mercy of the ship-owners. In 1939, the SS appointed Berthold Storfer, a Viennese Jew and not a Zionist, as head of the Committee for Jewish Overseas Transports. He was therefore regarded by Zionist activists as an informer and Gestapo stooge.

The SS wanted to expel as many Jews as possible, be they young or old, healthy or infirm, without having to deal with Zionist ideology. They did not care whether the transports reached Palestine or not. In March 1940, Storfer became coordinator for Palestine transports from all parts of the Reich, including the Altreich and the Protectorate of Bohemia and Moravia. Thanks to his intervention, 2,042 people left Austria and he helped 7,054 people to escape from the rest of the Reich territory, including 1,740 people from Austria.[68]

The Zionist organizations were forced to cooperate with the Nazis in order to rescue the victims of persecution. They were powerless, trapped between the Nazi persecution, the cynical imperial policy of the United Kingdom and the indifference of neutral countries. There was certainly never any question of negotiations between equal partners.

— 6 —

NOVEMBER POGROM – OVERTURE TO MURDER

The pogrom in November 1938 appalled the Jews in the German Reich not merely because the barbarity exceeded anything that had happened previously but also because the orgy of blood gave a premonition of worse things to come. The hope that the witch-hunt against the Jews would run out of steam disappeared.

Weeks before the pogrom, the anti-Jewish policy had reached a turning point. The persecution of the Viennese Jews had given rise to an unprecedented exodus, prompting the international community to close its borders. Whereas the November pogrom marked a decisive turning point for the Jews in the Altreich, i.e., Germany, it differed in Austria not so much in terms of the nature as in the extent of the brutality that had preceded it. In most cities of the Third Reich, the synagogues burned in November for the first time. In Vienna, however, the windows of synagogues had already been smashed, Torah scrolls desecrated, prayer rooms destroyed and the Grosser Tempel in the 2nd district torched a month earlier in October.[1] On Yom Kippur, the highest Jewish Holy Day, hundreds of Jews had the keys to their homes confiscated. They were locked out for a whole night and were instructed to go to the Ostbahn, from where they were to be deported. It was not until the following afternoon that these families were given back their keys.[2]

In brief, it might be said that if Austria was annexed to the German Reich in March 1938, the November pogrom marked the assimilation of the Altreich to the Jewish policy in the Ostmark. The earlier excesses could well explain why the November pogrom was more brutal in Vienna than in many other cities: all inhibitions had already been overcome. The pretext for the killing, looting and arson was an act of desperation by Herschel Grynszpan, a stateless erstwhile Polish

Jew, who assassinated the German diplomat Ernst vom Rath in Paris on 7 November.

In the evening of 7 November, the IKG received a letter from the Reich Agency of the Jews in Germany in Berlin, instructing it to condemn the act and to exclude the perpetrator from the Jewish community. The Jewish representatives feared the vengeance of the Nazis. The board of the Vienna community met and condemned Grynszpan's action. 'A delegation consisting of Mr Engel and OLGR Orenstein was dispatched to Eichmann with this memorandum. When they entered the room, Eichmann shouted at them: "Three steps back!" '[3]

The condemnation of the act by the Jewish community was of no avail. The assassination gave the Nazi Party leadership a welcome pretext for the pogrom. The 'Night of Broken Glass', the name coined by the people of Berlin for the November pogrom and soon appropriated by the Nazis, recalled the shards of glass on the street. It was a euphemism for the eerily fascinating blood, burning and violence.

The pogrom was ordered by the Party and carried out by SA units, SS troops and Hitler Youth groups. Individual members of the public also joined in unofficially. Forty-two synagogues and prayer houses in Vienna were put to the torch, but the pogrom was not limited to places of worship: 1,950 apartments in the 1st, 2nd and 4th districts were cleared of Jews and members of the Jewish community were beaten up and arrested. The offices of the Kultusgemeinde were also ransacked. Several hundred officials were arrested. The food kitchens were demolished, the food mixed with glass and the soup poured away.[4]

The arrest and mistreatment of large numbers of women was something new. In Brigittenau, 200 women were forced to dance naked in a basement. A Jewish woman who refused was tied to a table and her fellow-victims were made to spit in her face.[5]

Twenty-seven persons were beaten to death in Vienna alone. A total of 6,547 Jews were arrested and 3,700 of them deported to Dachau. One of the deportees claimed that after his experiences of detention in Vienna, the deportation to Dachau concentration camp was 'almost like a holiday'.[6]

After the pogrom, SS guards were posted in front of the Kultusgemeinde offices and the entrance controlled. The Kultusgemeinde was required to pay for the guards.[7] Löwenherz managed to persuade Eichmann on 2 February 1939 to forbid the SS guards from entering the offices and interfering with the work of the officials but violations were common. It was not until 3 April 1939 that Löwenherz managed to have the SS guards withdrawn.[8]

The November pogrom marked a turning point for Jewish confidence. All hope of normalization had finally been destroyed. In the first few months, the Jews of Vienna had hoped that the anti-Jewish excesses would come to an end and that they could live in the same way as the Jews in Germany. The November pogrom made it clear that the anti-Semitic witch-hunt in Austria was not just a localized temporary episode in the aftermath to the Anschluss. On the contrary, the anti-Semitic policy of the Nazi leadership appeared no longer to care what the international community thought.

Whereas most of the emigrants to date had been people who could hope to find work in other countries, everyone, including old people, now sought a way out of the death trap. Major transports were organized for children. Parents did not know how their children would fare in other countries nor if they would ever see them again.

The non-Jewish population showed an ambivalent attitude to the events and even disowned them. Particularly in the Altreich and to a lesser extent in Austria, the non-Jews simply felt annoyed. Many feared for the property that was destroyed by such actions.

The Nazis embarked on a new tactic. At a conference on 12 November 1938 to discuss the Jewish question, they opted for a systematic technocratic solution. At the meeting, Göring raged at the excesses because 'people's property' had been destroyed. 'I would have preferred it if you had beaten up 200 Jews and not destroyed all this property.'[9,10]

The Jews were held liable for the damage caused during the pogrom, even though the confiscation of the insurance pay-outs made certain that they were the injured parties. They were also ordered to pay in retribution a 'contribution' of RM 1 billion. In the end, they were in fact obliged to pay 1.12 billion.

Shortly after the November pogrom, the Jews were forbidden from participating in any cultural events. On 28 December, Göring abolished rent control for Jews, paving the way for the Aryanization of home ownership. The law on rental agreements with Jews of 30 April 1939 meant that most Jews were evicted from their homes. They were herded together in 'Jewish houses' and 'Jewish districts'. Freedom of movement was also curtailed. The Jews had to give up their driving licences. The prohibition was extended to trams, buses and public telephones.[11]

By the time war broke out, 250 discriminatory and oppressive laws had been passed.[12] Most of those who were not able to escape in the months following the November pogrom were robbed of their assets and killed in concentration camps.

— 7 —

THE JEWISH COMMUNITY AFTER THE POGROM

Escape as a last resort

After the November pogrom, the possibilities of escaping from the Third Reich became even more slender. First, all countries had closed their borders in the face of the large wave of refugees; in addition, arrests, evictions and confiscations made the situation for the Jews so desperate that the idea of an organized mass emigration was no longer conceivable. Many men who already had visas and emigration papers for themselves and their families were now arrested and deported to Dachau or Buchenwald. The emigration department of the Kultusgemeinde was overrun, but the institution now had its hands full with those who had been arrested or evicted.

Eichmann knew that he could put pressure on the Jewish organizations and their officials by using those who had been arrested during the November pogrom and deported to concentration camps. He approved the release of inmates only if they had emigration papers and could leave immediately.[1] The Kultusgemeinde attempted to intervene with the Gestapo on behalf of the inmates and to obtain emigration papers for them.[2] The state authorities were caught in a dilemma: whether to take even more money from those trying to get away or to continue to expel them from the country. The greater the distress of the Jewish population, the greedier the authorities became.

The victims were continuously exposed to new forms of harassment, and their official representatives were also powerless to help them. For example, Josef Löwenherz informed Eichmann that people applying for passports were being given backdated tax clearance certificates valid from the date on which the passport was issued. This meant that the dates on their papers were weeks old, giving them much less than the six or eight weeks that had originally been allowed to arrange the move, ship their goods and depart.[3]

Löwenherz was criticized by foreign Jewish organizations in March 1939, who said that more people were being expelled from Austria than from Germany. He pointed out that only a few days previously, on 16 March, Eichmann had complained that the number of emigration applications had declined and that if the numbers did not rise within the following forty-eight hours he would instigate measures similar to those in November 1938. In other words, Eichmann was openly threatening another pogrom.[4]

From the first half of 1939, hundreds of Jews were systematically assigned to perform forced labour in Austria and the Altreich. The Hachshara camps were also successively turned into labour details. In Vienna, Jews were forced to carry out clearing-up work with no pay, just a midday meal. These measures were part of the general disenfranchisement of the Jews. They were paid lowly wages for even the most arduous of tasks. From July 1940, the forced labourers were no longer allowed to obtain free meals or welfare benefits.[5] Those who were in labour camps were no longer automatically released to enable them to emigrate.

The Jewish organizations endeavoured above all to help concentration camp inmates. On 5 December 1938, the Kultusgemeinde requested the release of 1,319 inmates to enable them to emigrate. In the same month, Löwenherz managed to persuade Eichmann to arrange for inmates with immigration visas for other countries to be released from concentration camps. On several occasions, he attempted to obtain the release of Desider Friedmann and Robert Stricker, the former president and vice-president of the Kultusgemeinde, who had been held in a concentration camp since early 1938. Friedmann was 59 years old with a serious heart condition and diabetes. The 60-year-old Stricker had severe pulmonary emphysema. The requests addressed to Eichmann and the Gestapo were finally answered in February 1939. Löwenherz and Rothenberg had to sign a statement in which they took personal responsibility for ensuring that the two inmates would not leave the territory of the German Reich without permission from the authorities. Stricker and Friedmann were also forbidden from working in the Kultusgemeinde management. The two Jewish politicians were not ultimately released until June 1939.[6] They were not allowed to emigrate and were to end up being deported and killed.

Eichmann could now force the Jewish and Zionist organizations to include the inmates in illegal transports to Palestine. Since 1939, all Zionist factions had been taking part in these visa-less enterprises. The Palestinian-Jewish leadership of the movement had also changed its mind. The Joint and the Kultusgemeinde continued offi-cially to disapprove of the illegal transports in 1939, but in secret they supported some of them.[7] In March 1939, Löwenherz sent Eichmann as ordered a list of transports leaving Vienna. It included the illegal transports that had arrived in Palestine. Officially a differ-ent destination was given so as to enable the required transit visas to be obtained.

The situation of Jewish children had also deteriorated. Many juve-niles whose parents had been deported to concentration camps and had then been forced to flee were left alone. Some parents had aban-doned the hope of being able to escape with their children and had to leave them with relatives and grandparents.[8]

The Youth Aliyah was one recourse available to children. Its school provided a general education as well as commercial and craft courses, and it also organized excursions to the countryside. This helped to cheer up the children and juveniles, and at the same time youth leaders reinforced their Jewish identity.[9] With the aid of the Youth Aliyah, 1,402 youths left Vienna in 1939. Not all of them got to Palestine: 335 ended up in Zionist training camps in England, Sweden and Denmark.[10]

Even before the November pogrom, the Jewish welfare authorities had a list of children whose parents wanted them to leave the country. After the November pogrom, however, parents who had previously hesitated to send their children abroad were now approaching the authorities, fully aware that they would probably never see their sons and daughters again. They had realized that it was no longer possible to remain in the German Reich. Rosa Rachel Schwarz, head of the juvenile welfare department, described the first children's transport of 10 December 1938, which took 700 children to England:

A lot of these children had lived in the Jewish centres near the temple and had witnessed the terrifying images of destruction with their own eyes. Many were only able to take leave of their mothers, because their fathers were in the concentration camp. It was a terrible scene, these 700 mothers saying goodbye to their children at the railway terminus in Hütteldorf. They were, of course, not allowed to enter the station. The children were joyful and full of hope. They were heading for a better life in the belief that they would be able to do something for their parents. Only in isolated instances were they to succeed.[11]

The Kultusgemeinde attempted to select those children whose emi-gration appeared to be most important for health, psychological or financial reasons. The children were tested and medically examined before passports were obtained for them.[12] Welfare officer Franzi Löw interviewed the candidates for the children's transports; the interview was based on a questionnaire provided by the foreign organizations, and it was the foreign recipient organizations that selected the children on the basis of the Kultusgemeinde reports.

The children were received by the Movement for the Care of Children from Germany and they were soon to be known as 'Movement children'. According to the Kultusgemeinde reports, 3,188 children managed to leave the country between 10 December 1938 and the end of 1939; according to Rosa Schwarz's record, 2,844 children left Austria before the outbreak of war.[13] Many more could have been rescued in this way, but it was too late: war broke out on 1 September 1939.

The IKG issued a report on the first sixteen months of Nazi rule. The brochure *Auswanderung – Umschichtung – Fürsorge* (Emigration – Regrouping – Welfare) appeared with a French and an English section. It was intended for Jewish and non-Jewish aid organizations abroad.[14]

In the brochure, the number of Jews in Austria at the time of the Anschluss was put at 180,000 – 165,000 in Vienna and 15,000 in the rest of Austria. By December 1938, the number of Jews, all of them now concentrated in Vienna, had been reduced to 118,000. By the end of July 1939, only 72,000 Jews remained in Vienna. Of the 104,000 Jews who had emigrated by the end of July, 41,500 had only been able to leave the country with the assistance of the IKG. The Jewish authorities had paid the travel costs if necessary. Altogether 62,500 people received support from the Kultusgemeinde, which financed the departure of Jews without means from donations by international Jewish organizations.

When war broke out with the German invasion of Poland, the situation changed dramatically. Only a few neutral countries remained open for refugees, who were now obliged to seek out destinations in the Far East, in the Soviet Union and in China. By the time the German borders were hermetically sealed for Jewish refugees in November 1941, around 128,000 Jews had managed to leave Austria. As far as it can be determined, around 55,000 ended up in European countries, where many were rounded up again by the Wehrmacht. Some 28,700 got to North America, 11,500 found refuge in South America, 28,500 in Asia, 2,000 in Australia and New Zealand, and 650 in Africa.[15]

Functionaries: victims and messengers of terror

'Dear Herbert,
Next Friday the first issue of the *Zionistische Rundschau* will be appearing. I had the manuscripts sent to me and am currently doing the tedious work of censoring them. I will, of course, send a copy of the newspaper to you. In a way, it will be "my" newspaper.'

This is how Eichmann described the Jewish newspaper that was to appear in Vienna after May 1938.[16] All eight Jewish newspapers in Vienna had been closed down on the day the Nazis came to power. Eichmann even chose the name of the new magazine. It was not to be called *Jüdische Rundschau* as in Berlin, but rather *Zionistische Rundschau*. Editor-in-chief was Emil Reich. The *Zionistische Rundschau*[17] published the Nazi regulations and explained the new legal provisions. It was strictly controlled by Eichmann. Paradoxically, as a Jewish magazine whose readers were not necessarily being indoctrinated with Nazi propaganda like the rest of the population, it was allowed to be more critical than any other newspaper in Austria. Publication was stopped by the Gestapo on 9 November 1938.

> Vienna, 26 May 1939. We received your letter of 25 inst. addressed to the *Zionistische Rundschau* and can only repeat what we stated in our letter of 9 March this year, in which we respectfully pointed out that the *Zionistische Rundschau* no longer exists, as it was closed down on official instructions on 9 November 1938. The requested issues are not therefore available.

This message was written on a postcard by the editorial board of the *Jüdisches Nachrichtenblatt* to the Vienna university library.[18] In their diligent love of good order, the librarians, who liked to ensure that all printed matter was delivered regularly, had wondered where the copies of the *Zionistische Rundschau* had got to.

The *Zionistische Rundschau* was closed down right after the November pogrom. In the Altreich, all Jewish newspapers that had appeared hitherto were banned, to be replaced by a circular informing the Jewish population of the new laws that were being promulgated every day. The Ministry of Propaganda decided that a *Jüdisches Nachrichtenblatt* should be published for the entire Reich territory. All Jewish newspapers published until then were required to make available their lists of subscribers to the *Jüdisches Nachrichtenblatt*.[19]

Kurt Löwenstein was appointed as editor-in-chief in Berlin of the *Jüdisches Nachrichtenblatt*. He had previously been in charge of the Zionist Berlin *Jüdische Rundschau*, managed until 1938 by Robert Weltsch. After the first issue came out, however, Löwenstein was removed from office and the issue pulped. 'It was not surprising that the issue was confiscated, because we had been trying in some way to continue the editorial line of the *Jüdische Rundschau*,' explained Löwenstein after the war.[20]

There are only two or three copies in existence of this first banned issue of the *Jüdisches Nachrichtenblatt*, a courageous attempt at self-assertion after the terror of the November pogrom. It came out on 22 November 1938 and consisted of two pages, for the most part containing reports on emigration efforts.

The Jüdischer Kulturbund was now required to publish the *Jüdisches Nachrichtenblatt*. This association was headed in Berlin by Werner Levie. A *Jüdisches Nachrichtenblatt* was also to be published in Austria. Until 1 February 1939, a joint issue for the entire territory of the German Reich was published with a supplement for readers in the Ostmark. Löwenherz wanted Vienna to have its own paper.[21] A branch of the Jüdischer Kulturbund attached to the Palestine Office was to publish the *Jüdisches Nachrichtenblatt*. The middle section of the Vienna edition came from Berlin. The Vienna section was wrapped around it like a cover and consisted of several pages with local news and regulations. Censorship in Vienna was the responsibility not of the Ministry of Propaganda but the Gestapo. The newspaper provided information about possibilities for emigration, welfare, free meals and winter aid, and also published the anti-Jewish laws. Particular emphasis was given to reporting on Palestine and on those who had managed to leave Germany and settle in another country. It was not allowed to advocate the creation of a Jewish state, however. In that regard, the change in the name of the newspaper from *Zionistische Rundschau* was deliberate. The Nazis wanted the Jews to emigrate to Palestine, but the Zionist organizations were no longer allowed to proclaim their self-assertive ideology. Emphasis was to be on emigration of any kind and not on the right to Jewish sovereignty. After the war broke out, it was forbidden to write about Palestine. Even the name 'Palestine' could not be mentioned and no reporting on the war was allowed.[22]

Shortly after the Polish campaign began, new anti-Jewish measures were promulgated. There was an 8 o'clock curfew, and Jews were no longer allowed to possess radios. Curiously, these two new regulations were not published anywhere, as the only Jewish newspaper in

Germany, the *Jüdisches Nachrichtenblatt*, was expressly forbidden to mention them.[23]

The Kultusgemeinde was required to notify its members of the prohibitions, instructions and emigration regulations in circulars and bulletins. It was the harbinger of bad news. It not only notified the prohibitions and instructions, but also gave reasons why the laws should be obeyed. All members of the community had to subscribe to the *Jüdisches Nachrichtenblatt*. Those who could not pay the postage had to collect the newspaper from the offices of the Jewish administration. No one was to be left ignorant of the notifications. The editors knew that they were writing the obituary of a community in its death throes. 'Where did the Jews of Vienna come from?' was the headline of the Vienna *Jüdisches Nachrichtenblatt* of 5 February 1943. The sentence was deliberately put in the past tense and left no doubt that the Jewish community of Vienna had been liquidated.

The last issue of the *Jüdisches Nachrichtenblatt* in Vienna appeared on 31 December 1943 and consisted of two pages with regulations and decrees. Without any further explanation – none was needed – it announced laconically: 'As of 1 January 1944 the Vienna edition of the *Jüdisches Nachrichtenblatt* will no longer appear.'

Administration during the terror

During the first year after the Anschluss, a change had taken place within the Kultusgemeinde with the focus turning to emigration at the expense of welfare. In the weekly reports, it notified the Nazi authorities of all incidents in the previous days, changes of address and the deaths of its members.[24] The secretary of a British aid organization who visited Vienna in 1939 reported that he had been under observation the whole time. When he visited Leopoldstadt, the Jewish district, he felt as if he was in a dead city.[25]

For the Jewish officials to enable their fellow victims to survive and get away, they had to work for the Gestapo and keep on the good side of SS-Hauptsturmführer Adolf Eichmann. If he was looking for a villa in Hietzing with five rooms, central heating and a garden, but costing only 100 RM rent for a colleague who had been transferred to Vienna, he would call the Kultusgemeinde, ordering that four or five houses be ready for viewing the following afternoon.[26]

What possibilities did the leading functionaries of the Jewish community have of resisting the blackmail and threats by the Nazi authorities? By being conciliatory, they hoped for some relief and favours for Jews. They were not the representatives of another ethnic group with equal rights but rather nothing but hostages, liable with their own lives for the other persecuted Jews. If one of them went abroad to negotiate with international aid organizations, the others had to sign a paper standing surety for his return.

After March 1939, the Zionist Association of Austria was also incorporated into the Kultusgemeinde, and the Palestine Office had to coordinate its activities with it as well. Löwenherz had to chair a committee representing the two offices, the Kultusgemeinde and the Palestine Office. On 31 July 1939, the Nazi authorities ordered the Jewish administration to close down the Palestine Office.[27] All of Jewish life was now controlled by a single administration that was itself controlled by the Gestapo. The Kultusgemeinde was merely an implementing body. The Nazi officials told the Jewish administration what to do.

Josef Löwenherz, head of the IKG, became caught up in a competence dispute between the individual Nazi authorities. On 3 August 1939, he was ordered to appear before Gestapo Obersekretär Kuchmann, who asked him on whose authority he had instructed all departments to address all submissions and applications to the Central Office for Jewish Emigration, i.e., to Eichmann. Löwenherz said that SS-Obersturmführer Eichmann had ordered him to do this, but Kuchmann then forced Löwenherz to sign a document in which he stated that he would refer all organizational matters to the Gestapo headquarters. Löwenherz signed, saying that he would inform the Central Office of this instruction; he also asked Kuchmann to contact Eichmann, as he did not know how he was to carry out these conflicting orders. Löwenherz told Eichmann of Kuchmann's order at an audience on 7 August, whereupon Eichmann told him that he should obey his, Eichmann's, orders until the matter had been clarified. It was not until 11 August, after Löwenherz had been shunted to and fro for some time by both authorities, that he was informed that the Central Office was responsible for emigration matters, but the Gestapo would deal with organizational and institutional issues.[28]

In December 1939, the assets of the Jewish communities in Austria and those of the Jewish foundations came under Eichmann's control as 'special agent'. He was responsible for seeing that the possessions of the Jewish communities were sold; officially, the sales were to be carried out by Kultusgemeinde head Löwenherz. The proceeds were to be paid into an account to which the Central Office would have access for the purpose of implementing the Nazi Jewish policy.

A Central Office for Jewish Emigration was also to be established in Berlin. In contrast to Vienna, the Jewish functionaries in Berlin already had advance warning of what to expect because of what had gone on in Vienna and so they tried to prevent it. The situation in Berlin was not comparable to what was happening in Vienna. The German Jews were not willing to acquiesce to the mass expulsion. Heinrich Stahl, president of the Jewish Community of Berlin, was quite forthright in his opinion about the practices in Vienna and had expressed his abhorrence to representatives of the Kultusgemeinde and the Palestine Office during a visit to Vienna. On his return to Berlin, however, he was obliged to write the following letter to the IKG and the Palestine Office in Vienna:

Dear Sirs,

On the occasion of my visit to Vienna, I was able to satisfy myself that the Central Office set up in Vienna to promote and expedite Jewish emigration is a very practical institution that considerably facilitates the emigration formalities.

During the visit I criticized the way *you* organized the emigration procedure and expressed the opinion that preconditions of this type would make it more difficult to identify new possibilities for emigration and to maintain the ones already in existence.

I should like to stress explicitly that this criticism was not justified.'[29]

Eichmann presented Stahl's letter of apology to Rothenberg and Löwenherz on 9 March 1939.[30]

From 1933 to 1938, the Reich Agency for German Jews – from 1935 it was renamed Reich Agency of the Jews in Germany by order of the Nazis – was the central representative body for German Jews. From the beginning of 1939, the Viennese experience was applied to the Old Reich. Göring had given Heydrich an official order on 24 January 1939 to establish a Reich Office for Jewish Emigration in Berlin which was to employ a Jewish organization answerable to the Reich Office.[31] The Reich Agency of the Jews in Germany started work in February 1939 under the constant supervision of the Reich Office. Although the Reich Agency was subordinate to the Reich Security Head Office and, unlike its predecessor, no longer represented the Jews but functioned as an instrument of the Nazi authorities, most of the former Jewish functionaries remained in place. From December 1938 to March 1939, the Jewish representatives were summoned three times to the Gestapo to 'discuss' the establishment of a

Central Emigration Advice Centre and the Reich Agency of the Jews of Germany. In 1958, eyewitness Benno Cohn described the third summons in early March 1939:

It began with a violent attack by Eichmann on the representatives of the German Jews. He had a file with press cuttings, foreign of course, in which Eichmann was described as a bloodhound who wanted to kill the Jews. He read us extracts from the *Pariser Tageblatt* and asked us whether it was correct, saying that the information must have come from us. . . . Then a new subject: 'You were in Vienna. You were strictly forbidden from contacting the representatives of the Austrian Jews. You disobeyed our explicit order. Contrary to your instructions you had meetings with the Austrian Jews.'

Stahl or Eppstein said: 'The situation is grotesque. Our brothers are being persecuted there by you and we are not meant to speak with them. That is simply inhuman. We did not approach them; they came to us to hear from us, because we had been in the same situation as them for some years already.'

Eichmann said: 'It was strictly forbidden. If it happens again, you will be put in the "concert" camp.'

Then Heinrich Stahl, president of the Jewish Community of Berlin . . . went onto the offensive against Eichmann. He said: 'We are all in favour of emigration. But you are ruining the chances of emigration with your deportation system. By sending people en masse across the border you are making it impossible to emigrate to neighbouring countries. For that reason they don't want to issue visas any more.'

After this criticism, Eichmann yelled: 'You miserable creature, you old piece of shit, it's quite a while since your were in the "concert" camp. Who do you think you are?' Stahl went pale and kept quiet.

Then Paul Eppstein stood up and said: 'The gentlemen sitting here before you are representatives of German Jewry and not the recipients of orders from the German Reich. . . . We are accountable to our people for our behaviour. If you speak to us in this way, we cannot work with you. You can put us in the camp at any time and do with us as you please. But as long as we are free, you must respect our human dignity and treat us accordingly.'

This speech apparently made a deep impression on the other Nazis. Eichmann, however, yelled: 'This impertinent outburst will have to be dealt with. Leave and wait outside!'[32]

The Jewish representatives had to wait for half an hour in the anteroom and, as they expected to be arrested, they destroyed all the papers they had with them. After thirty minutes, the interview continued and it appeared to the Jewish functionaries that Eichmann had been ordered by his superiors to moderate his tone. But Eichmann's behaviour had had its effect. While waiting in the anteroom, the Jewish representatives had prepared themselves for the worst and were relieved to discover that nothing would happen to them and that in four days' time, on the following Monday, the Central Office for Emigration in Berlin would open. They were ordered to present a certain number of Jews every week to the new office for emigration. The Jewish officials would be informed every Wednesday how many would be required the following week. They could expect dire consequences if they did not meet the required quota. They were told to indicate the number for the following Monday by the next day.

Benno Cohn and his colleagues were surprised. Cohn attempted to explain that no one could guarantee a specific number. He demanded dignified treatment for the Jews but Eichmann started yelling that the stories of mistreatment were just untruthful propaganda. That evening, the Jewish functionaries met.

> It was clear to us that we had to cooperate and that pressure to emigrate was great. The running hither and thither between the different offices had been terrible and they were all crowded and overworked. The concentration of the emigration procedures in a single office made sense.
> [. . .]
> Decision: Eppstein . . . to indicate that we are interested in setting up the Central Offices for Emigrants and normalizing the emigration procedure. It is our understanding that in this way the expulsions across the border will cease.
> [. . .]
> We also knew that a new world war was imminent and feared the worst for the Jews. Emigration meant salvation.[33]

This meeting effectively installed the Vienna model in Berlin.

In 1958, Erich Frank, at the time head of Hechalutz in Berlin, described the meeting with Eichmann in March 1940 with Jewish representatives from Berlin, Vienna and Prague:

> 'He had cracked down from the start in Vienna and the Viennese were already used to this method. We in Berlin were not yet familiar with it and asked ourselves seriously whether we could cooperate. We had to . . . stand and the Viennese addressed Eichmann in the third person, 'If the Sturmbannführer will allow', for example. We found that terrible.[34]

In fact, the lawyer and 'Austrian-Israelite' official Josef Löwenherz was using the typical Viennese third-person language of an old imperial subject currying favour with his superiors, even if he intended to ignore their instructions.

The powerlessness of the Jewish institution was seen by the Jews as an unwillingness to help and their lack of authority as indifference. The bitterness turned into mistrust and anger against the IKG. A Jew who wanted to flee with his child complained to Löwenherz because he had not been able to emigrate to date; he said that an official had intrigued against him and his child. This official, continued the anonymous letter writer, was a 'vile murderer of the worst kind', a 'disgrace to Judaism'.[35] A Jewish woman, wife of a war invalid, wrote a letter in July 1940 to the Viennese Zionist functionary Sofie Löwenherz, wife of Josef Löwenherz.[36] The couple had attempted to obtain passage in a transport to Palestine through the Makkabi association, an illegal escape route organized by the revisionist Zionists. The husband had paid money, given notice in his apartment, and on the basis of the assurance that he would be leaving in a few days had even cancelled his pension. But the visa-less emigration was unsuccessful and the Jews were sent back to Vienna.[37] The couple had lost all of their money, missed other opportunities to get away and now felt betrayed by the Jewish functionaries to such an extent that they threatened in their despair to go to the Gestapo. They blamed their own representatives for the situation that they and other Jews had been put into by the Nazis.

Every argument within the Jewish authorities and organizations threatened to explode into a life-threatening dispute. The Jews in their desperation threatened repeatedly to go to the Gestapo, but at the same time they all feared Gestapo informers. In this atmosphere of panic and need, the pressure under which the leading functionaries worked could not but grow. They were summoned, sometimes several times in a single day, to the Gestapo headquarters, which were just a few buildings away from the Kultusgemeinde offices. At the same time, they had to look after several thousand victims and see hundreds. They were barely up to the task. Apart from the welfare officers who looked after the needs of individuals, the bureaucrats among the officials, who worked with figures and quotas and were therefore less sensitive to the fate of individuals, became increasingly important in view of the need to organize escape under the more difficult conditions that now existed. The scholar and rabbi Benjamin Murmelstein, who was later to become the Jewish elder in Theresienstadt, became a vital figure at this time within the Jewish administration, a technocrat of the administration of terror.

Benjamin Murmelstein

Benjamin Murmelstein, born in Lemberg (Lviv) in 1905, came from an orthodox family. After the First World War, he came to Vienna where he studied philosophy at the university and also attended the Israelite Theological Institute. He completed his theological rabbinical studies in 1927 with the second-best performance in the Institute's history.[38] In the same year, he completed his doctorate, writing a thesis entitled *Adam. Ein Beitrag zur Messiaslehre.*[39] His supervisor was Professor Viktor Christian, who after the Anschluss became the administrative dean of the Philosophy Faculty at the University of Vienna. In this position, he was responsible for removing all Jewish academics from the department and also issued the order on 23 April 1938 that lecturers and students were to give the Hitler salute at the beginning and end of lectures.[40]

After 1931, Murmelstein held the position of community rabbi at the synagogue in Kluckygasse, Vienna-Brigittenau. He also taught religious instruction at various secondary schools and lectured at the Israelite Theological Institute.

Following the assassination of the Austrian Austro-Fascist chancellor Dollfuss during the attempted Nazi putsch in 1934, Murmelstein was asked to make a speech because, as he subsequently noted, 'apparently no one else could be found to perform this delicate task'.[41] Murmelstein repeatedly spoke out against anti-Semitic propaganda. In 1935, he wrote the pamphlet *Einige Fragen an Prof. Dr. P. Severin Grill*, which was published by the Union of Austrian Jews with an introduction by chief rabbi David Feuchtwang.[42] In the old anti-Semitic tradition, Severin Grill had cited extracts from the Talmud out of context that gave a defamatory view of Judaism. Murmelstein's pamphlet rebutted these assertions. In a time of virulent anti-Semitism under the authority of the Austro-Fascists and in the shadow of the Third Reich, it was not without risk for the young rabbi to speak out publicly against anti-Semitism.

In 1935, he wrote a commemorative pamphlet on the Jewish scholar rabbi Moses ben Maimon, known as Rambam. It was dedicated to Jewish youth. Apart from other studies of Judaism, Murmelstein also wrote a book entitled *Geschichte der Juden*, which appeared in early 1938. At the end of the book, he wrote about how the Jewish people should now act:

'One thing is clear: many Jews will receive a serious warning in the coming decades: "Anyone of his people among you – may the Lord his God be with him, and let him go up." The history of the fourth millennium ends with God's appeal to Abraham that had introduced the first millennium: "Go to that land." [43]

After the German troops entered Austria and the Nazis came to power, Murmelstein had to stop teaching secondary school religion and curtail his rabbinical work in the Kluckygasse synagogue. However, he continued to receive a salary as rabbi of the community. As luck would have it, he lived in the same building, Nussdorferstrasse 42, as Josef and Sofie Löwenherz. After Löwenherz had been arrested, Murmelstein knocked on Sophie Löwenherz's door and asked whether he could do anything for her or for the community, since he was still being paid without having to work for it. Mrs Löwenherz soon appreciated Murmelstein's organizational talents and recommended the young rabbi to her husband after he was released. [44]

Löwenherz asked Murmelstein if he would like to work in the emigration department of the reopened Kultusgemeinde. After the Anschluss, Murmelstein applied for a position abroad but received only rejections. [45], Murmelstein stated after the war that he had wanted to stay in the Vienna community and like a soldier did not want to desert his post. [46] We do not know whether this was a later justification or whether it was his real motive. It is true that to remain in Vienna in 1938, to assume a responsible position within the Jewish administration, to be summoned to appear before SS men like Eichmann, was a dangerous and precarious affair. At all events, he did not slacken his attempts to emigrate. [47] The fact remains, however, that most other rabbis emigrated while Murmelstein remained and did valuable work to encourage mass Jewish emigration.

As an administrator, Murmelstein was in an awkward position. The Jewish representatives had a veneer of authority, which in reality only confirmed their powerlessness. They were held liable by the Gestapo for every Jewish transgression, but they could not be held responsible by the Jews for anything that happened. And yet they appeared important and were respected, admired, feared and hated by their fellow victims.

The scholar became an administrator, the intellectual a bureaucrat and the man of god a manager of misery. He demonstrated his capabilities when he compiled statistics at Löwenherz's request on Jewish emigration and welfare. Murmelstein also wrote descriptions of the Kultusgemeinde for foreign aid organizations. On 10 October 1940, Löwenherz wrote in a letter full of praise to Emil Engel, who by that time had already emigrated to New York:

'Dr. M. continues to work hard and is now preparing a report for the Joint, which will have a different form and will be very impressive.'[48]

For Eichmann, Murmelstein wrote summaries of Jewish history and religion and about the various Jewish organizations. It is possible that Murmelstein had already come to the attention of the Nazi anti-Semites through his pamphlet rebutting the anti-Jewish opinions of Grill. No doubt his speech for Engelbert Dollfuss had not gone unnoticed either.

Now Murmelstein was recruited as an expert to hold a bibliographical course on Hebraica for staff of the National Library on the premises of the Kultusgemeinde.[49] The Jews were being persecuted, their books stolen; and now the non-Jewish librarians were to be taught how printed matter in a foreign alphabet was to be indexed and registered.

Murmelstein's lectures gave Eichmann the possibility of creating an impression for himself among high-ranking Nazis as an expert on Jewish affairs. During his interrogation in Jerusalem, Eichmann stressed that of all the Jewish representatives he had got on best with Murmelstein.[50] This statement should not be misunderstood: Murmelstein was well aware that the Nazi official was a deadly enemy but he hoped to be able to humour him.

Many of the staff of the Kultusgemeinde got on less well with Murmelstein. He was feared as a supervisor because he was strict and irascible. In his standard work on Theresienstadt, the historian H. G. Adler described him as 'a Falstaff'.[51] His corpulence also made a bad impression in this time of Jewish penury. Murmelstein appeared cold and arrogant and he was of compelling and for some intimidating intelligence.

Willy Stern, who was Murmelstein's subordinate, relates that Löwenherz became increasingly reliant on Murmelstein.[52] The Gestapo terrorized the administrative director of the Kultusgemeinde unceasingly, and he responded by pushing forward his head of department and giving him more and more responsibility.

In the order of services for September and October 1938, Murmelstein was still one of several rabbis. The chief rabbi Taglicht conducted the services in the City Temple in Seitenstettengasse.[53] After the pogrom, all of the other synagogues were destroyed and closed down and Murmelstein now led the services in Seitenstettengasse.

He was head of the emigration department as well and his rise was an indication of the growing importance of emigration at the time. Willy Stern recalls: 'He was an extremely learned man, too young for

74

this responsible position, and too unscrupulous. That doesn't mean that he collaborated, but he behaved as if he belonged to the ruling class: he yelled, he was rude, he threw people out; it was very unpleasant.'[54]

The former welfare officer Franzi Löw-Danneberg also recalled in 1991:

> I had nothing to do with Murmelstein, thank goodness. He yelled. He was always yelling. I don't know whether he was evil . . . He was criticized even during the war. It started when the first transports were put together. He was a scholar. He had an unending fund of knowledge and was put in a position that he could not handle. He was forced into it.[55]

Rosa Schwarz, in charge of juvenile welfare until 1940, said of Murmelstein: 'I don't know how many of the bad things said about Murmelstein in Theresienstadt are true. I know him from Vienna and can only say how I found him to be. He was petty, pedantic and in no way helpful to people.'[56]

Murmelstein issued the permits for Kultusgemeinde employees who had to go out during the Jewish curfew. He refused to issue one to a young woman employee who was leaving Vienna the following day and wanted to say goodbye to her friends on her last evening after work. 'I asked him why he had refused. He replied that since midday I was no longer an employee of the community. Under the prevailing circumstances anyone else would have issued the permit.'[57]

Murmelstein understood how to cooperate with the Gestapo. He went about his work with a coldness that other Jewish officials did not have. To a certain extent, his behaviour was indicative of an attitude of submission to the logic of terror. He had accepted intellectually that it was necessary to cooperate with the Nazis. If many Jews were to be rescued, the Gestapo orders would have to be obeyed. He bowed to the system and knew no scruples at an individual level. He was accused of having no sympathy for his fellow victims. But even after the war he remained convinced that an unbending approach was the only way to have dealt with the problems at the time. The SS were not to be offered a handle on the Jewish community. The Jewish administration had to ensure discipline and order on its own.[58] At that time, it appeared inconceivable that cooperation would foster the organized mass murder and that the Nazis were interested not in exploiting the Jews but in exterminating them. The SS did not follow a particular rationale; it broke agreements and changed them at will.

The good behaviour of the Jews did not propitiate the anti-Semites. Murmelstein's attitude was no different to that of other Jewish functionaries; it was just his deportment, his systematic untouchability, that differed. Murmelstein's work saved the lives of many people between 1938 and 1940, but he used his position to gain superiority over others. His demeanour and his imperiousness brought him into discredit.

In addition, Murmelstein's work demanded that he take an authoritarian stance. Mass emigration in the shadow of Nazi terror called for military logic and organizational talent. Jewish emigration administrators had to appear confident and needed to be able to negotiate with Reich offices, travel agencies and banks. They had to organize the transports and keep order.

One of Murmelstein's staff was Robert Prochnik, born in Vienna in 1915. After the Anschluss, he had had to break off his law studies and, after unsuccessfully attempting to escape from Vienna, he worked from October 1938 in the Kultusgemeinde. His first job was to issue questionnaires in the passport department, but after a few weeks he was transferred to the special department under Murmelstein. In order to arrange trains and emigration transports, he had on a number of occasions to appear before the authorities as if he were a Gestapo official responsible for the expulsion of the Jews. He must have been very credible in this role. The non-Jewish officials did not always realize immediately that Prochnik was a Jew himself and they only started stepping on him when they noticed that he was in fact one of the people to be persecuted. Fortunately, he was never denounced, which would have meant certain death.[59] Prochnik's lordly manner was also noticed by the Jews. Willy Stern said of him: 'He yelled at people. . . . I said: "Robert, all that's missing is the riding crop to beat against the table." '[60]

In those years until November 1941, Murmelstein helped to enable some 128,000 Jews to leave Austria. From early 1941 onwards, the Kultusgemeinde and Murmelstein were recruited to assist with the deportations to the extermination camps.

In 1938, before the Anschluss, Murmelstein published an anthology of texts by Josephus, the leader of the Jewish rebels in Galilee and later chronicler of the defeat by the Roman Empire. His place in Jewish history is disputed: the Jewish general who ran over to the enemy when he realized the hopelessness of the Jewish cause, he was also the faithful commemorator of the Jewish rebels and defender of the traditions of Judaism. Murmelstein ended his introduction with the sentences: 'While faithful to Judaism, he was also enthralled by the great idea of the Roman Empire. His riven and ambiguous essence epitomizes the Jewish tragedy.'[61]

Today this reads like an autobiographical prediction, as if Murmelstein had written his own obituary in 1938: as a future Jewish functionary under Eichmann and a Jewish elder in Theresienstadt.

The employees in the system

On 13 March 1938, the IKG had 537 paid employees. There were 565 unpaid employees, including 36 elected committee members.[62] During the first year of Nazi rule, the number of employees increased. To provide relief, organize emigration and carry out the work of the Jewish associations that had been closed down, some 860 Kultusgemeinde employees had to be paid in September 1938, and there were also 303 unpaid members.[63] The Kultusgemeinde needed new staff and many Jews applied as they were no longer able to continue in their old jobs after the Anschluss.

On 16 October 1938, Josef Löwenherz, Emil Engel, Benjamin Murmelstein and director Stössel determined who should be hired and on what salary, and who was to be dismissed because they were not up to the task, could no longer work for personal reasons or intended to leave. It was decided to hire around 100 employees and to dismiss ten.[64]

The Kultusgemeinde was short of money and the Nazi authorities forced the Jewish administration to cut down on administrative expenses so as to be able to finance the expulsion. Further employees were dismissed in May 1939.[65]

In spite or perhaps because of their destitute circumstances, Jews agreed to work for the Kultusgemeinde without pay, hoping to be taken into account when new staff were recruited. The work for the IKG was important and respected; to carry it out employees – welfare workers, for example – were given permission to go out after 4 p.m.[66] Those who worked for the Jewish administration could also hope to be supported in an emergency by the board of the Kultusgemeinde.[67]

Recruitment after August 1939 was controlled by the Gestapo. An instruction was given on 14 August to appoint the Aryan doctor and SS-Untersturmführer Dr Eduard Sponer as supervising doctor in the hospital.[68]

At the beginning of 1940, the former Jewish public health officer Dr Emil Tuchmann was appointed Kultusgemeinde medical examiner for the entire health service. Tuchmann submitted monthly reports to the Gestapo. He was summoned to appear before the Gestapo every time there was a complaint about a Jewish health facility or its employees. He also had to appear whenever members of the non-Jewish population and NSDAP complained about Jewish patients or the danger of infection by Jews.[69]

At the beginning of June 1940, the Gestapo decided to further reduce the number of officials and demanded a list of employees with the salary structure. Löwenherz reported that 1,518 people worked for the IKG, including the Gestapo supervising doctor at the Rothschild Hospital, Dr Eduard Sponer. Sponer had a gross salary of RM 1,032.10.[70] It should be noted that it was the Kultusgemeinde that had to pay the doctor, who did nothing except keep an eye on the hospital for the Gestapo, out of its own funds. The average salary of office workers in 1940 was just RM 125 a month.[71] Because the war had made it almost impossible to continue expelling the Jews and no funds were being received from abroad, the Nazi authorities now sought to make savings at the expense of their Jewish assistants. In early June 1940, Eichmann ordered the Kultusgemeinde to cut pensions[72] and to dismiss 141 persons by 1 July 1940.[73]

Among those dismissed was the orderly Ignatz Marlé. Since October 1938, he had been paid RM 15, later RM 20, per week.[74] Marlé was a war invalid – but only 40 per cent disabled – and did not qualify for an invalidity pension. In 1939, he lived with his two brothers and two sisters in a miserably furnished apartment for which he had to pay RM 30 in rent; one of the two rooms was sublet to another family for RM 17. One of his two brothers was single and had been unemployed since 1928. The second had had no revenue since the Anschluss. Neither of the sisters was married; the younger one kept house; the older one was 64 years of age and poorly. Ignatz Marlé's salary had to do for the whole family. They got their food from the soup kitchens. On 3 October 1939, Ignatz Marlé fell sick with a lung ailment and suffered a haemorrhage. He had still not completely recovered when he broke his ankle on 7 February 1940. He returned to work on 4 March 1940.[75] On 1 July 1940, he received a letter of dismissal from the Kultusgemeinde.[76]

Ignatz Marlé wrote an immediate reply to Josef Löwenherz: 'As the only support for my brothers and sisters, the dismissal will mean the most severe hardship for me.'[77] Marlé's immediate colleagues enclosed a very good reference with the letter.[78] But it was to no avail; Marlé lost his job.

The continuous risk and consequences of dismissal on fourteen days' notice meant that the employees worked under the heaviest pressure. They were strictly forbidden from using their positions to plead for advantages for themselves from the Nazi authorities. Out of fear for their lives, however, the employees intervened in their own interests and, in spite of warnings from Löwenherz, begged for support and ship passage in the various departments of the Kultusgemeinde.[79]

A small group of employees was directly responsible for dealing with orders from the Gestapo. In 1940, they were already having to deal with 'Jewish resettlements', as they were called, inside and outside Vienna and in this regard were required to 'handle the relevant orders from the Gestapo headquarters in Vienna and the housing department of the city of Vienna'.[80]

The Nazi authorities also sought out informers from within the ranks of the Kultusgemeinde. Willy Stern recounts a failed attempt to recruit him:

I was very often at the Gestapo headquarters on Morzinplatz because we had to get the Gestapo to sign for all institutions such as old people's homes, soup kitchens, hospitals and food vouchers. That was my job. We even had to get a signature in order to send a telegram abroad. One day I arrived at the Gestapo and there was a German Obersekretär, Kuchmann, who said to me: 'Yes, that's all very interesting, but first go to Hollandstrasse 10, where a Jew called Israel Soandso is leaving today for Prague. Ask him what his arrangements are and then come back and tell me.' I said: 'Herr Obersekretär, you misunderstand my function here. I am a messenger of the Kultusgemeinde and not an informer.' 'What do you mean, "informer"? I want information from you.' I said: 'Information – that's a euphemistic way of saying it.' 'So are you going?' I said no. 'All right, wait outside.' When we went to the Gestapo we had to have a pass to leave the building. I waited there from 10 a.m. until 1.30 p.m. He asked me if I had reconsidered, but I said no. At 3.30 p.m. he asked me the same question and I said no again. Then he said: 'Go downstairs to the exit in Salztorgasse.' We all knew what that meant: that's where the van took prisoners away. So I went downstairs and he came down ten minutes later and said: 'I will ask you one last time. Do you want to go there or not?' 'No.' Then he said: 'Very well' and signed the pass so that I could leave. There must have been some kind of protective mechanism because I wasn't afraid. I knew what to expect, but I wasn't afraid, and that's the strange thing.[81]

Before he let Stern go, Kuchmann pointed out that the Gestapo needed informers but did not hold them in high regard.[82] The former welfare worker Franzi Löw-Danneberg confirmed this in an interview: 'They were tools and when you don't need a tool any more you throw it away. And that's what they did with these people.'[83]

The Kultusgemeinde had to report all cases of corruption to the Gestapo. On 21 July 1940, Wilhelm Bienenfeld, head of the Kultusgemeinde technical department, reported to Gestapo Obersekretär Kuchmann about a woman employee who had been accused by Murmelstein of accepting bribes. Murmelstein fired her immediately and had the affair investigated by Bienenfeld, who discovered that she had been forging bank transfer slips to prisoners so as to steal money. If the post office could not send money to the desired addressee and returned it to the sender, she kept the money for herself.[84] Would it have been possible for the IKG to keep this matter from the Gestapo and its informers? It was probably too late because the charge had already had ramifications. Bienenfeld wrote to Kuchmann:

'In carrying out the investigation the undersigned discovered the discrepancies with which the Herr Obersekretär is already familiar.'[85]

The Kultusgemeinde and its employee Murmelstein had to be very hard on corruption so as to deter other employees, since those who accepted bribes enriched themselves at the expense of other concentration camp inmates and their families. Murmelstein did not want to give the Nazi authorities any occasion to take action against the other Kultusgemeinde departments. But it had become repeatedly evident that the Gestapo did not need any pretext for taking action against the Jews, and the industriousness and discipline of the community did nothing to hold them back. Devotion to duty and 'good behaviour' were not sufficient to save lives.

The war invalid Ignatz Marlé discussed above, who had worked in the Kultusgemeinde until 1940 to the satisfaction of his supervisors, was deported to Theresienstadt on 10 September 1942, together with his older sister Laura. Neither survived.[86]

Lateral entrants

Political representatives of the Kultusgemeinde community before March 1938, like Desider Friedmann and Robert Stricker, were not reinstated by the Gestapo. Others like Josef Löwenherz were intended to maintain a certain continuity and operate under Eichmann's control. Selfless welfare workers risked their lives to help those in need. Other young employees like Benjamin Murmelstein and Robert Prochnik organized emigration. Mention should also be made of employees who worked for the Jewish community, not within the Kultusgemeinde but in cooperation with the Nazi authorities.

The juvenile functionaries in the Palestine Office, for example, were able to act in liaison with Zionist organizations abroad. Their policy was based on their own ideological principles. The Zionist functionary Georg Überall, who later changed his name to Ehud Avriel, planned visa-less immigration to Palestine in collaboration with the Jewish leadership there. Moshe Agami was sent from Palestine to Vienna to handle Jewish emigration on the spot.[87] The presence of an emissary of this calibre and the focus on the Jewish settlement area in Palestine boosted the self-confidence of the young Zionist functionaries. Those who were willing to fight for a state and hoped for an independent future in a Jewish national homeland did not escape persecution but felt liberated from the eternal curse of being nothing more than victims. The assertion of Jewish national rights on its own was a way of doing something to overcome the sense of powerlessness. The young members of the Youth League and youth movements lived effectively in an extraterritorial region; they were fixed on their vision of a Jewish homeland. In their centre and in the agricultural training camps, they were protected from the terror on the streets.[88] The Zionist leaders helped young Jews to maintain their identity. When SA cohorts and Hitler Youth groups attacked Zionist homes in October and November 1938, they were met with resistance by the occupants, who were arrested as a result.[89]

One of the selfless and charismatic youth leaders was Aron Menczer, born in 1917 and head of the Youth League in Vienna. He managed to communicate to the young Jews that, despite what the Nazi ideology might say, they had a right to human dignity.

Menczer left the German Reich on a number of occasions. In February 1939, he accompanied a group of young people to Palestine. He visited his former comrades in kibbutzim, his parents and his brothers in Haifa. Family and friends tried to persuade him to stay, but Menczer said that his place was with the Jewish children in Vienna. He remained firm in his decision even after he had met his brother in April 1939 in Trieste on his way to Palestine. He wrote to his family saying that he wanted first of all to be sure that every single one of the children for whom he felt responsible had left Vienna. He consoled his relatives by telling them that he already had an immigration certificate for Palestine. This was true, but Menczer never used the certificate; he gave it to someone else. Aron Menczer remained in Vienna. As late as December 1940, he turned down an offer to travel to Palestine.[90]

Frank van Gheel Gildemeester, son of a Dutch preacher and missionary, dealt with those who were termed 'non-Mosaic Jews' or 'non-Aryan Christians' in the nomenclature of the time. Before 1938, he had helped imprisoned Nazis. He now used his earlier contacts in the interests of emigration.[91] The real driving force behind Gildemeester's activities was Hermann Fürnberg, a persecuted Jew.[92] Fürnberg invented the 'Abyssinia project'. The Fascist government in Rome was said to want to make Italy 'ethnically pure' and was therefore planning to settle Italian Jews in Abyssinia. Fürnberg dreamed of enabling 15,000 to 20,000 people, including concentration camp inmates, to leave Austria for Abyssinia. The Italian Foreign Ministry could not be convinced, however. In an attempt to harness support, Fürnberg distributed a leaflet describing the fate of the victims in the Third Reich. He was accused as a result of 'disseminating stories of atrocities abroad' and was obliged to flee in early 1940 to Barcelona. Gildemeester, who was forbidden to return to Vienna, remained in Lisbon.[93]

The Zionist functionaries led by Moshe Agami, Willi Ritter and Georg Avriel-Überall, who were working on behalf of Mossad, also had to resort to people they would not normally have had anything to do with in order to create a network for escape. Staunch Nazis and foreign diplomats had to be approached and bribed to obtain forged visas. For many people, the mass exodus was a profitable business.

Other Jewish individuals also contributed to the emigration activities. The businessman Berthold Storfer had not only commercial experience and organizational talent but also excellent business links, particularly in the Balkans. He was born in Czernowitz in 1889 and was persecuted as a Jew under the Nuremberg laws, although in 1938 he was not a member of the IKG but a Protestant. He had occupied various functions as a financial expert and businessman as far back as the days of the Austro-Hungarian monarchy. After the collapse of the Österreichische Kreditanstalt in 1933, he was employed by the government as an advisor on the necessary major financial transactions.[94] After the Anschluss, he was encumbered by his Jewish origins but refused to allow himself to be regarded as 'subhuman'. He hoped that his knowledge and experience would still be useful. At all events, in April 1938 his Help Committee for Jewish Emigration offered to manage the liquidation of Jewish assets and to raise funds to enable poor Jews to emigrate. The Committee proposed to take over the affairs of the Jewish organizations that had been closed down and to represent the Jews in their dealings with the authorities in connection with emigration. The Kultusgemeinde had been reopened in the meantime and until the end of June 1938 Storfer received no response to his proposals.

In July 1938, Berthold Storfer and Heinrich Neumann von Hethars travelled to Evian as members of the Vienna Jewish delegation, along with Josef Löwenherz, to take part in a refugee conference at which the international community discussed the question of aid for Jewish refugees.[95] Storfer and Neumann von Hethars wrote a report on their mission:

> To our knowledge there was no unfriendly criticism of Germany during the conference. . . . It is superfluous to mention that we were aware at all times . . . that we were carrying out our mission not only in the interests of all emigrating Jews but also bearing in mind the intentions of the state authorities, whose support we regard as exceptionally valuable and therefore ask for.[96]

In the report, they also proposed the creation of a central office in which all Jewish emigration affairs and the interests of all state authorities would be handled. Storfer urged that the Jewish emigration from Austria be properly organized. He intended to write a memorandum on the problem for the migration office.[97]

As the creation of the Vienna Central Office for Jewish Emigration was being planned at the time, Storfer's proposals were initially ignored.[98] His busy activities did not go unnoticed, however, and his appeals and applications were finally heard. Storfer and his office, the Committee for Jewish Overseas Transports, were to deal in particular with illegal transports to Palestine. In contrast to the Zionist movements, Storfer did not take into account the suitability of applicants for emigration to Palestine. Eichmann appreciated Storfer as a transport expert and finance specialist capable of getting a large number of Jews out of the country. In March 1940, he made Storfer the sole mediator in Vienna, Berlin and Prague for all overseas transport affairs, particularly illegal emigration to Palestine.[99]

Everyone had to cooperate with Storfer, an almost intolerable situation for the revisionists and in particular for Mossad, whose functionaries regarded him as a traitor and Gestapo agent. Ehud Avriel-Überall described Berthold Storfer unsparingly:

> Storfer belonged to the class of international businessmen who were convinced that it was they who actually run the world – regardless of the regime of the day.
> [. . .]

As mass emigration was the order of the day, he, and he alone, was capable of managing this new order on a scale satisfactory to the new masters, and he offered Eichmann his services in the 'purification' of Austria. Storfer was ruthless, ready to shove everybody else aside. He had no time for amateurs and for idealists. He competed, quite clumsily, with the hard-won contacts of the Mossad in the shipping business and caused the price of boats – in such short supply already – to skyrocket.[100]

Storfer's offer to Eichmann to organize the Jewish emigration did not set him apart from the other Jewish representatives. They all had to cooperate with the Nazis in order to make escape possible. Storfer did not work within the Jewish political framework, however, but did indeed push himself forward because he believed not in ideologies but in individual initiative, financial clout and professional management. Be that as it may, all of the Jewish functionaries had to deal with the growing pressure from the Nazi authorities, which could now determine how the illegal transports were to be put together.

Schicko Torczyner, a leader of the Vienna Makkabi, a Zionist sports organization, reported in his memoirs that Eichmann ordered the Makkabi to subordinate itself to Berthold Storfer. Torczyner wanted to check Storfer's credibility; he related stories that he had invented under the seal of confidentiality. Shortly afterwards, he was summoned to appear before Eichmann because of these invented reports. 'We became more and more convinced that Storfer was a traitor working for Eichmann.'[101]

The main difference of opinion between the Zionist activists and Berthold Storfer was that Storfer supported Eichmann's strategy of making wealthy Jews pay for poorer ones and that he saw the illegal transports as a way of getting old, sick and infirm Jews out of the Third Reich as well. Other countries were unlikely to accept these people legally. The arrangements with fictional visas offered Eichmann the opportunity to get rid of them. Storfer was also primarily interested, albeit for different reasons, in how many people could emigrate, and it was the older established Jews who would be most useful in financing his plans. The Zionists by contrast wanted to select the pioneers for Palestine. But even Mossad was unable to maintain this point of view; they also had to take a few rich Jews on board because of their money in order to finance the voyages.[102]

There was mistrust on both sides. It would doubtless have been better if the differences between Storfer and the Zionist functionaries could have been settled in their mutual interests. It is also interesting to note that some Zionists subsequently changed their opinion of Storfer. After the war, they recognized that they had misjudged him. After he arrived in Palestine, Erich (Ephraim) Frank, head of the German Hechalutz who accompanied one of the ships organized by Storfer, had only bad things to say about him.[103] Years later, however, in a report written in 1958, he changed his opinion, saying that Storfer had been at the 'extreme limit of cooperation with the Gestapo, but on the right side'.[104] Even during the war, some Jewish representatives spoke against the denunciations of Storfer.[105] Otto Hirsch from the Reich Agency of the Jews in Germany, Franz Lyon, head of the Palestine Office in Berlin, and other Jewish functionaries, including Josef Löwenherz, also spoke up for Storfer.[106]

Storfer's work enabled many Jews to escape. At all events, he refused in his way to be classified as 'subhuman'. After the Palestine transports ceased, he no longer held a prominent position. He appears to have been involved in another transfer. Even while he was working on Jewish emigration, he was accused by Schicko Torczyner of transferring money stolen from Jews as reinsurance to Switzerland for Adolf Eichmann.[107] Benjamin Murmelstein also said later that Storfer had worked too closely with the SS and had opened accounts for them abroad, which was strictly forbidden. He was later killed, Murmelstein claimed, so that he would not be able to testify.[108] Johann Rixinger from the Vienna Gestapo Jewish department said after the war that Storfer had been involved in 'secret Reich affairs' as a confidential financial adviser.[109]

Although he had been assured that he could remain in Vienna, Storfer was deported to Auschwitz in summer 1943. Eichmann spoke during his interrogation in Jerusalem about Berthold Storfer, revealing the unashamed cynicism and corrupt self-righteousness of the former Gestapo official. Storfer, said Eichmann, requested to speak with him.

I went to Auschwitz and asked Höss to see Storfer. 'Yes, yes [Höss said], he is in one of the labour gangs.' With Storfer afterwards, well, it was normal and human, we had a normal, human encounter. He told me all his grief and sorrow. I said: 'Well, my dear old friend [*Ja, mein lieber guter Storfer*], we certainly got it! What rotten luck!' And I also said: 'Look, I really cannot help you, because according to orders from the Reichsführer nobody can get out. I can't get you out. Dr. Ebner can't get you out. I hear you made a mistake, that you went into hiding or wanted to bolt, which, after all, *you* did not need to do.' . . . I forget what his reply to this was. And he said, yes, he wondered if he couldn't be let off work, it was heavy work. And then I said to Höss: 'Work – Storfer won't have to work!' But Höss said: 'Everyone works here.' So I said: 'O.K.' I said, 'I'll make out a chit to the effect that Storfer has to keep the gravel paths in order with a broom,' there were little gravel paths there, 'and that he has the right to sit down with his broom on one of the benches.' [To Storfer] I said: 'Will that be all right, Mr. Storfer? Will that suit you?' Whereupon he was very pleased, and we shook hands, and then he was given the broom and sat down on his bench. It was a great inner joy to me that I could at least see the man with whom I had worked for so many long years, and that we could speak to each other.[110]

Why did Eichmann visit Storfer? Did he want to squeeze out some final information from the Jewish finance expert, the accountant responsible for bank accounts in Switzerland? Did Eichmann want to be sure that Storfer could not give anything else away? Did he want to satisfy himself that he would really be killed? Six weeks after this 'normal, human meeting', Storfer was dead; shot.[111]

— 8 —

BEGINNING OF THE END

Nisko or the dress rehearsal for deportation

The German invasion of Poland in September 1939 brought about a radical and sudden change in the situation of the Jews in the German Reich. The persecutions in Poland surpassed all previous inhumanities. The Jews were now concentrated in ghettos in one part of the city. The term 'ghetto' was used to recall the traditional medieval ghetto in which the Jews had been secluded for centuries until their emancipation as citizens. By contrast, the Nazi ghettos into which the Jews were now herded were places of hunger, deadly epidemics and planned wastage, the first step on the way to extermination. The Polish territory became the exercise ground for the Nazi Jewish policy.

On 21 September 1939, Heydrich gave the official order for the formation of 'Jewish councils' or 'councils of Jewish elders'. These two terms also come from the time before the legal emancipation of the Jews.

The Polish Jews had an even lowlier status for the new rulers than the Jews in their own country. On enemy territory it was possible to be even more pitiless; in Vienna or Berlin, non-Jewish relatives or friends of the victims had to be considered. The Nazis did not want to harm their own 'ethnic community' by discriminating against the Jews. The victims included former front soldiers and officers, and the wishes of the Wehrmacht, who felt a loyalty to their former comrades and deserving soldiers, had to be taken into account.

The occupation of western Poland presented a new problem for the Reich. In one fell swoop, almost two million Jews had come under Nazi control, over half a million alone in the conquered territories that Germany annexed at the beginning of October. The Nazis had been driving out the Jews for years and now they had more of them than ever to deal with. Warsaw had 400,000 Jews, more than remained in 1939 in the entire Reich and Reich Protectorate.

At the same time, Jewish emigration had come to a standstill because of the war, which provided some cover for the persecution and extermination. Events at the front diverted attention from what was going on in the hinterland. The regime no longer had to take account of criticism from the West. The Jews were regarded as an enemy from within and without, a 'counter-race'. At a meeting in the Central Office for Jewish Emigration, Josef Löwenherz pointed out that the Jews in Vienna had always been loyal and yet since Britain had entered the war they were being beaten up on the streets because Jews, such as those in Palestine, had volunteered to fight for the British. Löwenherz even proposed to suspend transports to Palestine and with a heavy heart suggested that the transports be stopped so as to avoid giving any possible offence. Fortunately, Adolf Eichmann did not hold the same view. He ordered that the emigration to Palestine should continue, not omitting to add that the necessary foreign exchange must still be provided by other countries.[1]

The anti-Semitic mob did not require a war to beat up the Jews. Spurious excuses were found to justify the mass killing as being necessary on account of the war. The so-called 'world Jewry' was not at war with the Third Reich, but, directly after the invasion of Poland, 1,408 Jewish men who were or had been Polish citizens were arrested in Vienna on 9 and 11 September. The majority were under 18 or over 60 years of age.[2] They were detained for three weeks in the stadium, which had been converted into a camp. At the end of September, they were deported to Buchenwald concentration camp and the first urns with the ashes of the dead soon started coming back to Vienna. By early 1940, over two thirds had been killed.[3] Only twenty-seven of over one thousand men lived to see the liberation in 1945.[4]

Even before the war, the Nazi Jewish policy strategists had dreamed of a 'territorial solution to the Jewish question'. There were plans for them to be sent to Madagascar, far from the Third Reich and from Europe. With the conquest of territories in the east, a different solution offered itself. On 21 September 1939, Heydrich revealed to Adolf Eichmann and the commanders of the Einsatzgruppen in Poland that Hitler had approved a plan whose short-term goal was to herd the Polish Jews into the cities and from there to deport them to the east, to the territories that were not to be 'Germanized'. At the end of September in a pact between Germany and the Soviet Union, the Germans were granted sovereignty over the area around Lublin. At this time, the idea of a 'Jewish reservation' in that area came about.

On 10 October 1939, Josef Löwenherz was ordered by SS-Obersturmführer Rolf Günther to appear with the Jewish representatives Berthold Storfer, Benjamin Murmelstein, Mosche Grün and Julius Boschan before Adolf Eichmann in Mährisch-Ostrau (Moravská Ostrava). The Kultusgemeinde was to make a list of 1,000 to 1,200 healthy men for resettlement in Nisko. There was a particular need for craftsmen. All of the Jews to be deported, said Günther, had to fill out an official form, for which they had to pay RM 5.00. In addition a lump sum of RM 5,000 had to be provided to cover the transport costs. They should take with them work clothes, spirit burners, food for three to four weeks, and also saws, axes, nails and other tools.[5] The Kultusgemeinde was to notify the participants. It was ordered to select a person to manage the transport and to provide supervisors and orderlies.[6]

Günther added that men fit for work from these transports could be sent to Nisko. He also decided that inmates in Dachau and Buchenwald with emigration papers who were not stateless could also be included. Only poor Jews should come with the transport and they should give up all of their valuables before departure.[7] The Nazi strategy was clear. Poor Jews were more difficult to expel to other countries because they did not have sufficient funds and were therefore to be deported to the east.

Many Jews thought that an autonomous Jewish settlement south of Lublin would enable them to survive the war safely. Löwenherz decided to invite all eligible men on 14 October to the destroyed foyer of the City Temple and to include only those who volunteered for the transport. Former members of the Association of German Front Soldiers also responded to the appeal, although it had been specifically indicated that older persons were ineligible for this transport.[8]

Günther wondered why 830 people were originally scheduled for the first transport and much fewer were listed. Löwenherz remarked that the Kultusgemeinde had drawn up the list on the basis of voluntary applications. On further investigation, however, it transpired that a considerable number of the candidates – around 300 – were ineligible for the transport because of their physical condition. Günther ordered these people to be replaced. If that was not possible, everyone who had volunteered would have to travel, regardless of their condition.[9]

The fact that there were volunteers at all indicates that the Jews had no idea what was awaiting them in Nisko. Many preferred an uncertain future to the terror in Nazi Vienna. Willy Stern, at the time

19 years old and employed by the Kultusgemeinde, volunteered for the third transport, which did not take place. Luckily for him, the deportation to Nisko had been suspended hitherto.[10]

As mentioned above, there were not ultimately as many volunteers as the Nazi authorities had demanded. The Central Office therefore had to look to its own files. Former concentration camp inmates who had no emigration papers and Jews expelled from Burgenland, for example, were included in the transport list.[11] Further deportations, each containing 1,000 people, were planned for the following Tuesday and Friday. Entire families were scheduled for the fourth transport. Every train was to be accompanied by armed police to prevent the deportees from escaping.[12]

The first train to Nisko was to depart on 18 October, not from Vienna but from Mährisch-Ostrau. A second transport of 875 men assembled in Katowice was added to the 901 men in the first transport. Benjamin Murmelstein and Julius Boschan from the Kultusgemeinde, Moses Grün from the Palestine Office in Vienna and Berthold Storfer, head of the Committee for Jewish Overseas Transports, travelled to Mährisch-Ostrau to meet Eichmann. They also met two representatives of the Prague community, Jakub Edelstein and Richard Friedmann, a former Kultusgemeinde employee who had moved to Prague in July 1939 to help there with his Austrian 'experience'. The Jewish representatives were obliged to accompany the first transport, which left Mährisch-Ostrau on 18 October.[13] Josef Löwenherz had already asked Rolf Günther on 10 October for Murmelstein to be allowed to remain in Vienna and for another IKG employee to be sent to Mährisch-Ostrau in his place. Günther asked Löwenherz to put his request in writing.[14]

Löwenherz did not know what would happen in Nisko. Nor should it be forgotten that Löwenherz tried in a small way to resist the instructions of the Central Office. For example, when on 27 September 1940, almost a year after the deportations to Nisko, Alois Brunner, head of the Jewish department, ordered that twenty people of up to 40 years of age be selected for the camps Doppl and Windhag, Löwenherz replied that it was not possible for him to make the selection. Brunner then said that he would do it himself.[15] Löwenherz's attitude was very courageous because he could not know whether his refusal would be punished.

In his letter of 11 October 1939, Löwenherz sought arguments to keep Murmelstein in Vienna. His efforts show that he depended on Murmelstein's work and considered him irreplaceable. The request was unsuccessful.[16]

The first transport left Vienna on 20 October 1939. At the station, Obersturmführer Rolf Günther told Löwenherz that the people leaving now would be 'grateful' to him. They would have 'regular work' and 'good and sufficient food'. He said that Löwenherz need not worry about the fate of the people. Löwenherz was in no way reassured, however, but asked for an audience with Eichmann, which was granted on 27 October. The Kultusgemeinde, said Löwenherz, was aware that it had to obey all orders, but there had been problems. The Jewish population accused it of having suggested the action and of sending the people into an uncertain future. The people also believed that those who had been sent to Nisko from Dachau and Buchenwald would be sent to concentration camps again. They also complained that it was no longer possible to leave Poland. Löwenherz reminded Eichmann that not all of the Jewish population could be resettled in Poland because the old and the sick were ineligible. Eichmann assured Löwenherz that the action would apply to most of the Jews from the Altreich and the Ostmark and Protectorate and would be carried out 'as humanely as possible'. The Jews would be able to move freely, he insisted, and build a life for themselves because the region was practically depopulated and was now to be developed. Eichmann promised that the Jews would be housed initially in the newly built barracks in Nisko and would be provided with food and medical care. He cynically invited Löwenherz, Rothenberg and functionaries of foreign Jewish organizations to travel to Poland to convince themselves of the advantages of 'resettlement' at first hand. He even intended to permit journalists and representatives of major foreign associations to find out for themselves how humanely this action in Poland was being carried out. When the war was over, emigration from the region would be possible, but not beforehand.[17]

The first 901 Jews from Mährisch-Ostrau arrived in Nisko on 19 October 1939.[18] They had been ordered by Eichmann to erect a camp with watchtowers. Eichmann gave a speech on 20 October, ordering them to erect barracks and to organize an administrative and health service. Benjamin Murmelstein recalls: 'After the speech he looked at us ironically and added softly: "Otherwise you would die". The words were icy but the tone like velvet, almost friendly.'[19]

The camp was called Central Office for Jewish Resettlement in Nisko on the San. Around twenty SS and SD men with machine guns guarded the inmates. An additional twenty young 'ethnic Germans' joined them in November 1939. The 'regular work' that Günther had promised involved carrying building material from the banks of the

San day and night to the camp, up a three-kilometre muddy slope, while the guards laid into them.[20]

The delegation of Jewish functionaries from Prague and Vienna who had accompanied the first transport to Nisko to verify the conditions realized right from their arrival that they had been deceived. The area could not be used for a 'Jewish reservation'. The marshy land had been devastated by the war. The Jewish commission was shot at several times. Bands of locals patrolled the area and attacked the Jews.[21] Julius Boschan remained in Nisko and had to write a report to Löwenherz making no mention of the real conditions in the camp. He wrote that the atmosphere in the camp was good, there were no infectious diseases and minor problems had been dealt with. He even praised the food.[22] While Boschan awaited the Vienna transports in Nisko, the other functionaries had contacted the Lublin community to discuss settlement projects. The Jewish council of Lublin did not know that a 'Jewish reservation' was to be established in the area. The Gestapo representatives and the local council knew nothing about it either. The commandant in Lublin, SS-Oberst Strauch, was horrified by Eichmann's plan to set up a 'Jewish reservation' in his area. He ordered the Jewish delegates to return to Nisko.[23]

Benjamin Murmelstein remained in Nisko until early November. On his return, he refused to make an official report to Löwenherz about the visit. In any case, however, all illusions within the Viennese Jewish community about the 'Jewish reservation' had already been shattered.[24]

Two trains from Vienna and two from Mährisch-Ostrau and Katowice arrived in Nisko. Most of the completely unsuspecting Viennese Jews did not remain in the barracks where the Jews from Mährisch-Ostrau were already working. On their arrival in Nisko, the guards did not distribute the luggage to the victims, except for small bags and rucksacks. The Jews were ordered to establish themselves on a wet meadow near the village of Zarzecze. They were watched over by SS men with guns. Craftsmen and the leaders of the Jewish transport were ordered to step forward and were directed to the camp. Most of the deportees were driven by the SS men, Viennese police and soldiers to the German-Soviet demarcation line. Julius Boschan was not allowed to mention these incidents in his report. He wrote that most of the Viennese had settled in local villages.[25] On 10 January 1940, one of the deportees described in a letter:

I can no longer describe exactly what happened next because we experienced hours of enormous panic and uncertainty. The SS began suddenly to fire and yell: Get a move on! Forwards! Anyone who is found in an hour in a radius of five kilometres and anyone who tries to return to Nisko will be shot! Go across to your red brothers![26]

Some of the Jews escaped across the border to the Soviet Union. The men who arrived in Soviet-occupied Poland were ordered to opt for the Soviet Union. In January 1940, an appeal for help from Nisko reached Emil Engel from the Vienna Kultusgemeinde. 'Members of both Nisko transports' had asked via Lemberg (Lviv) for an 'urgently needed intervention'. They begged to be allowed to return to Vienna for a short while to be able to escape from there with their wives.[27] The German authorities in Lemberg refused. As the men had not opted for the Soviet Union, they were now regarded by the Soviets as enemies of the regime and deported to labour camps in Siberia; few of them survived. Those who remained in Soviet-occupied Poland fell into the hands of the advancing Wehrmacht a year later; practically all of them were killed in Belzec extermination camp.[28]

Only 198 of the Vienna Jews who had remained in Nisko were still alive in April 1940 and were allowed to return to Austria when the camp was closed. They also brought back to Vienna all the details of the deportations.

The men and women who had applied for the third transport to Poland were no longer deported to Nisko. Instead they were brought from Aspang railway station to a homeless shelter in Gänsbachergasse. The SS interned them and separated the men and the women. They were not released until early February 1940. Most of the Jews had given up their apartments before the date of deportation. They were now homeless.[29]

The Nisko undertaking was badly planned and hastily organized shortly after the outbreak of war. It was soon abandoned because of the objections by Generalgouverneur Frank, who would not accept a 'Jewish reservation' on his territory. In addition, the Nazi leadership was concentrating at the time on the resettlement plans from the Warthegau and the search for jobs and accommodation for 'ethnic Germans' from the Baltic. But the basic deportation concept had already been revealed in Nisko. Many of the organizational details had been established for the future deportation to the extermination camps that were to start in autumn 1941. The future exploitation of the IKG also followed the Nisko model.

Until February 1941, however, there was a period of respite. Löwenherz attempted to dissuade Eichmann from further deportations. The bargaining between the perpetrator and the victim can be studied in the reports he was required to write about his meetings. On 13 November 1939, Eichmann stated that the 'emigration' of Viennese Jews had to be completed by 1 February 1940. He promised in addition that the leaders and employees of the Kultusgemeinde would also be able to leave as soon as this task had been successfully completed. Anyone who had not left the country by then, Eichmann threatened, would be deported to Poland. Löwenherz retorted that between 20,000 and 30,000 Jews could not emigrate under any circumstances because they were sick or too old. Eichmann ignored these objections. On 2 December 1939, Löwenherz reported to Eichmann that the American Joint Distribution Committee had informed him that further funds would be forthcoming only if the emigration continued. If the Polish transports were started up again in March 1940, all money transfers would have to cease. Löwenherz added that no special measures were required for the *Entjudung* (eradication of the Jews) from Vienna. There were only 58,000 Jews left in Vienna and only 22,000–24,000 could not emigrate and would need to be looked after. The rest wanted to and could leave Austria by the end of 1940. Thereupon Eichmann authorized the head of the Kultusgemeinde to inform the Joint that the deportations would stop. The Joint should continue until the end of the year to provide funds, and the Kultusgemeinde must undertake to ensure that a defined number of Jews emigrated every month so as to complete the liquidation of the Jewish community by the end of October 1940. The American Joint Distribution Committee set three conditions before it would continue to transfer money to the Kultusgemeinde. First, the Poland transports had to be stopped. Second, the status of the Kultusgemeinde as a public-law institution should be upheld at least until the end of 1940. And third, the Central Office for Jewish Emigration should help the Kultusgemeinde in its emigration efforts.[30] The Jewish organizations hoped that these negotiations would enable them to prevent further deportations. In truth, the Nazis had decided themselves to suspend the transports to Nisko and to continue with the expulsions. Thus, the plan to deport the Jews of Vienna had not yet been discarded.

On 26 January 1940, after consultation with the director general of the Joint in Budapest, Löwenherz proposed a transfer project to Eichmann. The Joint had promised to send more money to Vienna. The Kultusgemeinde received US$ 100,000 and transferred the equivalent amount in Reichmarks and zloty to an institute in Warsaw for the benefit of Polish Jews. The money financed relief in Warsaw; the dollars in Vienna, however, were used for emigration.[31]

Löwenherz sought ways of making it possible for the Jews to escape and survive. The difficulties with emigrating to other countries grew as the war progressed, however. The Gestapo pursued its resettlement plan. In early December 1940, it was finally decided to deport the Jews remaining in Vienna to the Generalgouvernement.

Segregation, concentration and theft

The anti-Semitic laws were designed to segregate the Jews from society, to remove them from the rest of the population and to herd them into areas designated for that purpose. They were not permitted to enter public parks and were only allowed on the streets at certain times. Before the policy of mass extermination was finally decided, however, came segregation, which in retrospect must be seen as part of the extermination process. Even the perpetrators could not anticipate the inner logic of the process that was to end in systematic, comprehensive and professional genocide. There was no far-sighted plan, but nothing happened without a purpose.

In Austria, the concentration of the victims began shortly after the Anschluss. The Jews outside Vienna were forced to move to the capital. The Vienna Kultusgemeinde became responsible for the affairs of all local Jewish communities. This phase of concentration also included the increasing unification of the Jewish community organizations.

This model was copied in other cities. The idea was to bring all of the organizations under the control of the Gestapo. As mentioned earlier, Richard Friedmann, a Kultusgemeinde employee, was transferred in July 1939 to Prague to organize the Jewish administration there on the Viennese model. On 18 March 1941, two further Kultusgemeinde officials, Wilhelm Biberstein and Leo Israelowicz-Ilmar, were sent to Paris by SS-Hauptsturmführer Theodor Dannecker, who worked in Department II-112 together with Eichmann and was soon to represent him in the preparations for the deportation of Jews from various countries. Here, Dannecker, with the help of Biberstein and Israelowicz-Ilmar, attempted to build up a uniform Jewish organization, a Committee for Welfare Situations, under Nazi control and based on the Viennese model.[32]

In those cities in which the structures of the Kultusgemeinde and the Central Office for Jewish Emigration in Austria were copied, the Viennese Jewish officials Friedmann, Biberstein and Israelowicz-Ilmar must have appeared to the local Jews as the prototype of Jewish cooperation. They were German-speaking foreigners who had come with 'Eichmann men' to replace the established independent Jewish organizations by a centrally controlled institution.

The emigration that had been imposed as a result of the organized terror and that had seen the departure of 104,000 Jews from Vienna by the end of July 1939[33] had tailed off rapidly, particularly since the outbreak of war. In 1939, the Jews of Vienna were already being forced into Jewish houses and Jewish quarters. In January 1940, Jews were still allowed to shop in their own Jewish stores at certain times of the day. Here they were at the mercy of the anti-Semitic mob. Shopping became a perilous affair.[34] Jews were unwanted on the streets. Even IKG director Josef Löwenherz, or Josef Israel Löwenherz, as he was now obliged to call himself, had to have permission from the Gestapo endorsed by his deputy Engel if he wanted to go home after the start of curfew.[35]

At the same time, the Kultusgemeinde attempted to attenuate the segregation through petitions and meetings with the authorities. On 17 May 1940, the Kultusgemeinde wrote a letter to the Vienna police headquarters in which Löwenherz asked that two parks be opened to the Jews.[36] The request was refused.[37]

In his countless meetings and reports, Löwenherz pointed out that the concentration of Jewish families in confined spaces increased the risk of epidemics. When he made an appointment with Dr Leopold Tavs, a deputy in the Vienna city administration, on 25 November 1940, he was unable to see Tavs directly because for ideological reasons the deputy did not receive Jews. Löwenherz got no further than an outer office, where he complained that Jews were being concentrated in inadequate premises. Married and unmarried, young and old, men and women were living in the same room. They were being forced into premises without bathrooms, heating or cooking facilities. Some had been assigned to apartments that were already occupied; many had to leave accommodation that they had only just moved into.[38]

The dispossessed and evicted Jews lived in extremely cramped conditions. The housing situation changed the mental state and outward appearance of the victims, who began to resemble the stereotype of the abject ghetto Jew. The victims of eviction were moved from one place to another. The Kultusgemeinde often had to settle quarrels when Jews were not allowed to move into the rooms that had been allocated to them. The victims of forced eviction made serious criticisms of the Kultusgemeinde. The Jewish administration was accused of collaboration. The Kultusgemeinde registrar of the time, Julius Rosenfeld, received a list of apartments that had to be cleared within two weeks, after which he was to return the list to the Gestapo indicating where the Jews had moved to or which apartments had not been cleared. Rosenfeld warned everyone who refused to move that he would have to inform the Gestapo in two weeks because he couldn't leave the relevant column in the list empty. If a Jew did not move out of his apartment, his furniture would be put out onto the street and he would be arrested and deported to a concentration camp.[39]

Often the officials in the housing department did not provide a new address. Jews who had not been allocated new accommodation and whose apartments had already been promised to non-Jews were in danger of being left homeless.[40] Sometimes they were set upon in their own four walls and forced at gunpoint to sign an undertaking to leave their apartment within one day.[41] As they could not usually take their furniture with them, their affairs generally ended up in the Furniture Disposal Office of the Gestapo Administrative Office for Jewish Property Removals, or 'Vugesta'. This department had originally been set up to collect valuables from Jews leaving Austria. The Jewish possessions were sold cheaply to museums and to Nazi clients on the basis of a distribution plan. In 1938, Jews were still allowed to export some of their belongings after payment of a tax equivalent to the real value. When war broke out, all removal goods had to be left behind. The furniture belonging to the evictees was bought for next to nothing by the Gestapo treasurers Bernhard Wittke and Anton Grimm and taken to the Furniture Disposal Office. The dealers acting for Vugesta employed forced Jewish labour to clear the apartments and their warehouses, paying them a pittance for it.[42] The systematic plundering was completely effective. The system had been set up originally to take possession of the valuables and belongings of Jews who were leaving; then the Nazi client community plundered the evicted; and finally the possessions of deportees were sold off cheaply.

After the outbreak of war, there was a shortage of labour. Jews were now exploited for road works and rubbish collection. They were treated as slaves, being paid minimum wages and being allowed only to carry out menial work. The plan to construct a Jewish labour camp near Vienna was abandoned because of the cost.[43] The creation of an open semi-ghetto consisting of isolated streets and blocks of houses was thought to be cheaper.

The rehousing phase was only an intermediate stage on the way to final deportation of the Jews to the extermination camps. Between 1938 and 1942, around 70,000 apartments were vacated through the expulsion and forced emigration of Viennese Jews. This was 10,000 apartments more than had been built under the Red Vienna housing policy until 1934.[44] This is not to say that the economic motive was of decisive importance in the extermination. In later phases, financial and strategic considerations even became subordinate to the prior aim of extermination.

Without a doubt, however, the Nazi's Jewish policy, the expulsion and terror, had been highly profitable. Many people benefited from the powerlessness of the victims. The concentration, segregation and ghettoization were a preliminary to deportation. On 16 June 1940, Josef Löwenherz again appeared before Eichmann and reported on a directive by the Ministry of the Interior calling for the Kultusgemeinde registers to be handed over to the city administration on 30 June 1940.[45] There was no talk of deportation in this regard. Löwenherz was still trying to enable Jews to get away. On 13 October 1940, he was informed by the Gestapo that a ration card register was to be established for the 60,000 Jews, including the non-practising Jews. The Kultusgemeinde was to provide 30 people to set up this central register. From 1 November 1940, the ration cards of all registered Jews had the word 'Jude' stamped on them.[46]

Anyone, young or old, who wanted to eat had to be registered. The Jewish administration was successfully deceived. The register that had been ostensibly created to centralize the organization of food rations was used to keep a record for the exploitation of the Jews, their deportation and murder, for the machinery of extermination.

— 9 —

DEPORTATION AND EXTERMINATION

I can only tell you that it would have been better if they had lined us all up against the wall in Vienna. It would have been a good death, we are dying in greater misery.
A deportee in a letter from Opole to Vienna on 18 February 1941[1]

On 3 July 1940, Adolf Eichmann told the head of the Jewish community Josef Löwenherz that a 'total solution to the European Jewish question' would have to be found after the war. The problem concerned four million Jews, he said. Eichmann wanted to know whether any plans to that end had been discussed. Löwenherz said no, whereupon the SS-Hauptsturmführer ordered the Jewish functionary to provide a list by the next day of the general considerations that would have to be taken into account in such a plan. Löwenherz replied that a plan of that sort could be considered only with reference to a specific settlement region. In addition, the financial resources would have to be known. Eichmann said he wanted only some approximate guidelines. Emigration should be completed without hardship in three to four years. Palestine could be taken as the destination country. Löwenherz set about the task immediately and handed in his report the following day, 4 July 1940.[2]

In reality, however, the Nazi leadership did not intend to wait until the end of the war to remove the Jews from the territories they were ruling over. 'On October 2, 1940, the after-dinner conversation in Hitler's apartment turned to the situation in the Generalgouvernement. Governor [Hans] Frank reported that "the activity in the Generalgouvernement can be described as successful. The Jews in Warsaw and other cities now are isolated in ghettos. Kraków soon will be 'clean' of Jews." '[3]

The new Reichsstatthalter and Gauleiter of Vienna, Baldur von Schirach, remarked that in Vienna 'he still had 50,000 Jews whom

Dr. Frank needed to take off his hands. According to Frank this was impossible.'[4] Frank did not want all of the Jews to be deported to the Generalgouvernement, mentioning the lack of space and population density. Hitler told Frank succinctly that the population density in the Generalgouvernement was of no consequence to him. On 3 December 1940, Baldur von Schirach received a letter written by Heinrich Lammers, head of the Reich Chancellery, on behalf of Reichleiter Martin Bormann, informing him that Hitler had approved the deportation of the Jews from Vienna.[5]

On Thursday, 23 January 1941, over a month after this decision, Löwenherz made an oral and written report to Hauptsturmführer Rolf Günther, head of the Central Office at the time, on his trip to Lisbon. He attempted to paint the possibilities for Jewish emigration in as optimistic a light as possible. The meeting suddenly took an unexpected turn, however; Löwenherz reported that the Jewish population was very worried. There were repeated rumours of an imminent resettlement of the Jews in Poland. Löwenherz asked that this plan be abandoned as it would not merely be a disaster for the Viennese Jews but would also mark the end of support from the Joint, not just for the Ostmark but also for the Altreich and the Protectorate. He added that after the war a major emigration plan could be completed only with the help of the Joint. The problem of evacuating the Jews (*Entjudungsproblem*) could be solved only by legal means, he told Günther. The SS man's only reply was to say that he knew nothing of a resettlement plan to Poland and if one existed he would know about it. He promised to enquire and to let Löwenherz know.[6]

On 1 February 1941, nine days after this conversation, all of the fears and rumours within the Jewish community were confirmed. Summoned to appear at the Gestapo headquarters at 12 noon, Löwenherz was informed by Regierungsrat Karl Ebner, head of the Jewish department of the Gestapo in Vienna, in the presence of SS-Obersturmführer Alois Brunner, Günther's successor as head of the Central Office, of the plan to resettle some of the Jews of Vienna in the Generalgouvernement. In a memo of this meeting, Löwenherz noted: 'The Kultusgemeinde is to be kept out of this action and will only have to carry out the instructions it is given. – Each transport is to contain around 1,000 persons. . . . The intention is to resettle 10,000 Jews in the General-Gouvernement by May 1941.'[7]

Five thousand people were deported that spring. Although it had been promised that the Kultusgemeinde would not be involved in the action, the instructions to the Jewish administration are precisely indicated in the director's memo. It was made clear, however, that the Central Office would draw up the deportation lists. 'Each emigrant may take two suitcases or bundles of a maximum 50 kg weight.'[8]

Those targeted for deportation had to report to a collection point in a former school at Castellezgasse 35. A school at Kleine Sperlgasse 2a functioned as a second collection point.[9]

The deportees were to bring their ration cards to the collection point and hand them in. Löwenherz was informed that Jews could take any amount of cash with them; an official of the Reichsbank at the collection point would change the marks into zloty. A precise list of assets, property rights and entitlements was to be delivered to the collection point and the Gestapo was to be informed of the name and address of the property administrator. 'The proceeds from the sale of these assets will be used to defray the expenses of resettlement and emigration and the definitive solution of the Jewish problem.'[10] The Jews had to pay the cost of deportation and extermination themselves.

The Kultusgemeinde was to notify those selected for deportation. In addition, the Jewish administration was to clear the building to be used as a collection point as quickly as possible, remove the furnishings and have a telephone installed there. It was also responsible for providing food for the internees in the collection points. The emigration of the Viennese Jews was to be continued by the Jewish authorities but the retraining courses in which refugees learned new professions were to be discontinued immediately. Members of the Kultusgemeinde and its institutions could be removed from the deportation lists. The Kultusgemeinde was to decide which officials were indispensable and which not. The teachers of the school in Castellezgasse and the persons responsible for retraining were to be dismissed immediately.

The Jewish community was required to produce an updated list of those supported by it. The list, arranged by families, had to be presented to the Central Office for Jewish Emigration. The Central Office had included a large number of Kultusgemeinde employees in the first deportation. Löwenherz therefore asked SS-Obersturmführer Brunner to remove them from the list as he required them urgently for the smooth running of the work of the Kultusgemeinde. Brunner agreed to exempt IKG employees from deportation if all of the other persons on the list were present as arranged at the collection point. Under these circumstances, he also told Löwenherz that he would be willing to remove persons capable of emigration in the very near future.[11] The promise to exempt some people from the transports and to allow a few to emigrate made it easier for Brunner to blackmail the community into cooperating.

The deportations in early 1941 helped the Jewish leadership in Vienna to define its strategy with respect to the mass deportations by the Nazis. As emigration was still possible, they complied with the orders of the Nazi authorities so as to prevent worse. In 1941, more than 6,000 Jews were able to escape from the Third Reich in this way.

All that remained for Löwenherz at the end of his meeting with Brunner was to plead for better provisions for the journey, to give each deportee a bar of soap and to distribute breakfast and supper, tea or coffee, soup and cheese to the internees at the collection point. Brunner agreed to these requests.[12]

In the weekly reports that Löwenherz was required to present to the Nazi authorities, he made his position quite clear. In the report of 4 February 1941, he repeated that the community would be responsible 'only' for the preparation and feeding of those selected.[13] In the weekly report of 11 February, he stressed the need not to deport indispensable Kultusgemeinde employees.[14]

The community leadership had to make a selection from within its ranks. They determined who was irreplaceable in Vienna. For every employee who was to remain in Vienna, however, the IKG had to provide a substitute, the selection being made not by the Jewish administration but by the Nazi authorities.[15]

On 15 February, the first train departed for the Generalgouvernement. By 12 March, four further transports had left. Around 5,000 Viennese Jews were deported in these transports. They were settled in small rural towns – Opole, Kielce, Modliborczicze and Lagow – where they lived in wretched conditions with little food. This under-provision was deliberate. At this time, the Reich Security Main Office wanted 'merely' to starve the Jews.[16]

On 17 June 1941, Löwenherz requested that the deportees be returned to Vienna and also mitigated for the release of Jewish inmates from Buchenwald and Dachau. He told SS-Obersturmführer Alois Brunner that he had received letters from the Generalgouvernement and that all efforts to send aid had been insufficient, but Brunner said that the deportees could not under any circumstances return to Vienna.[17]

By April 1941, thirty of the deportees from Vienna had died in Opole because of the inadequate supplies. A few had been able to return illegally to Vienna; others had been classified by the SS as fit for work and sent to labour camps. Most fell victim from early summer 1942 to the combing out operations in the Polish ghettos and were killed with Polish Jews from the various towns in the extermination camps of Belzec, Sobibor and Treblinka.[18]

After the fifth transport from Vienna in early 1941, the Nazi organizers suspended the deportations. In Vienna, the Nazi authorities used this pause to further segregate the Jewish population. On 1 June 1941, all changes of address by Jews without the prior authorization of the Central Office were forbidden. From September 1941, Jews had to wear a yellow star distributed to them by the Kultusgemeinde. Jews were not allowed to leave the community in which they lived without police permission. The use of public transport and indeed all freedom of movement were increasingly curtailed.[19]

Following the invasion of the Soviet Union on 22 June 1941, the Nazi rulers embarked on the mass extermination of the Jews. Initially, small SS and police units were sent to the occupied Soviet territories to kill the local Jewish inhabitants. Whereas the perpetrators in the Soviet war zone were brought to the victims, in other parts of Europe the victims were brought to the perpetrators to be killed in extermination centres – after September 1941 in trucks converted into mobile gas chambers. Then came a demand from on high for 'more rational' methods of extermination. The decision to exterminate the European Jewry was thus taken long before the Wannsee conference on 20 January 1942, which merely coordinated and defined the different responsibilities and interest groups within Nazi society for the purpose of the Final Solution; the mass murder was already well under way.

On 6 September 1941, the same day on which Josef Löwenherz heard at a meeting in Berlin of the introduction of the yellow star, he asked Adolf Eichmann whether recent rumours of further deportations were true. Eichmann said that he was not aware of any such intention.[20] As with the first wave of deportations, this denial was promptly followed by a confirmation of the rumours and the order for deportation. On 30 September, Alois Brunner informed Löwenherz that some of the Jews from Germany, Vienna and the Protectorate were to be deported to Litzmannstadt, as the Nazis renamed Lodz.[21] The lists for these transports were once again compiled by the Central Office for Jewish Emigration and the Kultusgemeinde was once again able to have individuals exempted. It was responsible for notifying and feeding the deportees.[22]

Löwenherz was informed of this on the morning of 30 September. That evening was the start of Yom Kippur, the highest Jewish Holy Day. Löwenherz had told only a few functionaries of the terrible news. When he was called up to read the Torah and stood before the community, however, he could no longer hold back the tears and all the Jews gathered in the temple in Seitenstettengasse understood what had happened. The rumours that had been circulating for weeks had proved to be true.[23]

In autumn 1941, some 20,000 Jewish men, women and children from the Altreich, Ostmark, Protectorate of Moravia and Bohemia and Luxembourg, as well as 5,000 Roma and Sinti from Austria, were deported to the ghetto in Lodz. Five transports of more than 5,000 Austrian Jews left for Lodz in less than three weeks: on 15, 19, 23 and 28 October and 2 November 1941. For three weeks, the new arrivals wandered through the streets of the ghetto looking for somewhere to stay. Many were quickly classified as 'unfit for work' and deported from January 1942 onwards to Chelmno (Kulmhof) where they were murdered in the mobile killing machinery. Thousands died in the ghetto of hunger, disease or exhaustion. By the beginning of summer 1942, the SS had killed around half of the 20,000 Jews deported in October/November 1941 to Lodz. In autumn 1942, only 2,503 were still living.[24]

At the end of October 1941, the order was given for the deportation of 50,000 Jews from the Altreich, Ostmark and Protectorate of Moravia and Bohemia to Riga and Minsk, shifting the focus to the occupied eastern territories where the *Einsatztruppen* or mobile killing units were to be found. On 27 October 1941, Brunner informed Löwenherz of the new deportations. Löwenherz urged that the orphans in the Jewish community homes be exempted from the transports until the following spring. Brunner agreed not to deport the orphans for the time being. He also allowed employees of the Jewish administration and Jewish health workers to be removed from the transports. Refugees with emigration papers were no longer exempted, however. When Löwenherz informed Brunner on 5 November once again of 150 individuals and their families with immigration visas and the possibility of leaving in the near future, Brunner decided that emigration was no longer an option. On 10 November 1941, the borders of the German Reich were closed for refugees; with very few exceptions, emigration was no longer possible; all means of escape had now been blocked.[25]

On 13 November, Löwenherz was ordered to see to the deportation of persons who had returned from the Generalgouvernement. These were Jews who had been deported in early 1941 but had managed to return to Vienna. As these 200 or so persons had nowhere to hide in Vienna, they were quickly rounded up. The Central Office sent them to the collection point in Castellezgasse from where they were to be deported again in one of the next trains. Löwenherz asked that the returnees be exempt from deportation but that they be included in the 1,000 people calculated for each train. Brunner refused, saying that the required quotas had to be filled in reality.[26]

The first five transports to the Reichskommissariat Ostland in November 1941 from Berlin, Frankfurt am Main, Munich, Vienna and Wroclaw ended not in Riga as had been announced but in Kowno. Here the deported men, women and children were shot immediately on arrival by SS units with the assistance of Lithuanian collaborators. After the murder of 20,000 Latvian Jews on 'Bloody Sunday' in the ghetto in Riga in early December, the deportees from the Greater German Reich were lodged in the emptied ghetto, an additional reception centre and a further barrack camp. Many of the deportees died as a result of the shortages, terrible living conditions, epidemics and cold winter. Selections began in early 1942 and thousands were killed. The sick were the first to be murdered and only around 800 of the 20,000 deported men, women and children survived the selections, the ghetto and the various concentration camps.[27]

On 7 November 1941, the SS killed around 12,000 White Russian Jews in Minsk. The massacre served as preparation for the deportations from the Greater German Reich. The deportees were housed in the premises previously occupied by those who had been killed; in addition a German ghetto was formed in Minsk. The conditions were terrible; many died of hunger or froze to death. From May 1942, the SS transported most of the deportees directly on arrival at the station to mass dug-out graves where they were killed.[28] Many died on the journey because of the terrible deprivations or were clubbed and beaten to death by the guards; several suffered nervous breakdowns and were completely disorientated. In Minsk, a few men were detained to unload the baggage, the other deportees being taken away immediately.[29] 'Windowless grey vans were waiting to take away the sick, old and infirm and those who had been driven mad by the journey. They were simply thrown in to the van on top of one another, men, women, the old, the sick, the crazy and the dead.'[30]

A very few deportees were selected for forced labour in the SS farm Maly Trostinec. The rest were shot or gassed. Four gas trucks were in operation. The Minsk ghetto was finally liquidated in October 1943. The SS did not forget to kill the inmates at Maly Trostinec before the Red Army approached. A survivor estimates that only twenty-five to thirty inmates of Maly Trostinec survived.[31]

On 19 February 1942, Eichmann summoned Löwenherz and Murmelstein to Berlin, where he informed them, together with six further members of the Reich Agency of the Jews in Germany and two functionaries from Prague, of the plan for the complete evacuation of the Jews from the Altreich, Ostmark and Protectorate. Löwenherz said that in his opinion a complete evacuation from Vienna would not be possible because, following the forced emigration, an above-average number of old and sick remained who were not fit for transport. In addition, Jews protected by being in mixed marriages would also remain. Eichmann said that the transports would be arranged together with the Wehrmacht but that he would bear in mind the Jewish functionary's request.[32]

From spring 1942, the Jews of Vienna were deported to Izbica and Wlodawa in the district of Lublin. Most were gassed with Polish Jews from these two ghettos in Sobibor and Belzec. In June 1942, a transport with Jews from Vienna went directly to Sobibor although it had originally been heading for Izbica. This deportation is described in an incident report by the accompanying police guards. A thousand Jews were herded into the wagons. The guards complained: 'Because of the shortage of wagons, the guards had to make do with a third-class carriage instead of a second-class one.'[33]

The train left Vienna at 7.08 p.m. and arrived in Lublin at 9 p.m. on 16 June 1942, two days later, where SS-Obersturmführer Pohl selected 51 Jews aged between 15 and 50 years who were fit for work to be transported to Trawniki labour camp. Here the accompanying unit handed over three baggage wagons with food and the money from the Jewish victims, 100,000 zloty. On the morning of 17 June 1942, some 949 deportees were transported to Sobibor and handed over to the Austrian security police Oberleutnant Franz Stangl and killed in the camp.

The Viennese police returned directly to Lublin after 'unloading the Jews', as it says in the incident report. 'No travel expenses were paid for this journey.'[34]

The Viennese police travelled to Krakow, where they remained for a day before continuing back to Vienna. No incidents were reported. But the executive officer, who had been in charge of transporting the Jews to their death, made a personal complaint:

> In future the members of the transport commando should be issued marching rations because the cold rations do not keep. By 15 June the sausage – it was spreading sausage – was already running and oozy and had to be eaten by the third day because it was in danger of spoiling. On the fourth day the men had to make do with jam as the butter had gone rancid because of the heat in the carriage. The quantities were also insufficient.[35]

The last great wave of deportations began in June 1942 and ended in October that year; the destination was Theresienstadt. Jews who had hitherto been exempt were now included in the transport. Jewish spouses in a mixed marriage (Mischlinge), the infirm and war invalids with bravery medals were told that they would be taken to an old people's ghetto.

Theresienstadt served as a facade to present an apparently 'humane' Nazi Jewish policy and was also a transshipment point for the death camps. Almost 70 per cent of the Austrian Jews deported there were ultimately gassed in Auschwitz. In 1942, 13,776 people were deported from Vienna to Theresienstadt.[36] The various deportation waves overlapped. In June 1942, a number of trains set off at the same time for Minsk, Izbica, Sobibor and Theresienstadt.

In October 1942, there were still around 8,600 people living in Vienna who were Jewish, according to the Nuremberg laws. Of these, 6,600 were in mixed marriages.[37] The IKG was closed in November 1942 and its work and that of the aid organizations for non-Mosaic non-Aryans was taken over by the Council of Elders of Jews in Vienna. There were financial reasons for the closure, since the German Reich was to take over ownership of the public-law institution. The IKG assets had served their function; welfare, emigration and deportation had been paid for in part from the assets of the administrative apparatus and the Jewish foundations.[38]

According to the Council of Elders, on 1 January 1943 there were still 7,989 people living in Vienna who were defined as Jews under the Nuremberg laws.[39] Most of them were in mixed marriages or were protected by having an Aryan parent. If the non-Jewish partner or Aryan parent died, the protection was removed. It was almost impossible for practising Jews who were not married to a non-Jewish spouse to remain in Vienna unless they worked for the Council of Elders. But the Jewish administrative apparatus was required to continuously reduce its staff, and every dismissal meant deportation and extermination.

Between March 1943 and October 1944, around 350 people were deported by the Gestapo in smaller transports to Auschwitz, and a further 1,400 to Theresienstadt.[40] On 31 December 1944, the Council of Elders reported 5,799 people still in Vienna who were persecuted as Jews on the basis of the Nuremberg laws. Of these, 1,053 were practising Jews. Research to date has revealed a further 600 or so 'submarines', i.e., Jews in hiding, who survived the Nazi regime in Austria.[41] This was all that was left of the former 200,000 Jews in the country.

In the last phase of National Socialism, the Jewish victims were to suffer not only from the far-reaching plans of the Nazi regime but also from the personal hatred of many individual anti-Semites. An anonymous denunciation received on 20 February 1941 by the *Rassenpolitisches Amt* (Office of Race Policy) was no isolated instance:

The authorities have become aware that Grete F. [address], married to Fritz F., is a Jew. . . . It is no doubt hard for individuals and in human terms, but who asks our soldiers and the mothers of the women if it is hard for them? And if they want to die? War is war. – Please check F.'s documents carefully! If they are in order, you need say nothing about the letter. I don't want to do anyone an injustice. But I cannot believe that she is Aryan. And if she is a Jew, why should she be allowed to cheat like this!![42]

—10—

THE ADMINISTRATION
OF EXTERMINATION

Segregation and identification or
a Jewish star for ten pfennigs

The Kultusgemeinde was required to cooperate in the segregation of
the Jews. As mentioned in the previous chapter, this process was by
no means complete when the deportations began. The aggression
against the few remaining Jews took the form of new regulations.
Freedom of movement was increasingly curtailed and the Jews were
branded by being forced to wear a yellow star. This star identified
those who had not yet been deported. Jews were attacked in public.
The Jewish star made them readily identifiable and easy prey. When
in winter 1941–2, an elderly Jewish war invalid slipped on the ice
and fell, he asked in vain for assistance from passers-by. They ignored
him. It took him three hours to get up on his own and he broke his
right wrist in doing so. None of the Red Cross ambulances, which
were still required at the time to transport Jews, would come to
collect him. He remained at home unattended for days before he
managed to get to a hospital on his own.[1]

How was the Jewish administration involved in the task of identifying the Jews? On 6 September 1941, Dr Paul Eppstein from the Reich
Agency of the Jews in Germany and Dr Josef Löwenherz were summoned to appear before Sturmbannführer Rolf Günther and
Sturmbannführer Regierungsrat Friedrich Suhr at the Reich Security
Main Office.[2] On 5 September, a police regulation on the identification of Jews was published.[3] The two Jewish functionaries were
informed that the stars would be handed to the Reich Agency in
Berlin on 16 September and to the Kultusgemeinde in Vienna the
following day. The Jewish organizations were required initially to
distribute one star to each person. By 15 October, there would be

four stars for every Jew. The issue, said Günther and Suhr, should depend on individual requirements. If necessary, a Jew could receive fewer or more than four stars.

The Kultusgemeinde in Vienna was responsible for distribution of the Jewish stars in the Ostmark. The Jewish administration had to ensure that the Austrian Jews would have stars by 19 September. This gave it very little time to organize and distribute the stars, as it was only to receive the yellow material on 17 September.

The Kultusgemeinde had to pay five pfennigs for every star; it was ordered to sell them for ten pfennigs each, the difference being used to cover the administrative costs resulting from the police regulation. Once again the Jews were being called upon to pay for the discrimination against them. Every person receiving a Jewish star was to sign a receipt.[4]

At the meeting on 6 September, Günther and Suhr also mentioned that Jews were prohibited from leaving the community in which they lived without permission from the local authority, which in Vienna was the Central Office for Jewish Emigration. The prohibition was part of the Police Regulation on the Identification of the Jews, which included a whole package of restrictions.[5]

The Jewish organizations were to publish the new regulation in the *Jüdisches Nachrichtenblatt*. In Vienna, the Emigration Aid Organization for non-Mosaic Jews was to distribute the stars to non-practising Jews. The Kultusgemeinde had to pass on the necessary Jewish stars to the Emigration Aid Organization. At the meeting on 6 September, Eppstein and Löwenherz were informed that all violations of the regulation would be punished by a fine and immediate imprisonment.

On 9 September, Eppstein and Dr Arthur Lilienthal from the Reich Agency of the Jews in Germany sent a circular to the district offices of the Reich Agency with the details of the identification order. It informed its members: 'We expect all Jews to respect the obligation to show the greatest restraint in public, which has now become even more important with the introduction of the identification, and to bear in mind more than ever their responsibility to our community at all times, particularly in their demeanour in public.'[6]

On 10 September, Benjamin Murmelstein sent guidelines on the police regulation to all departments in Vienna. The Jewish star was to be issued to all Jews in the German Reich; children over the age of six years also had to wear it.[7] The departments also received separate summaries of the specific tasks. The action called for the cooperation of the entire institution. The legal department was to issue an official statement on the regulation and provide an instruction leaflet on its implementation. This statement was to emphasize that there were no exemptions. Applications for exemption from wearing the Jewish star were pointless and should not therefore be attempted. Punishments for violations would be much more severe than indicated in the regulation. The education department was to distribute the 'Jewish stars' in schools. There were nineteen issuing offices in Vienna for practising Jews and three for non-practising Jews. The supply department was instructed to make receipts with the following text: 'I confirm receipt of one Jewish identifying mark as ordered in the regulation of 1 September 1941.'[8]

To ensure distribution in time, the Kultusgemeinde had to make 176,000 stars. The employees worked day and night; the Jewish stars had to be cut out of the bales of cloth.[9] They could be purchased in the issuing offices between 7 a.m. and 8 p.m.[10] Oskar Meisel, a voluntary employee, refused to issue the Jewish stars. Born in 1873, he was deported a year later on 1 October 1942 with one of the last major transports containing most of the Kultusgemeinde employees and workers to Theresienstadt. He did not survive.[11]

According to the guideline on the police regulation, the Kultusgemeinde had to inform all of its departments who was exempt from wearing the identifying mark. The complicated distinction between Jew and Mischling was explained. Countless individual cases had to be discussed. Foreign Jews were exempt from the regulation; the German Reich had to allow for international and diplomatic interests. Others exempt from wearing the Jewish star were

Jews married to Aryans if they have children from their marriage who are not considered Jews; this exemption also applies if the marriage no longer exists or if the only son of this marriage has fallen in the current war; Jewish women married to Aryan men whose marriage is childless but only as long as the marriage exists; the Jewish widow or divorced wife of an Aryan man has to wear the identification unless the marriage has produced children that are not considered Jewish.[12]

These regulations were designed to ensure that the Reich German 'ethnic community' was not affected by the anti-Semitic discrimination. A Wehrmacht soldier under Hitler's supreme command need not fear that his mother or father could be branded as a Jew in the event of his 'heroic death'. A non-Jew could protect his childless Jewish wife. A non-Jewess, by contrast, could not protect her Jewish husband from persecution if their marriage was childless. 'Mischlinge' were only exempt from wearing the Jewish star if they had not practised the Jewish religion or been married to a Jew since 15 September 1935, the day on which the Nuremberg laws entered into force.[13]

The Kultusgemeinde bore responsibility for the branding of its members. Moreover, it had to persuade the Jews of the need to observe the regulation strictly. A violation would mean immediate arrest and deportation. The Jewish authorities even had to distribute stars to victims at the collection points who had already been herded together for deportation.[14]

In April 1942, the Jews were ordered to affix a Jewish star to their doors. If Jews obliged to wear a star were living in apartments with relatives who were exempt, stars had to be attached to the nameplates of the Jews. Once again it was the Kultusgemeinde that announced the official order and issued the stars.[15]

The Jewish authorities also had to announce on 4 April 1942 that Jews could no longer use tram lines D and 40. This was a deliberate provocation since the Jewish cemetery, the Rothschild Hospital and the Central Office for Jewish Emigration were all on these lines. Travel on all other lines was forbidden after 2 p.m. on Saturdays and all day on Sundays and public holidays.[16] From May 1942, Jews were forbidden from using public transport at all within the area they lived, the only exception being if it took longer than one hour on foot to get from home to work, in other words if the distance one way was greater than seven kilometres. Kultusgemeinde employees, the infirm and sick, war invalids, schoolchildren, Jewish legal advisers and health workers were allowed to use the trams. The Kultusgemeinde was responsible for issuing the individual permits.[17] In spite of this entitlement, the young Kultusgemeinde employee Kurt Mezei was thrown out of a moving tram and his mother and sister were threatened because a non-Jewish passenger found it unacceptable to ride in the same tramcar as Jews.[18]

On 18 May 1942, a resistance organization, the Herbert Baum group, carried out an arson attack on the Nazi propaganda exhibition 'Das Sowjetparadies' against the 'Jewish-Bolshevist international enemy'. The Herbert Baum group was a Communist group, most of whose members were Jewish. On Friday, 29 May 1942, Josef Löwenherz and Benjamin Murmelstein were ordered to report to the Reich Security Main Office in Berlin together with two representatives of the Jewish authorities in Prague. They were made first of all to stand against a wall for six hours and were then informed that, in retaliation for the act of sabotage, 500 Jews were to be arrested in Berlin, 250 of them shot and 250 deported to a concentration camp.

Similar reactions could be expected, with the involvement of members of the board and their families, if acts of this nature occurred again. This information was to be communicated to all Jews 'in an appropriate manner', not through the *Jüdisches Nachrichtenblatt* but in a written circular.[19]

The Jewish administration in Vienna was unable to prevent these acts of discrimination but attempted through submissive requests for individual relief and complied with the official instructions so as not to endanger the Jewish welfare apparatus.

Liquidation – expropriation to the last

The dismissals, exploitation and expropriation of the Vienna Jews had begun in March 1938; the economic destruction was therefore undertaken by the Nazi authorities long before the physical extermination. The Jews were plundered and exploited through forced labour. Their homes were taken from them and they received limited food rations.

In 1941, further discriminatory regulations entered into force. In October 1941, Jews lost all labour law protection.[20] On 25 November 1941, the Eleventh Decree concerning the Reich Citizenship Law was promulgated, stating that a Jew with 'his normal place of abode abroad' forfeited his German citizenship and his assets.[21] This law covered not only those who had escaped but every deportee as well. The Nazi bureaucrats knew that the Jews would not be returning; they were greedy to get hold of the assets they had left behind. The property that had been taken from its Jewish owners, confiscated and held in trust was now to be raked in. The Eleventh Decree concerning the Reich Citizenship Law regularized the forfeiture of the assets of all deportees.

For non-Jewish German creditors, the law stated that the Reich would be liable for Jewish debts only to the extent of the market value of the confiscated assets and only if the payments did not run counter to 'popular sensitivities'. Non-Jews who had received support from Jews could claim compensation, which again could not exceed the market value of the confiscated assets. These provisions were intended for the non-Jewish relatives of deportees. Pensions and insurance payments were suspended as soon as the recipients had been deported. The deportees were allowed to take with them to Poland only the small amounts of cash and personal belongings they still possessed. This was done so as to maintain the pretence of 'resettlement' but was normally taken off them as well on arrival.

The Kultusgemeinde also had to cooperate in financial terms. It collected records of the accounts of deportees showing how much they had deposited in the bank. It did its best at least to pay the taxes from these accounts. This money was used to finance all Jewish institutions and the additional deportation arrangements.

The Jews remaining in Vienna were no longer permitted to dispose of their movable assets prior to their deportation. In a circular on 1 December 1941, the Kultusgemeinde was required to communicate the 'restrictions for Jews on the disposal of movable assets'.[22]

On 21 May 1941, Obersturmführer Alois Brunner informed Löwenherz that the Jews of Vienna were to be moved from the districts in which they lived and resettled in the 2nd, 9th and 20th districts. Löwenherz requested that Jews who had already been rehoused several times be allowed to remain in the accommodation that had been allocated to them, which was already cramped. On 29 May, Brunner reported that the request had been passed on but that the Jewish resettlement would nevertheless take place. As there were 53,208 people in Vienna registered as Jews in accordance with the Nuremberg laws, of whom 43,200 lived in the 2nd, 9th and 20th districts, 10,000 were affected by this rehousing.[23]

The Gestapo Administrative Office for Jewish Property Removals, 'Vugesta' for short, sold the property of those who had been rehoused and deported. All of the purchasers knew where the objects came from. Those items that had to be left behind were taken away by Jewish workers by order of the Gestapo treasurers Bernhard Wittke and Anton Grimm. A special department within the Kultusgemeinde, the 'search group', as it was called, was responsible for providing trucks to carry out this work.[24] The Jews who worked for Vugesta were not infrequently recruited from the collection point before deportation.

Apart from the valuables, which had without exception to be handed over to the Nazi authorities, some of the deportees' belongings were kept for Jews who had not yet been deported. On 16 December 1941, Löwenherz asked Karl Ebner, head of the Gestapo department for Jewish affairs, to permit the Kultusgemeinde to appropriate the furniture of the deportees and to apply for permission retrospectively. He also requested that Jews be allowed to donate textiles, shoes, mattresses and bedding to the clothing department.[25] The Kultusgemeinde clothing and shoe departments worked not only for Jewish welfare; Gestapo officers also had clothing and shoes made for themselves and their families. The Nazi functionaries made use of skilled workers from the Jewish community to decorate their villas and houses as well.[26]

The Jewish welfare organization had to look after those who had been transported to the collection points by providing them with food. At the same time, they sought out the belongings that they would not need in the camps so as to distribute them to Jews still living in Vienna who no longer had beds, mattresses or clothing. In this way the extermination and self-help and survival mechanisms overlapped.

The Kultusgemeinde kept precise records of the house evacuations. They had lists showing the street, house number and owner with a separate column indicating whether the key was missing or whether the evacuation levy had been paid or not.[27] Robert Prochnik wrote reports indicating how many apartments with how many rooms for how many persons were opened and made available in a month, who had paid for the work and to whom the objects in them had been handed over. Every box, every lid was listed; what had been given to Wittke, what to Grimm and what the Kultusgemeinde had kept itself. Old clothes, simple beds and cheap furniture were left with the Jewish welfare organization. The jewellery, gold and money, the ivory fans and silverware went to the Vugesta treasurer Anton Grimm.[28]

As the Nazi bureaucrats did not wish to wait for the Jews to be deported in order to get their hands on their property, and because some Jews were not yet scheduled for deportation, the Gestapo started to collect their belongings even before they were deported. It was also keen on raking in the booty without the Ministry of Finance knowing about it and therefore ordered the Kultusgemeinde to make regular collections. On 10 January 1942, the supervisory authority told the Gestapo that the Jews were to hand in their walking shoes, ski boots, skis, fur coats and woollens. If the coat had a fur collar, the collar was to be cut off.[29] Jews also had to hand in optical and electrical appliances such as stoves, heating pads, hotplates, vacuum cleaners, irons and also gramophones, records, typewriters, bicycles and accessories, cameras and telescopes.[30] Once again, it was the Kultusgemeinde that had to announce and carry out this order. It also kept records of the items, listing for example that it had collected 160 women's blouses weighing 37 kg or 164 pairs of men's underpants weighing 33 kg.[31]

The Jewish institutions were also to be plundered. The IKG itself was ultimately closed so as to gain access to its assets. In 1938, its status under public law had been left intact to enable it to receive foreign exchange. On 10 October 1942, Brunner informed Löwenherz that the Kultusgemeinde would lose its status under public law with effect from 31 October but would remain in place until the sale of the real estate registered in its name. Until that time, all claims were to be settled and a liquidation report submitted to the Central Office and the Gestapo.[32] On 1 November 1942, the Council of Elders of the Jews in Vienna was established to continue the work of the Kultusgemeinde; for the purposes of taxes and levies, it was now a private association.[33] It was allowed only around RM 300,000 out of the Kultusgemeinde's assets of RM 7 million. The rest was paid into the Emigration Fund for Bohemia and Moravia to maintain Theresienstadt concentration camp, i.e., to finance the extermination policy.[34]

The Jewish administration was transformed for financial reasons only. The new name had little special significance. The structure of the Jewish administration remained unchanged. As we have seen, the Kultusgemeinde had already functioned as a prototype Jewish council or council of elders since 1938.

The Nazi bureaucrats wanted a record of the assets of all Jewish victims. It disturbed them that they could not plunder the assets of those Jews living in mixed marriages. In summer 1943, the Thirteenth Decree concerning the Reich Citizenship Law was enacted; the assets of a Jew should revert to the state on his or her death; non-Jewish heirs were merely to be granted compensation. Jews could not inherit.[35] This closed up a last loophole in the law. The legal framework for the comprehensive plundering of the Jews was complete.

Designation and handing over of the victims

Deportation lists

The selection of the deportees and the drawing up of lists for Vienna were carried out in 1941 by the Nazi authorities themselves. The Central Office decided who would be deported.

Various groups were exempt from deportation at that time. Half-Jews or first-degree Mischlinge who were not members of the Jewish religion and not married to a Jew, and quarter-Jews, second-degree Mischlinge were not to be deported. First-degree Mischlinge were in danger and could be denounced at any time, however. Information that they were behaving 'like a full Jew' was sometimes sufficient for their arrest. Jews in privileged mixed marriages were also exempt. A mixed marriage was deemed to be privileged if it was between a

116

Jewish man and a non-Jewish woman provided they had children who were counted as first-degree Mischlinge or if they were childless. The Jewish father or mother of a Mischling was also privileged, regardless of whether the marriage with the non-Jew still existed, even if the Mischling son had fallen in the war. All childless Jewish women in a mixed marriage were privileged as well, in this case, however, only as long as the marriage existed. Privileged Jews were therefore persecuted, robbed and humiliated but not yet exterminated.[36]

Also exempt in 1941 were war veterans, former soldiers with more than 50 per cent disability, foreign but not stateless Jews on whom businesses and state offices were still reliant, and retired civil servants whose pension entitlements had not yet been clarified. These people did not at least appear in the lists first sent to the Kultusgemeinde. The Jewish administration could also ask for people to be removed from the lists. It could request the postponement of deportation for Kultusgemeinde employees that it considered to be indispensable. It could also provide other reasons for having a person removed from the list: imminent emigration, health reasons or the splitting up of the family.[37] These Jews were not regarded as privileged but were merely temporarily deferred. Every single case had to be submitted, the decision being made usually by Alois Brunner, head of the Central Office.

Finally, all deportees had to sign a form revealing their assets. At this time, the Nazi authorities carried out a procedure known as *Kommissionierung* (selection) at the collection points. In rare instances, individuals could yet be rescued from deportation.[38]

At the beginning of 1941, Alois Brunner ordered Löwenherz to provide an updated list of Jews supported by the Kultusgemeinde and to submit it to the Central Office.[39] Jews working in the health service, Jewish doctors (*Krankenbehandler*), pregnant women and the mothers of infants up to one year of age or single mothers with children up to fourteen years of age, the sick and physically infirm and everyone over sixty-five years of age were meant to be exempt from the first deportations. But the first transport consisted essentially of old, sick people and 60 per cent were women. Blind, deaf and dumb and handicapped persons were also deported. The Self-Help Group of Blind Jews wrote a letter to Löwenherz on 25 February 1941:

There can be no doubt that the resettlement is difficult for everyone of our faith. But there is even less doubt that it is much more difficult still for the blind. A blind person removed from a familiar environment

117

and placed in an unknown one is lost in every sense of the word. Three blind persons were on the first transport. Two more are currently in Castellezgasse and it is to be feared that more will suffer this indescribably difficult fate. We therefore ask you, Herr Doktor, to protect the poorest of the poor, the blind, from this most terrible fate and address to you the respectful and most ardent request: please help us!

All of the blind people in Vienna who belong to our group and on whose behalf we are making this request regard you as the only and, in view of your eminent personality, the most suitable person to help and save them.[40]

Löwenherz was unable either to help or to save them. The Jews that the Kultusgemeinde managed to remove from the deportation lists were simply deferred.

The lists of deportees were drawn up by the Central Office and, after its dissolution, by the Gestapo and handed to the Kultusgemeinde. The Jewish administration could remove individuals from the list but had to find someone to replace these deferred persons. It was not, however, obliged to select the persons to be deported instead of those who were deferred.[41] On the contrary, the Central Office already had a list of replacements. Wilhelm Bienenfeld, one of the leading Jewish functionaries, said after the war:

> In most cases a replacement had to be provided for those left behind. We always asked whether a replacement was absolutely necessary and were occasionally successful, so that instead of 100 Jews only 92 were transported. We did not select the replacements; they were pulled out of a Gestapo file. The Central Office always had a list of replacements. . . . We would not have given any names.[42]

The Nazi authorities did not need the Kultusgemeinde to replace the deferred persons. The collection points were usually overcrowded. In addition, the Nazi offices had their own files. If a Jew spoke up for a relative, however, the Gestapo would enjoy asking him whom he would like to be sent instead. In June 1943, for example, Emil Gottesmann was ordered to bring his two brothers to the Gestapo the following day. He intervened personally to the Gestapo functionary Johann Rixinger and begged him to allow his brothers to remain in Vienna. Rixinger claimed incorrectly: 'That will be difficult and in any case it's not me who is sending your brothers away but Dr Löwenherz, head of the Council of Elders.'[43]

Then Rixinger suggested that Gottesmann name a replacement for his two brothers. Gottesmann refused. At his trial after the war,

Rixinger admitted that Löwenherz had not 'sent away' anyone.[44] He could not have had anyone deported on his own initiative.

After the first deportations, the Nazi Central Office for Jewish Emigration noted that many Jews failed to heed the order to assemble at the collection points. The lists were also inaccurate. The list system was retained but in addition *Aushebungen* were introduced from winter 1941 on.[45] SS men from the Central Office accompanied by Jewish marshals visited the houses occupied by Jews. Streets were simply cordoned off and people hauled out of the houses for deportation. One Jewish marshal was left in the apartments to help the victims pack and accompany them to the collection point. He was liable with his own life for ensuring that the numbers were correct. The Kultusgemeinde did not know in advance who was to be deported but received a list of their entries in the land register after the *Aushebungen* had taken place.[46]

Indirectly, however, the Jewish administration had a say in who was deported. It had to decide which of its officials were indispensable and which not. Some employees attempted to save themselves by making donations. In October 1941, Dr Hermann Altmann sent a thankyou letter to Löwenherz: 'Herr Direktor, I should like to thank you with all my heart for removing me from the Poland transport. In keeping with our honourable commandments I have made a donation of 50 marks to the tax office for winter relief . . .'[47] Dr Altmann, a retired accountant born in 1884, hoped that this donation would keep Löwenherz well disposed towards him. But it did not help him for long: on 1 April 1942, he was beaten to death by an SS man on the street on his way to the collection point.[48]

Although the Kultusgemeinde did not draw up the transport lists and although the Central Office could no doubt have killed all of the Viennese Jews without the Jewish administration, the deportations and extermination would not have run smoothly without its collaboration. Benjamin Murmelstein organized the Jewish cooperation in the evacuation from Room 8 of the Kultusgemeinde office. Here the lists were sorted alphabetically, copied and transcribed. The young Kurt Mezei was employed as a clerk in this room. In his diary, he writes of his distress at the deportations during these weeks, but in spite or possibly because of this he worked very hard. He knew that his employment and the tedious copying of lists might save his life. He slowly got used to the work that kept him alive and distracted him from his fears. It became routine. On 23 November 1941, he wrote that he was now accepted by the other employees and that he 'enjoyed' his work.[49]

Room 8 was not just an administrative deportation centre. The decision was also made there which employees and patrons of Jewish institutions were indispensable. The Jewish heads of the various Jewish institutions met there to decide which of their employees to protect. After the war, in August 1945, Siegfried Kolisch, former head of the Association of Jewish War Victims, reported that in summer 1941 Josef Löwenherz had passed on an order requesting him to take part in these meetings with the heads of the other Jewish organizations. Kolisch went to Alois Brunner, known as 'Brunner I', head of the Nazi Central Office, to decline the request in person. He was not forced to cooperate but was released from doing so after he had pointed out that it was incompatible with his position and his conscience. It should be mentioned, however, that Kolisch did not refuse other forms of cooperation. He was responsible in the first months for the transport logistics, the allocation of wagons and rations.[50] Before he notified Brunner of his refusal to take part in the selection of indispensable individuals, he had observed the activities in Room 8 for two days. He said: 'The people in Room 8 discussed who should be put on the transport list and who should be exempt. I had the impression that they were not objective and merely took the point of view that the Central Office list should form a basis and that they should not play with destiny.'[51]

The other Jewish functionaries were not opposed to removing employees who they thought to be indispensable from the lists. Kolisch said in 1945 that it was not until he was in Theresienstadt that he discovered why the Kultusgemeinde had cooperated: 'In Theresienstadt I learned from Dr Desider Friedmann and Oberbaurat Robert Stricker . . . that the cooperation by the Kultusgemeinde in the evacuation of the Jews had been decided at a previous meeting as it was hoped in this way that more humane treatment could be achieved.'[52]

In reality, the Jewish functionaries were powerless in the face of the deceptions practised by the Nazi authorities. The Jewish administration was unable to offer an alternative strategy. It was not a serious partner for the oppressors and did not play a determining role in the Nazi calculations. The individual functionaries could adopt different points of view but the behaviour of the Jews no longer had any influence on the Nazi policies. On 29 September 1941, Siegfried Kolisch, who had refused in the summer to work in Room 8, stated at a meeting of the board of the Association of War Victims that Obersturmführer Brunner had demanded a list of the members of the Association. The same order had been given to the war veterans' associations in Prague and Berlin. An official from the Association named Fürth indicated that 2,071 veterans were listed in a file; he suggested in addition that the war widows of highly decorated soldiers and veterans who had left the Association could also be included in the list. Kolisch noted at the end of the meeting: 'Lists are important only because the Central Office wants them.'[53]

On 13 and 14 October 1941, Benjamin Murmelstein reported to the head of the Association of Jewish War Victims in Vienna that he had made an 'agreement' with the Central Office on the compilation of priority 'dismissal lists for the resettlement operation'. The list was to contain six categories of Jews exempt from deportation:

1 Employees and volunteers working for the Jewish administrative apparatus and parents, children, brothers and sisters living in the same household
2 Persons who had already made preparations for emigration to South America
3 Residents in old people's homes
4 Blind persons, full invalids and severely sick persons
5 Forced labourers
6 War invalids and highly decorated war veterans

He suggested that Kolisch provide a similar list for his association. The lists from the Association of War Veterans and the Emigration Assistance Programme had to be presented together with the list from the Kultusgemeinde, for which Murmelstein was held personally liable, so that they could be checked.[54] In reality, the Gestapo had not assented to any 'agreement' of this nature. It wished merely to postpone the deportation of these categories because Theresienstadt, the ghetto for elderly and more prominent Jews, had not yet been completed. Highly decorated veterans and war invalids were also to be held back for the model ghetto in Theresienstadt so as to conciliate the Wehrmacht. The Gestapo had no intention of making any agreements with the Jewish leadership and the document was designed solely to safeguard the cooperation of the Jewish administration in organizing the deportations.[55] Murmelstein and Kolisch nevertheless argued about this apparent agreement. Kolisch was annoyed that a far-reaching agreement of this nature could have been concluded without involving the Association of War Victims. While recognizing that the alleged agreement offered certain advantages, he could not accept it as it was not to apply to the first transport, which was due to depart two days hence, on 15 October 1941. He intended therefore to present his own list to Brunner for this transport. Murmelstein opposed this idea; if an agreement had been made one day, he said, it was unacceptable to go to the Central Office the following day with requests running counter to it. It would cause confusion and would make the Nazi authorities distrustful of those who were considered reliable and trustworthy. He claimed not only to have negotiated an agreement but also to be considered completely trustworthy for the Nazis. Kolisch replied angrily: 'In other words I should sacrifice the war invalids.'[56]

Murmelstein suggested that Kolisch could make a plea for a few individuals on compassionate grounds. Kolisch refused, pointing out that either he had an entitlement and did not need to solicit sympathy or he had no entitlement and would have to sacrifice the people. The two parted on bad terms.

On 15 October 1941, the day of the deportation, Murmelstein informed the Association of War Victims by telephone that the war veterans scheduled for deportation had been deferred at the last moment.[57] The following day a German Wehrmacht officer from the army headquarters, Hauptmann Dr Licht, phoned Kolisch to ask whether three Jewish veterans, Oberst Grossmann, Rittmeister Wollisch and Rittmeister Eisler, had been included in the 'resettlement transport'. Kolisch replied: 'I am not authorized to give information without the permission of my superior. I should also like to point out that the Association has informed its members that they are forbidden to approach Aryan offices.'

In his memo of this telephone conversation, Kolisch wrote that, of the Jewish officers, only Rittmeister Eisler was a member of the Association. The last sentence reads: 'I shall notify the Central Office for Jewish Emigration of this telephone call.'[58]

The ghetto in Theresienstadt was opened in early 1942. As far as the Nazis were concerned, there were no further obstacles to the deportation of the war veterans. But not all of the former Jewish soldiers ended up in Theresienstadt. Only the 'privileged' ones were deported to the 'ghetto for the elderly'; the rest were deported with most of the other Jews to extermination camps. When this wave of deportations started, Siegfried Kolisch was not in Vienna. His deputy Fürth was visited by Löwenherz, who asked him to divide the Association into four groups: war veterans with 50 per cent invalidity or more, highly decorated officers, highly decorated other ranks and all other members. He evaded Fürth's question as to the purpose of the list.

On 9 June 1942, after Kolisch's return, the board of the Association met again. The minutes of the meeting appear to indicate that the board members had intervened with the Central Office during Kolisch's absence and that Löwenherz had been put in an awkward position as a result, no doubt on account of the rivalry between the Central Office and the Gestapo. Fürth told Kolisch: 'I now know what it was about. I didn't know before because it was confidential. If I had, I would not have played off a Jew against an Aryan.'[59]

An official named Schatzberger explained why they had reported Löwenherz's request to the Central Office:

Schatzberger: We are answerable not to the Kultusgemeinde but to the Central Office and we thought that our leader would not want us to provide any information without the permission of the Central Office.

Kolisch: That's not correct. Amongst Jews themselves it's not the same. The Central Office would never interfere. The ban applies only to Aryan offices.

Halpern: It's clear that the Kultusgemeinde was only a messenger for the Gestapo. Löwenherz got what he deserved. He should have been honest.[60]

At this meeting, Fürth stated that of the 2,500 members of the Association, 1,100 had already been deported. In two months, he said, all of the members would be deported. The meeting discussed possible rescue strategies, whether special conditions should be sought for certain groups of members such as highly decorated veterans. Kolisch explained that any kind of exemption for a Jew 'is a favour by the Central Office. . . . The Kultusgemeinde is just an institution for implementation of all orders from the Central Office. . . . There is sure to be a reason why lists of war invalids and highly decorated front veterans are being asked for. At all events Berlin decides whether a Jew is to be exempted.'[61]

Kolisch was clearly of the opinion here that the Nazi authorities themselves should decide who was to be deported. At the board meeting on 4 August 1942, however, he changed his mind in view of the new circumstances. One of the items on the agenda was 'Reduction in the Kultusgemeinde personnel'. The Jewish administration was required to hand over a fixed number of its employees for deportation because most of the community had already been deported and the Gestapo no longer required such a large administrative apparatus. Among the Kultusgemeinde staff to be dismissed were war veterans.

Kolisch stated to his colleagues that the Kultusgemeinde was not likely to let him see the lists. In order to be able to help members of the Association, it would have to draw up its own list indicating which war veterans the Association considered worthy of remaining in Vienna. If one of these selected members were to be dismissed by the Kultusgemeinde, the Association could then appeal to the Central Office. Another possibility, said Kolisch, would be to give the list directly to the Central Office. During the ensuing discussion, several officials were in favour of giving the list first of all to the Kultusgemeinde. Kolisch said he did not want a war with the Kultusgemeinde. At the end of the meeting, a list of members for whom the Association wished to intervene was drawn up.[62]

The discussion was taken up again on 7 August 1942. Should the Association give the Kultusgemeinde a list of all members working for the administration, as Schatzberger suggested? Kolisch pointed out that the most important consideration was whether the Association should address itself from the outset to the Nazi Central Office or not. Was the Association answerable to the Kultusgemeinde? Could a confrontation with the Kultusgemeinde be risked?[63]

These discussions among the Jews had no effect on the extermination process. On 14 August 1942, one day before the dismissals were to take effect, Kolisch gave the Kultusgemeinde direction a complete list of all members of the Association working in the Kultusgemeinde, organized by departments with precise details of decorations and degree of invalidity. He added at the end of the list: 'Those to be dismissed effective 15 August 1942 are not included.'[64] In this manner, the Association cooperated in its way with the bureaucratic registration of its members for deportation.

From this discussion, it can be clearly seen that for all their differences of opinion and arguments, the Jewish functionaries had very little room for manoeuvre. The board of the Association of War Victims accused the Kultusgemeinde of passing on the orders of the Central Office, but in the end it was also obliged to cooperate, not because they were merely the recipients of orders from the Nazis but because the alternatives made available to them by the Nazi authorities gave them no real choice. If the Jewish functionaries hoped to rescue as many Jews as possible, they had to accept the 'agreements' and Nazi precepts; as a result, they were caught in a trap that the perpetrators had set to see as many Jews as possible deported. The Jewish administrators attempted to grasp the aims of the Gestapo and Central Office. They had to try to think like the perpetrators and anticipate them. They had to take every opportunity available to them and not to ignore any proposal, despite their mistrust of the Nazis. From the perspective of the Jewish functionaries, it was counterproductive to assume that the Nazis would in any case deceive and lie to them.

The mass deportation of the Jews of Vienna had been effectively completed by September 1942. Only a few thousand Jews still lived there, for the most part those who were protected by non-Jewish spouses, along with the remaining employees of the Jewish administration. Around 1,500 employees of the administration, along with their families, were deported in the last two transports on 1 and 10 October 1942.[65] At this point the notorious Central Office for Jewish Emigration had completed its work in Vienna and was closed in March 1943. Subsequent deportations were carried out by the Gestapo. For the most part, they consisted of transports of 100 to 150 people. The Gestapo ordered that a certain number of Kultusgemeinde employees who had been considered indispensable hitherto were to be included in these transports. The Jewish administration was to select and hand over the persons concerned itself. Leading functionaries decided who was to be deported. By that time, Benjamin Murmelstein had already been deported to Theresienstadt. The meetings were chaired by Josef Löwenherz. He announced how many employees the Gestapo required for deportation and how many from each department were to go. He was assisted in his deliberations by Wilhelm Bienenfeld, Dr Arnold Raschke, director of the Jewish hospital, Dr Emil Tuchmann, the medical examiner designated by the Gestapo who was required to write reports for the Nazi authorities about the Jewish health service, and Max Birnstein, who had been a prison governor before the war and on the basis of this experience had been appointed director of the old people's home.[66]

Tuchmann, born in 1899 in Jablonica, Bukowina, had lived in Vienna since 1915. In 1938, he had been medical director of the Kultusgemeinde welfare service and was designated head of the Jewish health service in 1940. He was appointed medical consultant to the Jewish Rothschild Hospital by the Gestapo and was effectively its director, as its nominal director, Arnold Raschke, was increasingly sidelined.[67] Tuchmann ran a tight ship, claiming that it was the only way of protecting the hospital from intervention by the Nazis. He managed to maintain the medical infrastructure and to circumvent the authorities and obtain necessary supplies.[68] He attempted to save the staff and patients in his charge but in doing so was obliged together with the other leading functionaries in the Council of Elders to surrender those employees who did not correspond to his requirements. At the same time, he managed to save patients who had already recovered from deportation, risking his life in the process.[69] He fought with all his energy against the Nazi plans, hoping to rescue people from extermination. But his harsh style and the strict regime that he maintained in the hospital were useful to the Gestapo, since he insisted that the Nazi orders be obeyed so as to save the hospital. He was responsible for ensuring that no Gestapo prisoners in the hospital escaped. He tried to protect as many of them as possible from deportation to a concentration camp.[70] Testimony about Tuchmann appears contradictory. The conflicting observations reflect the situation in which the Jewish functionaries found themselves; all of their values had been turned upside down. Acts that in 'normal' times might have appeared inhumane could now save lives. After the war, for example, Tuchmann was accused of designating sick persons for deportation in place of healthy ones. He claimed at his trial that he had indeed done so because healthy persons had better chances of survival than the seriously ill. Patients delivered to the hospital from the collection points were often in such wretched condition that they were in any case condemned to death.[71] The Nazi Jewish policy had inverted normal medical values. The moral dilemma arose not with the choice that Tuchmann and the other Jewish functionaries made but as a result of the paradoxical alternatives that they were left with as a result of the Nazi demands. They acceded to these demands so as at least to rescue as many Jews as possible but by doing so they helped the perpetrators to kill as many Jews as possible. They had been willing to sacrifice a few more so as to rescue as many as possible, but in reality they sacrificed most to rescue but a few. They were not able to make a real choice. They could at best have refused to cooperate at all with the perpetrators or have committed suicide. But would this not have been tantamount to abandoning those whom they still hoped to save? The perpetrators left the victims no way out of this moral dilemma.

Until Vienna was liberated, when practically all of the Jews had been deported, Room 8 was responsible for keeping an updated file of the Jews living in the city. The Jewish Department for Population was ordered by the Gestapo to continuously check the files. During the last years of the war, the noose tightened around the necks of the Mischlinge and those who had been protected by marriage to a non-Jew. From March 1944, all Jews living in privileged mixed marriages were summoned so as to provide a list of their family members, who were added to the file. A total of 3,026 persons were officially registered in 1944.[72] The Gestapo checked this file because twice a year

Rixinger, who was head of the Gestapo Jewish department, summoned all Jews in mixed marriages. Those who were no longer protected by non-Jewish relatives were deported forthwith.[73]

Convocation and Aushebungen

After it had been decided which Jews were to be deported in the next transport, the Nazi authorities needed to ensure that the victims assembled at the collection points. Since spring 1941, the Jews had been required to report to the collection points some time before the deportation to make sure that there would not be too few at the station. Initially, there were still so many Jews remaining in Vienna that it did not appear to be difficult to herd a predefined number of victims into the trains. The Jews received pre-printed postcards from the Central Office ordering them to go to the collection points. Prior to this, the members of the community had been informed of the procedure in a circular distributed by the Kultusgemeinde.[74]

The Jews were required to draw up a precise list of their assets and property, including the number of the entry in the land register. They had to lock their apartments and provide a cardboard tag for every key with the address and personal information written clearly on it. The keys were to be taken to the collection point. The Jews were allowed to keep RM 100; all other cash had to be handed over at the collection point together with the list of assets. Every victim was permitted to take two suitcases or bundles weighing a total of 50 kg, two blankets and a second pair of shoes. Each piece of luggage had to be labelled with the name and address of its owner in white oil paint. The Kultusgemeinde stated in its leaflet that the remaining clothes should be made available to needy Jews left in Vienna. The Jewish administration pointed out that persons who failed to obey the order to assemble at the collection point would be taken there by force and as a punishment would not be permitted to take any cash with them.[75]

The Kultusgemeinde was notified of the names of those who failed to obey the order to assemble at the collection point. Kultusgemeinde marshals were required by order of the Central Office to round up the victims and bring them to the collection point, unless they could produce a medical certificate indicating that they were unfit to travel.[76]

The headquarters of the Jewish marshal service was in Room 8 under Murmelstein's direction. His direct subordinate for organizing the marshals was Robert Prochnik initially, then Leo Balaban. The Jewish marshals had to help the victims to pack and bring them to the collection point. As long as they performed these duties, they were exempt from deportation. Murmelstein is said to have threatened those who did not wish to cooperate with deportation. He would hit those who allowed Jews to escape.[77]

The Kultusgemeinde printed out a leaflet for employees involved in the preparations for deportation. It explained how the Jews were to be collected from their dwellings:

> No one may leave the dwelling, nor may anyone enter it until it is vacated. No messages may be delivered orally, in writing or by telephone. Assistance is to be provided to the persons to be transported; the marshals are obliged to help them pack and unless otherwise instructed are to supervise the baggage until it is taken away. It must be ensured when the dwelling is vacated that the gas, water and heating are turned off. Pets must be taken care of and may not be left in the dwelling. The comment 'with' or 'without key' must be clearly visible on each inventory sheet. The persons leaving are to be informed that there is no possibility of retrieving forgotten items from the dwelling.[78]

The documents that have been mentioned so far in this chapter are administrative papers: instructions, leaflets, reports. The *Couplet von den Rechercheuren* by Walter Lindenbaum gives a different impression of the marshals as seen by the Jewish population of Vienna.[79] Lindenbaum, born in 1907, was a writer and cabarettist, a well-known political, Social Democratic author. When the Nazis came to power in Austria in 1938, he was employed in the Kultusgemeinde.

Lindenbaum's song makes fun of the marshals and their devotion to duty. Every marshal who came to the collection point knew that he could himself be deported at any time. He was liable with his life for ensuring that no one escaped during the packing or on the way to the collection point. Lindenbaum knew only too well what he was writing about and making fun of because he was himself not only an *Ausheber* but also a Gruppenführer, one of those who accompanied the SS men to collect the Jews from their dwellings and take them to the collection point.

He was deported to Theresienstadt on 1 April 1943 where he continued to perform in cabaret and write songs and poems. As in Vienna, his texts were designed to raise morale a little. He was deported to Auschwitz on 28 February 1944. His wife and daughter also arrived in Auschwitz-Birkenau on 6 October. He was evacuated to Buchenwald and registered there on 15 January 1945. Then he was allocated to a transport to the notorious satellite camp Ohrdruf in Thuringia, where the inmates were exploited under terrible conditions to build a secret headquarters for the Führer. Lindenbaum, who was classified as a political Jew, died a few weeks before the camp was liberated on 20 February 1945.[80]

On 22 September 1942, Murmelstein told Kollmann, a marshal, that the marshals would be deported with the last transport and would be notified eight days in advance. As a favour, they were being allowed to take all their effects with them. Moreover, he stressed 'explicitly on [his] word of honour that this group would be put to work there', and not hard labour but in jobs appropriate to the profession and skill of each marshal. He said that he was passing on this information on behalf of Sturmbannführer Alois Brunner.[81] Brunner had indeed told Löwenherz on 4 September that the Kultusgemeinde employees would leave in the last two transports and that they could take more luggage and even pieces of furniture with them. This 'reward' for the Jewish administration came to nothing, since the authorities had not provided sufficient wagons for the employees' belongings.[82] And as for appropriate work, the marshals, like all the other Jews in the ghettos and extermination camps, were deported and then killed.

As many Jews failed to obey the order to present themselves at the collection points, a further system was introduced to collect the victims: *Aushebung*, literally 'lifting out'. SS men from the Central Office accompanied by Jewish helpers cordoned off the streets, usually at night, in which Jews lived and selected the people to go to the collection point on the spot. A Jewish marshal was left behind to help the victims to pack and bring them to the collection point, being liable with his own life for ensuring that there was no one missing. This new system of *Aushebungen* was introduced by Alois Brunner in November 1941. He ordered Löwenherz to provide Jewish employees to help the SS men with the *Aushebungen*. Löwenherz refused to comply. Brunner threatened to have the work carried out without the Kultusgemeinde in his own way, using members of the Hitler Youth, for example. Robert Prochnik, Murmelstein's direct assistant in the Jewish marshal service, recalls in his memoirs that Brunner set about ordering a Jewish Gestapo informer to assemble a Jewish troop. Within a few hours, this man recruited a group of 40 Jews. Brunner ordered his SS men and this Jewish unit not to be squeamish in the performance of their duty. The results are said to have been terrible. Primitive, frightened and brutal men were selected and they treated the victims harshly and roughly. In a few days, says Prochnik, the

129

Kultusgemeinde was receiving complaints of theft, blackmail, bribery and even rape. Brunner refused to see Löwenherz at this time. When he summoned him on another matter, he permitted the Jewish functionary to voice his complaints about the *Aushebungen*. He informed Löwenherz that he had not intended the *Aushebungen* to take place in that way and that Löwenherz was responsible for the situation because of his refusal to cooperate. At this point, Löwenherz agreed to provide the SS with his own employees. He attempted to select particularly 'reliable and decent' persons for this task.[83]

But even these Jewish *Ausheber*, around 400 or 500 of them,[84] spread terror among the Jewish population because their appearance meant deportation. Some of them were hated and did not behave at all in a decent manner. On the contrary, it is possible that the work brutalized some of them; or else Löwenherz and Murmelstein were unable to find sensitive employees for this delicate work. A Jewish Gruppenführer was responsible for each unit of *Ausheber* that was commanded by an SS-Scharführer.

No one writing about the Jewish SS helpers should forget that all of them were fighting for their own lives. Survivors recall the different types of behaviour of these *Ausheber*. Some began in the course of their work to make anti-Semitic comments, calling the people at the collection point 'Jewish pigs' who deserved no pity. Others tried to help their fellow victims, risking their own lives in the process.[85] Whether they jeopardized their own existence in attempting to help the other Jews, whether they were corrupt or brutalized under the continuous pressure and dealings with their superiors and the SS criminals, all of them were under permanent threat of death.

The Jewish Gruppenführer Wilhelm Reisz, who was discussed in the first chapter of this book, described at his trial in 1945 how an *Aushebung* functioned.

> As the Jews were all registered – the Jewish housing department was also part of the Central Office – the Scharführer already had a list to hand. Not all apartments were searched, only those on the list. First the marshals were ordered to proceed to the building and then to the individual apartments. Two or three marshals were allocated to each apartment. They then had the task of making a list of the Jews living there and taking away their identity cards. Then the Scharführer came and I had to supervise the work of the packers while the Scharführer compared his list with mine.[86]

Reisz had to make a note of who was being taken. He had to ensure that no one escaped and had to inform the SS man if anyone had been forgotten. On the list, the reason the Jew was still allowed to remain in Vienna was noted. If a Jewish *Ausheber* overlooked someone who was to be deported, he was deported himself.

The Vienna *Aushebung* system appeared to the Nazi authorities to be so effective that three Viennese Jews were ordered to Berlin so that the system could be copied there. The group consisted of Wilhelm Reisz, his colleague Walter Lindenbaum, the famous cabarettist mentioned earlier,[87] and Josef Gerö, a member of the *Sonderdienst*. Reisz, who volunteered for the trip, related on his return from Berlin that the *Aushebung* system met with resistance there from the non-Jewish population.[88]

To escape the *Aushebungen*, many Jews stayed away from their dwellings during the day. For that reason the operations were carried out for preference at night. During the day, raids were carried out in cafés and parks. Jewish children playing there were taken and brought to the collection point where they were ordered to give the names and addresses of their parents.[89] To fill up the collection points and deportation transports, Jews detained in prisons, police stations or who had been arrested by the border gendarmerie, Gestapo and customs authorities were also handed over.

The *Sonderdienst*, unofficially also known as 'Jupo' (for 'Jewish police') and made up of Jewish helpers, was responsible for handing over hidden Jews or 'submarines' and was also given other special tasks. These Jews were answerable not to the Kultusgemeinde but to the Central Office and, after March 1942, the Gestapo. Because of their work, the 'Jupo men', six of them,[90] did not have to wear a star. They were recruited by the SS from among those destined for deportation and were allowed to stay in Vienna provided that they agreed to help find Jews in hiding to escape deportation. Brunner ordered that they be paid by the Kultusgemeinde. Murmelstein said in 1980 that he had been opposed to counting the 'Jupo men' as employees of the Kultusgemeinde and they therefore received support by the welfare centre as 'Jews without means'.[91]

Apart from the *Sonderdienst*, there were also Jewish Gestapo informers. Rudolf Klinger, for example, was able to uncover Jewish 'submarines' even when they were well hidden. He also infiltrated the Polish underground movement and an anti-Fascist group formed by Baron von Lieben, Baron Karl Motesicky and the doctor Ella Lingens. According to Lingens, he set a trap for the group and had the Jews and non-Jews who helped them sent to Auschwitz. As Klinger knew too many official Gestapo secrets, however, the Gestapo official had his Jewish informer deported to Auschwitz in 1943. Klinger did not survive.[92] To all appearances, the Gestapo wanted to get rid of its Jewish informers before the end of the war.

One or two Jewish doctors, selected for the task from the Rothschild Hospital, together with a few qualified nurses, were required to provide medical treatment at the collection points. Their medical certificates had to indicate whether the patients at the collection point, and the patients in the Jewish hospital and the residents of the old people's home, were fit to travel. They had to present their assessments to the commander of the collection point or the Gestapo. The Nazi authorities did not need the agreement of the Jewish doctors, however, when they decided to deport the sick and invalid. They could have the diagnoses of the Jewish doctors checked by the medical officer. In addition, the Gestapo raided the Jewish hospitals by day and night, dragging patients from their beds for deportation.[93] What then was the task of these Jewish doctors? Why was the Gestapo interested in their findings? The Jewish administration was interested in achieving humanitarian relief where it could and in buying time for a few people. The Nazi authorities were not interested in these matters and wanted merely to ensure the smooth and rapid deportation of the Jews of Vienna. The Gestapo did not want to have to deal with people who were not fit for transport as long as there were plenty of healthy Jews in Vienna. By acceding to the humanitarian demands of the Jewish administration, they secured their cooperation. When there were only a few Jews left in Vienna, the invalid residents of the old people's home were also thrown into the trains. In 1942, the Jewish old people's home at Malzgasse 16 was closed by order of Anton Brunner. A former Jewish nurse describes what happened on that day:

> The people struggled, of course, fighting for their lives. They were thrown roughshod into this truck without checking whether they had somewhere to sit or not. One wheelchair-bound patient was hauled from his wheelchair by two men, one at the shoulders and the other at the feet, and thrown in, without feeling, needless to say. They never had any feelings.[94]

The desire of the Nazi authorities to finish off the deportations as smoothly as possible and the hope of the Kultusgemeinde for 'humane deportation' formed the basis of this cooperation between perpetrators and victims. The Jewish doctors at the collection point gave their assessments; the SS commandant made his decision at the latest during the *Kommissionierung* ('selection') of the individual Jews. The

Kultusgemeinde was required to pass on the instructions. On 3 September 1942, Murmelstein informed the hospital management which of the operations it had asked to be approved could be carried out; with 'strict observance of the condition (date)'. The admissible duration of unfitness to travel after the date of surgery was listed for every name and diagnosis.[95]

The names of patients and their condition for operations that had not been approved were also listed in this document. On 4 September 1942, Murmelstein informed the children's hospital that a tonsillectomy had been approved for the eight-year-old Ada Blatt. 'Admissible duration of unfitness for travel from the date of operation' was one week. And in fact the girl was deported to Theresienstadt on 24 September 1942. From there, the eight-year-old Ada was loaded on a train to Auschwitz on 6 October 1944.[96]

Collection points and Kommissionierung

The Jews were herded into the collection points prior to deportation and it was here that the *Kommissionierung*, the selection of the 1,050 to 1,100 people to be deported in a transport, took place.

The collection point was full of desperate people. No one could enter or leave it without a pass. An electrified wire was fitted on top of the outer wall in Sperlgasse.[97] The collection point was run by an SS-Unterscharführer, *Dienststellenleiter* or duty officer, answerable initially to Alois Brunner, known as Brunner I. This SS-Unterscharführer was also in charge of the Jewish registration office, which was responsible for making lists of the people transported, keeping a register with the personal data, last address, date of arrival and date of departure, i.e., deportation, of the people at the collection point and noting whether they had been released or deferred. He had to provide a daily roll-call and give the Kultusgemeinde information about the supplies required for the inmates.[98] The Kultusgemeinde was also responsible for cleaning the collection point. The welfare worker Franzi Löw visited the collection points to look after the people there. She noted the important items that they had left behind and collected them from their apartments.[99] One or two Jewish doctors and a few qualified nurses provided medical treatment. They had a consultation room, sick bay, out-patients' room and quarantine room at their disposal. The Kultusgemeinde provided medical instruments and drugs. As mentioned above, the Jewish doctors were also responsible for determining whether a person should be released, deferred or admitted to hospital for health reasons.

133

A separate room was reserved for those who had already been deported on an earlier transport but had managed to return to Vienna. They were returned to the collection point but kept apart. They were no longer mentioned in the arrivals list and were not subject to *Kommissionierung*. Against the wishes of Josef Löwenherz, they were not deducted from the 1,000 persons required for each transport. They were not counted in the transport to which they were now allocated. They were not counted but were still taken off in the train.[100]

Every person detained at the collection point participated in the *Kommissionierung*, which determined who would be deported. The victims had to pass three or four tables. At the first table during the many mass deportations was Anton Brunner, known as Brunner II. There was also a secretary, a Jewish doctor and a Jewish marshal. At this table, the victim's documents were examined and compared with the file card. Then the certificate of origin and passport were taken away. Brunner particularly enjoyed ripping up documents that Jews had guarded so carefully before their very eyes. Then he stamped 'evacuated on . . .' on the identification card. It was at this table that decisions on deferral were made.[101] At the second table was the Gestapo official, two secretaries and a Jewish marshal. The victim had to hand in two copies of the list of assets and sign them over to the Gestapo. He (or she) was also ordered to hand over all valuables and money. Under Anton Brunner, this was also carried out at the first table and the second table abolished. The victim's valuables and money were handed in at the third table and a Kultusgemeinde employee took charge of the deportee's apartment key. The ration cards were also handed over.[102] A Jewish official wrote the *Kommission* number on a label. At the fourth and final table, the people to be deported were recorded on a list and transferred by *Kommission* numbers to a billet.[103]

After the *Kommissionierung*, the procedure was repeated and the duty officer or his deputy determined which of the up to 1,200 people who had been selected should actually be deported. There were always around 100 too many. The Nazi authorities did this in order to provide replacements for those who were deferred. This procedure was even more brutal than the first *Kommissionierung*. The victims were sometimes interrogated, tortured and beaten. Brunner II was particularly feared; he beat people himself and kicked them in the small of the back with the heel of his boots.[104] During this procedure, it was also decided which of the deferrees were to be released and which had to stay at the collection point.

There were around 2,000 people crowded into the collection point. The Jewish marshals were responsible for ensuring that no one escaped. They guarded their fellow victims. Löwenherz was told that for every person who escaped from the collection point, two guards would be deported.[105] The unlucky ones lay without blankets on the bare floor or on straw sacks. In these crowded conditions arguments broke out over every triviality. People who were insane or had suffered a nervous breakdown because of their suffering were also interned in a separate room.[106] Quite a few people in the collection point committed suicide in despair so as to escape deportation. Brunner had people who were half-dead or unconscious, having attempted to escape deportation by killing themselves, put on stretchers and carried to the train. He said of a girl who had taken poison but was still alive: 'Let her die in Poland.'[107]

The deportees were shorn. They were transported on open trucks to Aspangbahnhof. These journeys took place during the day. Passers-by in the busy streets shouted insults at the departing Jews.[108]

The Jewish administration provided a Jewish transport supervisor and a deputy who were subject to the orders of the official transport supervisor. There was also a doctor and nursing staff in the train. Every wagon had a wagon orderly and a deputy.[109] In a 'leaflet on the future transports to Poland', the Kultusgemeinde indicated that the wagon orderly had to ensure at the station that the Jews remained in their seats in the wagon. An hour before departure they had to take their leave of their families. Only officials and functionaries of the IKG with official passes were allowed to remain on the station platform. The wagon orderlies 'had to ensure that the train departed quietly. Demonstrations and loud behaviour are forbidden.'[110]

The Jewish functionaries at the time believed that by keeping order and quiet they could avoid additional hardship. The Jewish community therefore ensured that the deportation of its members was carried out in a civilized and disciplined fashion. Most of them were to be killed shortly after their arrival. At the time, however, the Jewish administration did not know this.

Welfare and burial service – administration in the shadow of destruction

During the first wave of deportations, it was still possible for Jews in Vienna to escape from the Third Reich. The Kultusgemeinde hoped to be able to continue its welfare services and emigration assistance.

According to the Jewish administration, there were still 44,000 Jews left in Vienna on 30 June 1941, of whom 19,691 or 44 per cent were over sixty; 34,076 or over 77 per cent were over forty-five; and 27,657 or 63 per cent were women.[111] These were the Jews left after the emigrations between 1938 and 1941. The young and healthy were most likely to have been able to get away. Women were disadvantaged; many mothers stayed behind with their children after their husbands had emigrated in the hope of earning enough money abroad to send for their families. Now they were trapped; the borders had been closed.

The Kultusgemeinde continued to attempt to encourage emigration and to find new channels for escape. It also sought to provide the needy with enough to live on. From early 1940 onwards, it also looked after non-religious Jews, persons who were Jewish according to the Nuremberg laws but were not members of the Jewish community.

Everyone sought ways of leaving the Third Reich. After the German army invaded the Soviet Union in June 1941 it was no longer possible to flee eastwards. The more hopeless their circumstances became, the more desperate their attempts and those of the administration to emigrate. Australia, Canada, in fact the entire British Empire and dominions were now enemy territory and were thus out of bounds. Palestine was unreachable. For refugee ships, the entire Mediterranean had become almost impossible to navigate because of the battles in south-eastern Europe and North Africa. It was difficult to obtain an entry visa for the countries of South America. Enormous brokering fees had to be paid to consular representatives, travel agencies and lawyers. Very few obtained a visa at the US consulates as the quotas for 1941 had already been filled by spring. Between January and June 1941, some 429 Jews were able to emigrate from Vienna to the United States of America. During this time, 1,194 Austrian Jews managed to leave, and thousands had already been deported.[112] On 10 November 1941, normal emigration was stopped except for a few exceptional cases.[113]

In 1941 and 1942, the responsibilities of the Jewish welfare service changed radically. As a result of the deportations, there were fewer welfare recipients. Whereas 140,000 meals had been dished out in January 1942 by the soup kitchens, in December of that year only 12,765 meals were served.[114]

It became increasingly difficult to send support from abroad to Jews in Vienna. The Kultusgemeinde acted as a contact and information centre. The welfare department answered questions from worried relatives abroad. And then in January 1942, the Nazi authorities banned the IKG 'from answering questions coming from abroad about the whereabouts of evacuated Jews. Enquiries by authorities and banks are to be responded to with the instruction that the required information is to be obtained from the police.'[115]

The only information it was allowed to give was the address of the Jews who had not yet been deported. As late as May 1944, a Jewish woman sent a postcard from the ghetto in Lodz to the Kultusgemeinde. The welfare department replied that 'the address of the woman . . . was not known'.[116] On the postcard from Lodz, the official had written the word 'East'. This information could not be provided in the answer from the Kultusgemeinde, but the correspondent in Lodz must certainly have known that her friends or relatives had been deported. The welfare department had used the blank reverse side of a pre-printed form for its reply, one of those forms on which the deportees had to sign that they had given over the personal belongings to the Jewish old people's home.

The welfare department took care of those who were interned by the Gestapo on Rossauer Lände or in Buchenwald, Sachsenhausen or Dachau. The Gestapo informed the Kultusgemeinde who had been arrested and which relatives were to be notified. The welfare department sent monthly support, food and clothing to the detainees and also tried to settle their debts. The dispatches could not be sent on behalf of the Jewish administration, however, but only in the name of the official. The welfare worker Franzi Löw was in contact with detainees and she visited those who had no relatives. Every day she carried a heavy rucksack into the prisons. She was allowed to bring the detainees a kilo of bread, jam, sugar, a shirt, underwear, a pair of socks and two handkerchiefs per week.[117] There are countless letters of thanks to the welfare department from inmates in prisons and camps.[118]

The Kultusgemeinde was also permitted to send packages and money to the concentration camps and ghettos, although again not as an official administrative body. It was in contact with the Council of Elders in the ghetto in Lodz, who provided addresses for the needy recipients from Vienna.[119] After January 1942, it was forbidden to send money and packages to the camps and ghettos.[120] As late as March 1943, however, the welfare department attempted to send letters and packages to Birkenau and Monowitz, part of the Auschwitz complex.[121]

Lily Neufeld, head of the welfare department, was deported in 1942 and Franzi Löw now had to run the department on her own.

She was also the official guardian for mentally handicapped Jewish youths. When she learnt that her wards were being taken to Steinhof, she attempted to intervene. The next day, she was informed that they had been taken away nevertheless. As the official guardian, she received the death notice, the cause of death being given as 'heart failure'.[122] She was also the official guardian for illegitimate Jewish children. Most of these children had been deported from the homes in 1942, together with the staff. Only one of the three homes in which these children lived was still running. Franzi Löw was able to rescue those who had a non-Jewish parent and were thus classified as half-Jews. They survived in Vienna. She even managed to obtain the release from the collection point of a child whose mother had been deported in 1941. Her ward had an Aryan father and Löw claimed that the boy, Harry Gelblein, had been baptised as a Catholic. Brunner said he would spare the boy if the Jewish welfare officer could produce a baptism certificate by the following day. She sought out Father Ludger Born in the archdiocese of Vienna, who was head of the Welfare Department for Non-Aryan Catholics, which provided food, medicine and clothes for Catholic victims of the Nuremberg laws. Löw managed to persuade Father Born to issue a fake baptism certificate for Harry Gelblein, whereupon Brunner had the child released.[123]

Of the seventy remaining residents in the Jewish children's home in 1942, around forty were subsequently deported so that some thirty survived until Vienna was liberated in 1945. The Kultusgemeinde knew that some of these children had a non-Jewish parent and Franzi Löw was given the task of obtaining proof of Aryan ancestry for them. In other cases, the paternity was unknown and it was possible to name a non-Jewish man as the father. These children owe their lives to the efforts of the Jewish administration.[124]

Franzi Löw also worked on behalf of Jews who had gone underground to avoid deportation. Many were hiding with non-Jews but did not dare to leave their hiding places. Löw brought them ration cards. Altogether she looked after around thirty of these concealed Jews in Vienna. To do so, she needed the assistance of non-Jewish offices and individuals. One such person was Sister Verena from Caritas Socialis. The Welfare Department for Non-Aryan Catholics provided food stamps, medicine and money until it was closed in 1942. There was also the Protestant aid association in which Mala Granat from Sweden worked. The persecuted Jews were helped as well by private individuals such as Primarius Dr Riese or the family of Dr Wilhelm Danneberg, who later married Franzi Löw.[125]

Those who accuse the administration of having collaborated in the deportations should also bear in mind the efforts Franzi Löw made on behalf of these underground Jews. Many of them would not have survived without the covert assistance of the Jewish welfare department. Obviously, there were only a few of them in Vienna, but those who attempted to help them nevertheless risked their lives doing so. Franzi Löw, the only Jewish welfare officer in the Council of Elders, ran all over Vienna with her Jewish star hidden, carrying forged documents and ration cards and hauling a heavy rucksack full of food, all of the time exposing herself to the suspicious glances of Gestapo officials and SS men. She and her superiors, such as Löwenherz, who knew about some of her activities, could have been deported if the Gestapo had got wind of what was going on.

As a result of the deportations, the Rothschild Hospital had to admit and treat patients who had previously been cared for by relatives and friends. On 26 December 1941, hospital director Dr Arnold Raschke complained that he was having to turn away seriously ill patients.[126] The hospital had 250 beds; without any structural alterations the number of beds was increased in 1941 to 450, thanks to the administrative skills of the medical examiner Dr Emil Tuchmann. In his annual report, submitted to the State Health Department, the Kultusgemeinde and the Gestapo, Tuchmann wrote that 45,141 patients had been treated in the out-patients' department in 1941, with 125 new cases every day. There were 2,286 permanent residents of both sexes in the old people's homes; 3,873 patients had sought admission, of whom 1,192 had been admitted on account of the severity of their condition. The old people's homes were overcrowded and the sanitary inspection officers pointed out that the maximum capacity had long been exceeded. The old people's home in Seegasse was meant for 430 residents and not the 611 who were living there.[127]

The Jewish administration was also responsible for organizing Jewish rituals. The Jewish holidays in 1941 were celebrated in the City Temple by Rabbi Benjamin Murmelstein.[128] In an interview after 1945, Murmelstein said that he no longer performed religious services in 1942 as he did not consider himself worthy. The fact that he had broken the Shabbat and had been in daily contact with Eichmann and Brunner 'ritually disqualified' him.[129]

On 31 October 1942, the Kultusgemeinde had its legal status under public law removed and its work from 1 November 1942 was to be carried out by the Council of Elders of the Jews in Vienna. All of the remaining Jews were obliged to join and pay subscriptions in accordance with their assets and income. Money was to be demanded of

Jews in institutions. All Jews were obliged to subscribe to the *Jüdisches Nachrichtenblatt*. On 31 October 1942, the Emigration Aid for Non-Mosaic Jews in the Ostmark was also closed and the work of this office was taken over as well by the Council of Elders. Likewise, the Association of War Victims was disbanded and the Jewish war victims still in Vienna came under the charge of the Council of Elders.[130]

Josef Löwenherz was officially appointed head of the Council of Elders on 1 January 1943. At his suggestion Wilhelm Bienenfeld, Heinrich Dessauer and Benjamin Murmelstein were also appointed as members of the Council. Murmelstein and Dessauer were deported a few weeks later to Theresienstadt. Dessauer was subsequently moved to Auschwitz in 1944, where he died.[131]

In the 1942 annual report, the Jewish administration drew attention to the achievements of the IKG since 1938. It pointed to its assistance with emigration, foreign currency, soup kitchens, medical care, education and welfare and claimed that it had helped 136,000 Jews to emigrate and had arranged 3,101 retraining courses for 20,432 men and 21,773 women. The report was submitted to the Nazi authorities: 'In the last annual report describing the work of the IKG, it may be said without pretension that: IT WORKED IN THE PUBLIC AND JEWISH INTERESTS AND MET ITS RESPONSIBILITIES TO THE FULL.'[132]

By the beginning of 1943, there were only 7,989 Jews left in Vienna and by December the number had dwindled to 6,259. Of these, 1,080 belonged to another confession, 85 were foreign, 3,702 lived in privileged mixed marriages and 1,392 in non-privileged mixed marriages. On 1 January 1942, the Kultusgemeinde had 1,088 paid employees and 558 volunteers. At the end of the year there were 254 paid and 80 voluntary employees. Of the Jews still living in Vienna, most had been recruited for forced labour.[133]

After summer 1944, the Council of Elders had to look after not only around 6,000 Viennese Jews but also 18,000 Hungarian Jews who had been interned in the camps. They had been sent to Austria as a result of an agreement between the Hungarian Zionist functionary Reszö (Rudolf) Kasztner and Adolf Eichmann. Kasztner attempted to rescue the Hungarian Jews in exchange for trucks and other material. They had been transported initially to Strasshof as security for this arrangement between Kasztner and Eichmann and were in the charge of the Vienna *Sondereinsatzkommando*. Around 8,000 were sent to Vienna and 7,000 to Lower Austria for forced labour. Dr Tuchmann was responsible for medical care in the camps and organized a staff of ten doctors who visited the camps and were supported by Hungarian personnel. He managed to set up a postnatal depart-ment for Hungarian babies at the children's home in Mohapelgasse. Through his contacts with the head of the employment department, he also arranged for the exemption from work of old and sick Jews. He set up a prayer house in Malzgasse and in March 1945 he enabled Pesach to be celebrated there. With the knowledge of the *Sondereinsatzkommando*, he managed through contacts with the International Red Cross to have shoes, clothing, underwear and food smuggled illegally to Vienna.[134]

Franzi Löw organized clothing for the Hungarian Jews without official permission. She was arrested on the way to the camps and brought before Siegfried Seidl, deputy head of the Vienna *Sondereinsatzkommando* and responsible for the Hungarian Jews deported to Vienna and Lower Austria for forced labour. Seidl yelled at Franzi Löw, who remained calm and managed to persuade the Nazi official of the need for her welfare work. He gave her written authorization to visit the camps and to deal as far as possible with the needs of the inmates.[135] Franzi Löw reports:

> The camps were closed in March 1945. Some of the inmates were deported. On the day of the deportations, twelve Hungarian Jews sud-denly turned up at the Kultusgemeinde asking me to hide them some-where. I managed with great difficulty to find hiding places for them in the cellars of apartments belonging to non-Jews in the 1st district, on Tiefer Graben and elsewhere. I provided them with the most urgently needed food supplies. In this way I was able to save these Hungarian Jews until Vienna was liberated.[136]

In the last few months before liberation, long after the Jewish com-munity in Vienna had been destroyed, the Jewish administration continued to work. Why did the Council of Elders continue to exist after 1943? Why was there a Jewish cemetery and a Jewish hospital? Those who believe that the Jews throughout Europe were all killed at the same time might be surprised to know that there were Jewish institutions in Vienna and a Jewish hospital in Berlin until 1945. In contrast to the occupied countries, the Nazi authorities appear to have believed it particularly important to cleanse the population of the Third Reich of everything Jewish but without frightening or harming their own 'Volksgenossen'. There were still Mischlinge, Jews married or related to non-Jews, and their families living in Vienna whom the Nazis had to allow for. The remaining Jews had to be looked after in the interests of the population as a whole. They needed medical care so as to prevent infections and epidemics in the non-Jewish environment. They still needed to be segregated, however, and to be looked after by Jewish institutions rather than in Aryan hospitals. They were still tolerated, but the machinery of extermination was waiting for them. As soon as an Aryan husband died, his Jewish widow was deported unless she was protected by other relatives.

──11──

THE KULTUSGEMEINDE – AUTHORITIES WITHOUT POWER

The administrative murder of millions made of death a thing one had never yet to fear in just this fashion. There is no chance anymore for death to come into the individuals' empirical life as somehow conformable with the course of life. . . . Since Auschwitz fearing death means fearing worse than death.

Theodor W. Adorno, *Negative Dialectics*[1]

Individual stories

What kind of behaviour by the victims during the Nazi extermination can be regarded as normal? How much ignominy can a person endure and how many members of their families do they need to lose? If the enemy is no longer interested in subjugation but in death, isn't every obstruction and every effort to save the lives of as many Jews as possible already a form of resistance? The victims took all possible measures to escape persecution. This chapter looks at some personal survival strategies, the efforts of the individual to avoid extermination.

Some turned to the state authorities, to the all-powerful perpetrators, in their desperation. They wrote appeals to the Gauleiter. They begged, protested or pointed out that they were German nationalists. Their letters were neither answered nor heeded.[2]

Between March and September 1938, only 1,702 people attempted to convert to Catholicism. Most were women who had converted to Judaism after marrying a Jewish man and now hoped to protect him and their children by reconverting.[3] According to statistics by Leo Goldhammer from the year 1927, it was usually the Jewish spouse who abandoned his or her religion.[4] In the Third Reich, these pairs were now discriminated against as mixed marriages. Claudia Koonz has studied the different reactions by Jewish men and women to the Third Reich until 1938.[5] The men first felt the economic anti-Semitism through being prohibited from working, while the women were more exposed to everyday anti-Semitism. Men persisted longer in attempting to defend their social territory. They hoped for a change in the situation. Women were more willing to live in another country. As mentioned earlier, however, it was easier for men to emigrate. Women had less chance of being accepted as immigrants. The victims did not allow themselves to be led like 'lambs to the slaughter'. They did not simply resign themselves to their fate. They conducted a personal struggle merely to survive. They wrote to aid committees; they contacted remote acquaintances; they looked in foreign telephone directories for potential relatives; they scurried from embassy to embassy trying to obtain visas; they acquired countless emigration papers and learned new professions so as to be accepted as immigrants.[6] Many applied for organized emigration, others tried to reach freedom on illegal transports or by being smuggled over the border. Illegal escape was a form of non-conformist behaviour.[7]

Attempts to avoid discrimination by dissimulating their Jewish identity were perilous. The Vienna Gestapo files contain reports on violations of the various regulations for Jews. Those who hid the Jewish star with a piece of clothing or a bag, those who did not include the names 'Sara' or 'Israel' on forms, risked being brought to the collection point for deportation.[8]

A few Jews attempted to escape from the SS and Gestapo by going underground. Some attempted to create a logistical infrastructure for these 'submarines'.[9] Some refused to accept the humiliations without resistance. On 25 April 1938, Easter Monday and the last day of Pesach, since the Middle Ages a favourite day for anti-Jewish pogroms, hundreds of Jews at the Reichsbrücke were compelled to spit in each other's faces. One young man refused, saying that he would rather be shot than to accept this torment. He was killed a short time later in a concentration camp.[10]

The Vienna Gestapo reports of anti-Nazi utterances by Jewish defendants should be considered with caution. Not infrequently the cases were the result of anti-Semitic denunciations. The reports nevertheless contain some clear examples of protestation.[11]

There were organized resistance groups in Vienna that were active in the underground. Some of these circles contained a relatively large number of people who were persecuted as Jews. When the Nazis came to power in 1938, the Austrian Communist Party called on comrades of Jewish descent to break off contact with other members of the movement so as not to imperil anyone.[12] Jewish Communists therefore founded their own clandestine groups. A distinction should be made between Jewish resistance and resistance by Jews. Communist anti-Fascists of Jewish descent did not want to be identified as Jews. In spite of their conception of themselves, however, they still belonged to the group of persecuted Jews. They should not be denied their perception of themselves, but the fact remains that everyone who suffered the fate of Jews or was regarded by outsiders as being Jewish on account of their origins must be included in the historical study of German and Austrian Judaism.

The Jewish functionaries attempted to warn the Jewish population against resisting. When Leo Baeck heard that the resistance by the Herbert Baum group was continuing, he is alleged to have said: 'To be honest, I did not believe that reason would prevail in these circumstances. . . . From the outset their actions were madness. . . . Now at least they realize it. . . . There is nothing else we can do.'[13]

During the deportation phase, the leaders of the Jewish community adhered to the principle of legality and warned against resistance to the Nazis. The administration feared that resistance by individual Jews would have repercussions for the Jewish community as a whole. They did not know that the death sentence had already been pronounced in any case on all Jews. The Jewish anti-Fascists did not seek the support of the Jewish community. They were only too well aware that the Jewish administration could not help. This aspect should not be overlooked. The resistance fighters recognized that the only way that the regime could be countered would be through large-scale resistance by the population as a whole.

A Jewish anti-Nazi resistance group also formed in Vienna. In 1943, decimated by the deportations, some of the persecuted Jews joined forces. As most full Jews had already been deported, the activists called themselves the 'Vienna Mischling League' or WML, although not all of its members were Mischlinge. It contacted Yugoslav partisans and in 1944 it was prosecuted as a secret military organization and its members sentenced to imprisonment.[14]

The conservative opposition in Germany, the bourgeois underground, fought against Hitler, but the prevailing anti-Semitic sentiments meant that Jews were excluded from it.[15] Many Jews were politically active in left-wing groups and in the Communist and Social Democratic resistance. Others fought in Spain against Fascism. Many joined the Allied armies after emigration and contributed in this way to the defeat of Nazism.

Those who ask why there was no armed Jewish resistance in Vienna are being naive. To believe that the Jewish population could have functioned as a sovereign unit within Austrian society and have rebelled against it is to succumb to the anti-Semitic cliché that the Jews of Vienna were a homogeneous block, a conspiracy, isolated and hierarchically structured. Most Jews lived dispersed throughout Vienna and had more contact with their non-Jewish neighbours than with the Jewish authorities. The persecution cut off every single victim from his or her social network. The Jews could scarcely hope for solidarity and it took more than courage to dare to resist. There was no major anti-Nazi movement in Vienna at the time with which the Jewish organizations could have made contact. Where there was no anti-Nazi resistance within the non-Jewish population, the European Jews could not organize an armed underground. All rebellions need support. In other European cities, in the ghettos of Warsaw and Vilna, for example, the victims were able to argue how they should react to the Nazi persecution of the Jews. Some called for Jewish resistance. But only those who were not too old or too young, who did not have to look after a child, a sick person or needy relatives, could decide to resist. Without power centres, without territory, without support from non-Jews and without a logistical infrastructure, rebellion against the state authorities was doomed to failure. A community like the Viennese Jewish community with a surfeit of older members because of the departure of so many young people, one that was politically and socially heterogeneous and in no way autonomous, was not in a position to put up militant resistance.

It was not possible for the resistance by the Jews of Germany to have any impact on the power politics of the time, but that should not detract from the respect that the activists merit. Of the 200,000 Jews living in the German Reich after 1939, around 2,000 young persons were active in the anti-Fascist underground at various times between 1933 and 1943.[16] If the non-Jewish population had resisted to the same extent, it would have created a mass movement of 600,000–700,000 activists against the Nazi regime. As history has shown, no such mass movement rose up.

Many were unable to outwardly express their despair and anger at the injustice. The number of suicides among Jews rose in 1938 from five in January and four in February to seventy-nine in March and sixty-two in April.[17] The previous year, three Jews had committed suicide in March and seven in April.[18]

It was simply impossible to explain to anyone outside Austria the matter-of-fact resignation with which the Austrian Jews of the time spoke of suicide as a quite normal way of escaping from their terrible situation. Jewish friends would inform you of their decision to commit suicide in the same way as they would formerly have told you that they were going on a short train journey.[19]

The suicide rate rose whenever particularly terrible events such as pogroms and deportations occurred.[20] Orthodox Jews seldom opted for suicide. Germans who had long renounced their Jewishness and adopted other religions were in despair at the inexplicable fate that had befallen them. Some would take their leave of friends as if they were departing on a long journey. Everyone then knew that they were planning to kill themselves.[21] It was not a suicide of choice. These people were driven by society first to exclusion and then to death. They killed themselves but not freely. And yet suicide was still a demonstration of free will and a determination to resist the criminal acts and the process of persecution and extermination, the ultimate strategy of refusal.

The victims' perspective

Historians attempt to describe what happened in a particular place at a particular time. To a large extent, the previous chapters have followed this historiographical approach. They contain a description of what happened to the Vienna Jewish community between 1938 and 1945 and how it reacted. The present chapter does not attempt merely to describe what happened, but what could have happened; what alternatives were available to the Jewish leadership and its administration. It also looks at the strategies pursued by the Jewish functionaries and the hopes that they entertained. This approach runs contrary to a historiographical principle that claims that there are no facts other than those that actually occurred, effectively a capitulation to the power of facts. But it is also interesting to study the uncertainties that were later to crystallize fatefully into historical reality. In the late 1930s, for example, the countries of the West could have prevented the extermination if they had reacted differently to the Nazi persecution and expulsion, had willingly accepted the refugees and provided humanitarian assistance or sought an alliance with the Soviet Union against the Third Reich. Nazi Germany could have been defeated earlier. Perhaps Berlin would have surrendered if one of the assassination attempts against Hitler had succeeded. It is not a question of speculating what would have happened if events had taken a different course but of describing the prospects and insights of the Jews and their representatives. What were the victims' perspectives?

First, we should consider how much they knew about the crimes. This has been the subject of numerous discussions and also oral history. On occasion, one and the same person might claim to have known nothing, only to assert a short while later that he or she was fully informed. One of the reasons for this haziness is the way questions are asked. The persecution of the Jews in the Third Reich was already well known before the Nazis came to power in Austria. No one can claim to have known nothing about the pogroms in 1938. But when did the Jews of Vienna find out about the conditions in the Polish ghettos? When did they first hear about the mass shootings? When did they realize that they were all to be exterminated?

One survivor claims to have known nothing about Auschwitz until summer 1944. Only through more persistent questioning does it become evident that this eyewitness had heard about this camp earlier and feared it more than any other and that, even without knowing the precise details, he was aware of crimes that were being committed.[22] The revelations of the details of the gas chambers and crematoriums that became known only between 1943 and 1945 were so inconceivable that quite a few people were unwilling and unable to believe that something like that could occur in twentieth-century Europe. Primo Levi wrote on this subject:

> Many survivors . . . remember that the SS militiamen enjoyed cynically admonishing the prisoners. [Rest of quotation from Levi: 'However this war may end, we have won the war against you; none of you will be left to bear witness, but even if someone were to survive, the world would not believe him. There will perhaps be suspicions, discussions, research by historians, but there will be no certainties, because we will destroy the evidence together with you. And even if some proof should remain and some of you survive, people will say that the events you describe are too monstrous to be believed: they will say that they are the exaggerations of Allied propaganda and will believe us, who will deny everything, and not you. We will be the ones to dictate the history of the Lagers.']

He is referring indirectly to Simon Wiesenthal's account of an encounter with SS Rottenführer Merz in September 1944, who said:

> Just imagine, Wiesenthal, that you are arriving in New York, and the people ask you 'How was it in those German concentration camps?

What did they do to you?' . . . You would tell the truth to the people in America. . . . And you know what would happen, Wiesenthal? . . . They wouldn't believe you. They'd say you were mad. Might even put you into an asylum. How can *any*one believe this terrible business – unless he has lived through it?[23]

What does it mean to 'know' about a crime? A long time can pass from the first rumours of an atrocity to the day on which these rumours turn into a certainty. In the meantime, doubts may arise as to whether the misdeed is really as bad as that. The victims were not subject to the same suppression mechanism as the perpetrators, accomplices and fellow travellers. The crime was kept out of the public eye as far as possible. Awareness by Nazi society of the anti-Jewish persecution was ambivalent because most people had an idea of what was happening but at the same time were not allowed to speak about it.

The Jews of Vienna, by contrast, were eager and anxious for all news of the crimes being committed in the east, since their lives were at stake. Rumours spread like wildfire. The victims were aware of the inhumanity of the regime but, even if they had a foreboding of what awaited them after deportation, the anxiety was mitigated by hope and the fear of death by a will to live.

The Vienna Jews knew that their community was to be dissolved. They fled from the discrimination in terror to save their lives. At the beginning of 1939, Hitler spoke of the 'extermination of the Jewish race in Europe' should war break out. Peace could be assured, he said to the Reichstag on 30 January 1939, only if the Jews were driven out of the continent and settled somewhere else in the world.[24] The same year, he began to attempt the deportation of the Jews of Vienna to Nisko in the newly conquered territories. The Jewish administration did not know what would happen to the deportees. Although a group of Jewish functionaries accompanied the first transport to Nisko, they did not return to Vienna until the plan to settle the Jews in the Lublin region had already been abandoned.[25] The details of the deportation became known within the Jewish community when the survivors of Nisko arrived back in Vienna in April 1940.[26]

Josef Löwenherz hoped that there would be no further deportations of the Vienna Jews. He attempted to persuade Eichmann not to continue the deportations. On 13 November 1939, Eichmann stated that the emigration of the Vienna Jews had to be completed by 1 February 1940, threatening that those who had not left by then would be deported to Poland.[27] The Vienna Jewish administration set its sights on winning this race against time. Two thirds of the community had already left in 1938 and 1939, and it seemed that it ought to be possible to rescue the last third in the third year. But the war made it more difficult to emigrate and the Nazi authorities hatched their 'resettlement' plan. It was only on 1 February 1941 that Löwenherz learned that the first transport was to take place fourteen days hence.[28] Once again, the leaders of the Jewish community did not know what awaited the Jews in the small Polish towns. The first letters arrived very soon afterwards. However disquieting the measures appeared, no one could yet grasp the significance of the transports. In an interview, the Zionist youth functionary of the time, Martin Vogel, said that many young people believed when the deportations started that the Jewish population would indeed be settled in defined areas of Poland and be recruited for labour details. Some even seriously considered the possibility of volunteering to go.[29] The Zionist youth movement sent food and clothing to Opole and Kielce to help the deportees. When it received no replies from the east in early autumn 1941, Vogel asked the Kultusgemeinde about the whereabouts of the deportees. He was told that it would be better not to ask any more questions.[30] The Jews of Vienna and the leaders of the Jewish administration were beginning to realize that for many people, particularly the old and sick, deportation meant death. But they still knew nothing of the systematic killing.

In the course of 1941, word got back about the mass shooting of Jews on the Eastern front. On 3 September 1941, the leaders of the Kultusgemeinde received a report from its legal office. Officials had reported that a letter from a soldier at the front had been posted on a notice board next to the Nordsee fish restaurant on Radetzkyplatz at the corner of Löwengasse:

> The letter describes that the soldiers had heard how the Jews had behaved towards the soldiers at the front, after which they still treated them humanely, lining up 1,000 Jews against the wall and shooting them. The next day, however, they learned again that worse atrocities had been committed, whereupon they had the Jews retrieve the corpses and clean them up. Then they assembled the Jews on a square and beat them with truncheons, deservedly so.[31]

The Jews in Vienna were aware of the massacres and pogroms on the Eastern front. The extermination had already begun in the occupied Soviet territories, but the Viennese Jews could not yet imagine anything of the future killing machinery and the systematic extermination in the camps.

Rumours circulated in September 1941 of another wave of deportations. Löwenherz was informed on 30 September, the eve of Yom Kippur.[32] When he was called up to the reading desk he was unable to hold back the tears. The congregation in the crowded temple on Seitenstettengasse understood; the rumours that had been circulating for weeks within the community were true.[33] Although the Jews did not know exactly what would happen to them, they already realized that deportation meant destruction and death. Everyone attempted to avoid transportation as long as possible. During 1942, a few more detailed reports reached Vienna but the extent of the extermination was still not apparent. In addition, it was strictly forbidden to talk about the terrible events. The dissemination of information of this nature in the Third Reich was regarded as 'vicious rumours'. More and more news filtered back to Vienna, however. In April 1942, Munisch (Menashe) Mautner, a Kultusgemeinde official, received a letter from his two nephews, Yossele and Mendel, from Lanczyn.[34] They wrote that the town had been occupied on 11 April. After a massacre lasting four days, 270 of the 300 Jews had been killed. The thirty survivors had been left destitute. Non-Jewish peasants had moved into their homes. Mautner wrote a letter on 19 April to his brother-in-law Karl Seidner in Tel Aviv and described what his nephews had suffered. He added: 'Dear Karl, I don't know what tomorrow will bring, even for myself, because there are fewer of us every day. We are picked out and sent to an uncertain destination under terrible conditions.'[35]

Mautner asked his brother-in-law to hand over the letter to the American press but it never got to Palestine. Mautner told Josef Löwenherz about the killings in Galicia. When he suggested asking the advice of Benjamin Murmelstein, Löwenherz is said to have replied: 'Anything but that! Murmelstein must hear nothing about it!'[36]

Mautner inferred from this comment that it must somehow be dangerous to ask for Murmelstein's aid. Did Löwenherz fear that Murmelstein would denounce Mautner to the Gestapo? At all events, Löwenherz and Mautner did not pass on their information to the Jews of Vienna. Mautner had read about pogroms and feared the worst, but even he had no idea about the systematic extermination.

On 14 September 1942, Martha Weissweiler, who worked at the Bondi children's home, wrote a letter to Sofie Löwenherz, the wife of the Kultusgemeinde director. She knew that she was to be selected and deported from Vienna.

It was a difficult decision for me not to volunteer to go with my eighty-year-old mother with today's transport to Theresienstadt, which should at least be better for her than Riga. I regret it twice as much now that I heard today that Dr Friedland, Dr Burchardt and Dr Löwenstamm are with their mothers and parents. But this is not a good time to tempt the fates.[37]

Theresienstadt was known to be the ghetto for elderly and prominent Jews, but Martha Weissweiler knew a lot more: 'For the time being I have every reason to be doubly thankful. My job has kept me safe so far and above all protected me from going to Oswiecim – our house (Flossgasse 4) was picked out on 4 July, the date of the worst transport so far.'[38]

Oswiecim, Auschwitz. The word was already out that this place was worse than the others. Even so, Martha Weissweiler was probably ignorant of the mass extermination.

In some cases, the international Jewish organizations knew more about the situation in the Third Reich than the victims in Vienna. Letters from Switzerland to Zionist organizations in January 1942 contained descriptions of the conditions, hardship and epidemics in Lodz.[39] On 8 August 1942, Gerhart Riegner, representative of the World Jewish Congress in Geneva, sent a telegram to Stephen Wise, president of the World Jewish Congress in the United States, and to Sidney Silverman, member of parliament in the United Kingdom, about a report he had received of plans to exterminate all of the Jews in the European territories occupied by Germany. He also mentioned that prussic acid was to be used. The telegram was received initially with doubt and disbelief; American undersecretary of state Summer Welles asked Stephen Wise not to publish the information until it had been confirmed. On 3 September 1942, Jacob Rosenheim, chairman of Agudat Israel in New York, received a similar telegram from Isaac Sternbuch, representative of the Jewish aid organization Waad Hazala in Switzerland. In response, Wise and Rosenheim founded an emergency committee. When the American government had persuaded itself that the information was correct, Wise contacted the press on 24 November 1942.[40]

The Jews in Vienna were completely isolated, without telephones or access to free newspapers. The extermination camps were far away in the east of Europe. Correspondence by the administration was limited and subject to censor. Despite this, the first rumours of systematic extermination appear to have reached the Viennese Jews at the end of 1942.

To understand the situation of a leading Jewish community functionary, it is necessary to take account of the daily terror and the hardship, blackmail, lies and promises by the perpetrators. Löwenherz could not analyse the situation dispassionately. He and his family were in constant peril and he was exposed directly to the threats and demands of the Gestapo. At the end of 1942, fewer than 8,000 Jews remained in Vienna. At that time Löwenherz sought out Karl Ebner from the Vienna Gestapo to find out about the fate of the deportees. Ebner described the incident after 1945:

> He came to me one day after 1942, presumably in 1943, an utterly broken man, and asked for a meeting with Huber. I asked him what he wanted, and he told me that the Jews were already being put to death and he wanted to be sure that this was in fact the case. I thought that he was going to have a bad time with the chief and that he might conceivably be charged with spreading enemy radio reports. Löwenherz said that it was all the same to him, and thereupon we went to Huber. When Huber was put in the picture, he then called the chief of Office IV in the Reich Security Main Office (Müller) on a direct line while we waited outside. As we went in again, Huber said to us that Müller had dismissed these allegations as evil reports. Löwenherz was visibly relieved.[41]

Thus it would seem that Löwenherz did not learn about the systematic extermination until the deportation of the Vienna Jewish community had been completed. But he had already known about atrocities and mass shootings since summer 1941. After the war people often wondered why the Elder of the Jews had not told the Jews that the deportations meant death. In reality, the Jewish representatives in many regions did not know much more than the other Jews. The accusation that they deliberately left the other Jews in the dark is based in Vienna and elsewhere on a false premise. Whether people understood the situation clearly and without embellishment depended not on their position but their character. The way in which an individual dealt with the information was a question of personality. As a jurist and official, Löwenherz sought to establish the truth through official channels. Despite the fact that he had been consistently deceived and betrayed in the previous years by the Nazi and state authorities, he nevertheless turned to the police, i.e., the perpetrators, for confirmation. He was systematically deceived. In fact, it was easy to deceive the victims because what was happening ran contrary to all reason and anything that they could have imagined before. They expected to be starved and exploited but why would the enemy want to systematically exterminate them? Did Löwenherz expect a truthful answer? Was he really 'relieved' when he left Ebner and was he comforted because he trusted the persecutors, or because any pretext was better than believing the full extent of the crime? Löwenherz asked the Nazis, although he must have known that he would not receive an honest answer from them. It should not be forgotten, incidentally, that he showed impressive courage by daring to confront Ebner with the reports of mass killing. His demand to speak to Huber could have resulted in immediate arrest.

No one willingly joined the transports, but no one could or wanted to imagine what was happening in the extermination camps. There is nothing surprising or pathetic about this. When Hannah Arendt heard about the extermination for the first time in 1943, she blocked it out because

> militarily it was unnecessary and uncalled for. . . . And then a half-year later we believed it after all because we had the proof. That was the real shock. Before that we said: Well, one has enemies. That is entirely natural. Why shouldn't a people have enemies? But this was different. It was really as if an abyss had opened. Because we had the idea that everything else could somehow be made good again, like in politics when everything can be made good again. But not this. This should never have been allowed to happen. And I don't mean just the number of victims. I mean the method, the fabrication of corpses and so on – I don't need to go into that. This should not have happened.[42]

No one can be accused of not believing what was going on in the extermination camps. Retrospectively, the hopes cherished by the Jewish functionaries might appear far-fetched, since the crime associated with Auschwitz has been etched in our consciousness since 1945. Those who do not want to believe how the mass murders by the Nazis were carried out are denying the crime and step over the line that separates us from barbarism and the collapse of civilization. At the time, however, people could not imagine it because they didn't believe that anyone, even the Nazis, were capable of such atrocities; it is no shame not to have anticipated this lack of enlightenment, this capitulation of European culture before the primacy of the anti-Semitic desire to exterminate the Jews. Far from it.

If anyone is to be criticized for not divulging this knowledge of the extermination, then it is the Allied powers. They knew at an early stage of the crimes committed by the Nazis against the Jews. Richard Breitman has shown that the British secret service had already decrypted the German radio transmission codes in summer 1941 and knew everything about the mass shootings. Almost three months before the first extermination camp started operations and over four months before the Wannsee conference, the secret service knew what the Nazis had in store for the Jews in the occupied regions of the Soviet Union. But the fight for the lives of the Jews was not a priority for the Allies.[43]

During 1943 and 1944, it became clear to everyone in the Jewish community in Vienna that the Jews were being systematically killed. People who had been at the front, foreign slave labourers, including Jewish ones from Hungary, for example, were telling stories about what was happening in the east.

Samuel Storfer deputized from 1939 for his brother Berthold Storfer as head of the Committee for Jewish Overseas Transports. In March 1943, he learned that all of the Jews in Romania were to be rounded up and deported. He warned his sister, whose husband was Romanian, and his nephew and his wife. Anton Brunner at the Central Office appears to have got wind of this. He ordered a search of Samuel Storfer's house by a member of the Jupo (Jewish police). When no one was found, Brunner gave an order by telephone that Samuel Storfer and his wife were to be arrested. Berthold Storfer was taken as a hostage and was not to be released until Samuel Storfer and his wife had arrived at the collection point. Berthold Storfer appealed to Eichmann on behalf of his brother and, on 1 April 1943, Samuel Storfer and his wife were released. On 31 August 1943, however, Gestapo official Johann Rixinger informed Berthold Storfer that his brother and sister-in-law were to be deported and were to report to Aspangbahnhof the following day. The two brothers decided to go underground; the gassings in Auschwitz, said Samuel Storfer after 1945, were already an open secret.[44] Samuel Storfer managed to survive, but his brother Berthold was soon discovered and deported to Auschwitz.

In March 1938, the Jewish administration was closed down and its leaders arrested. Thereafter the Jewish functionaries endeavoured to have the Kultusgemeinde reopened. From the outset, it was under the absolute control of the Gestapo and SS. Welfare and escape were possible only in cooperation with the Nazi authorities. At the time there were no thoughts of a policy of obstruction. By cooperating, the administration enabled over two thirds of the members of the Jewish community to escape the terror of the Third Reich. Until November 1941, the Jewish functionaries still hoped to be able to assist Jews in emigrating. To understand the situation in Vienna, it is important to bear in mind that emigration continued even after the deportations started. The first deportations to Nisko took place in 1939 and the deportation of the Jewish community continued in spring 1941. When it became clear in autumn 1941 that all of the Jews in Vienna were to be deported, most of the young men had already emigrated or been deported. For the most part only the weakest and neediest were left. It is rapidly evident from the age and gender structure of the Jewish population between 1941 and 1943 that this community did not have many defence strategies left open to it – even if its members knew what awaited them.

What would have happened if the Kultusgemeinde had refused to cooperate when the deportations started? They would not have taken place so smoothly, but would have been unruly, probably accompanied by much greater brutality on the part of the Nazi and state authorities. At all events, a refusal to cooperate would not have saved any of the Jews of Vienna.

All of the lists and files were already in the hands of the authorities. The administration had provided the files containing details of its members in 1940 because it had been told that they were needed to issue ration cards. The Jewish functionaries could not suspect that these lists would be used to organize the transports.

Where could all of the Jews, the thousands of sick, old people and children flee to? How could they have fed themselves, where would they have found shelter? They were trapped, surrounded by the enemy. Should the Kultusgemeinde simply have abandoned its responsibility for these people? The Jewish administration had no choice. There was no way out of the dilemma. It had to cooperate in the deportations in order to be able to provide for its members. It hoped to be able to rescue at least those who were deferred. With its time running out, these authorities without power attempted to gain as much of a respite as they could. They had continuously to find new ways of protecting individual victims. The Jewish functionaries and officials cooperated in order to gain some relief and exemptions where they could. They succeeded in individual cases, but through this cooperation the murderers were able to work more quickly towards their goal of deporting all of the Jews.

Ironically, the individual victims began to see the employees of the Kultusgemeinde and the searchers as their main danger. Those who wanted to go underground had to stay out of the way of the Jewish administration, which was merely an additional threat. When the emigrations came to an end and the deportations began, the victims started to avoid Seitenstettengasse, where the Kultusgemeinde offices were located.[45] Some of the Jewish community workers, like Franzi

Löw, helped those who had gone underground as far as they could, but those who received the instructions, orders and summonses from the bureaucratic apparatus saw it as an extension of the Gestapo authority. In retrospect, it is easy to see why the strategies employed by the functionaries failed and how the perpetrators triumphed. At the time, however, when people did not know what we know today, when the victims still believed that the exploitation of their labour was more important to the Nazis than their extermination, the Jews did not really have any alternative but to cooperate. By the time the extent of the crime became known, the community was on its last legs; most of its members had already been killed.

The administration and its employees

When the deportations started, the administration was also restructured. Departments that had formerly worked for emigration and rehousing were now recruited to assist with the deportations.[46] At the same time, the Kultusgemeinde instructed its employees to devote themselves to the new tasks.[47]

The decisions regarding deportations were sent to all offices and departments of the Jewish administration. All employees were informed, for example, that the Jews were to be notified that enquiries to the German Red Cross on the whereabouts of the deportees were forbidden.[48] The victims were enmeshed in the concealment strategy of their murderers. On 20 May 1941, the director of the old people's homes wrote an instruction to the employees: 'I request all staff members to refrain from political discussions of any kind on the premises of the homes. Non-compliance with this order will be reported to the management and could result in dismissal. . . . Every employee must confirm that he or she has been informed of this order.'[49]

When the deportations commenced in early 1941, the directors of the administration stepped up their efforts to maintain discipline and calm. Political discussions would inevitably involve discussion of what was happening and what could be done to prevent it and were therefore to be avoided. The employees were to obey orders on pain of serious consequences. Dismissal at that time meant the loss of protection and hence the threat of deportation. On 15 December 1941, Löwenherz demanded extreme punctuality, subordination and obedience from all employees in carrying out their official tasks. He added: 'Employees coming into contact with official bodies through their work shall maintain a suitable distance and avoid causing any nuisance.'[50]

Löwenherz further ordered the officials to treat Jews who came to the offices and families visited in their homes with courtesy and to provide them with all possible assistance.[51] How helpful and courteous is it possible to be when one is taking people from their homes and bringing them to the collection points?

While the deportations were taking place, a position in the Jewish administration could be life-saving, and for this reason Jews continued to apply to work for the Kultusgemeinde.[52] But even this cooperation within the administration merely postponed deportation and was not usually sufficient to prevent it altogether. On 27 July 1942, Löwenherz informed the Jewish agency in the Vienna Employment Department that, in view of the reduction in staffing levels, the Central Office for Jewish Emigration had ordered that employees who were dismissed should not be made available to the Employment Department and would be resettled in Theresienstadt.[53]

By the end of 1942, the vast majority of the administration employees had been deported. On 17 January 1943, there were only 318 employees left, of whom 248 were paid, including two non-Jews or Aryans, one first-degree Mischling and 47 protected through marriage to non-Jews. Thus 198 were subject to persecution as Jews and were still in Vienna only because of their work, in this way also protecting 155 relatives. Every employee was allowed to keep one other person in Vienna. There were 39 voluntary employees, of whom 16 were protected through marriage to non-Jews. The other 23 were subject to persecution as Jews and were allowed to remain in Vienna along with 15 relatives because of their work. A further 31 volunteers worked in the office of the Council of Elders.[54] Some of the positions vacated by employees who had been deported because they were not deemed to be indispensable were filled by other Jews.

Even after the major deportations had ended, discipline did not let up. Löwenherz could punish serious violations of discipline with fines or threats of dismissal and he had to report them to the Gestapo. Disobedience of orders, hiding the Jewish star or persistent lateness could result in dismissal, deportation and death. Even when there were barely any Jews left in Vienna, employees of the Council of Elders had to work seven days and 60 hours a week. Administrative employees worked from 7.30 a.m. to 7 p.m. On Saturdays and Sundays, they were obliged to remain in the office from 8 a.m. to 1 p.m.[55] The hours of work had to be strictly complied with under threat of arrest by the Gestapo.[56] In this way, the Jewish administration carried out its work punctually and in a disciplined fashion until 1945, by which time most of the former Jewish community had already been killed.

The conditioning of leading functionaries

The Nazi authorities did not replace the entire leadership of the Jewish organizations in Vienna. They reopened the Kultusgemeinde under their control, completely restructured it and converted the Jewish administration into their tool. The most prominent members of the Kultusgemeinde, president Desider Friedmann and vice-president Robert Stricker, were arrested and were no longer allowed to work within the administration, but they were not in conflict with the new leadership. They both remained in contact with Löwenherz and did not oppose the strategy of cooperation in any way. Even in Theresienstadt, Friedmann and Stricker defended the reaction of the administration and its cooperation during the deportations; they had agreed at a meeting that a 'more humane procedure' could be achieved in this way.[57] Thus there was no friction between Löwenherz and Friedmann, and it cannot be assumed that the former president and vice-president would have reacted differently to the Nazi authorities. The Gestapo wanted to be able to rely on the leaders of the Jewish administration. Josef Löwenherz, Alois Rothenberg and Emil Engel had already been working there for many years. The rise in the administration of Murmelstein, who had also worked for years in the community, was not opposed by Löwenherz. On the contrary, Murmelstein became Löwenherz's closest associate.

For all the continuity within the Kultusgemeinde at the personal level, the structural discontinuity should not be forgotten. The Jewish political leaders were no longer elected representatives but merely functionaries appointed by the Nazis. This immediately restricted their power and scope for action. After the Kultusgemeinde reopened, Löwenherz and Engel were the dominant figures. The technocrat and organizer Murmelstein rose in importance in 1938. Engel emigrated in 1940.

The community was trapped. The wretched conditions created by the Nazis forced the persecuted Jews into subordination. The Jewish administration had to organize welfare and escape according to the Nazi guidelines. The meetings by Jewish functionaries with the Gestapo were merely to receive orders. The administration was inundated with instructions. The leading functionaries were hostages to the Nazis. They were liable for their colleagues who were required to travel abroad to discuss Jewish emigration.[58] For a journey of this type of a few days on behalf of the Nazi authorities, for example, Löwenherz had to indicate to the foreign exchange department how many pairs of pyjamas, underwear and handkerchiefs he was taking. He even had to indicate whether he had a wedding ring.[59]

Löwenherz attempted to improve the situation of the Jewish community through individual applications and appeals to the 'common' interest in successfully organized emigration, even if the motives varied considerably. As soon as the number of emigrants began to drop, however, Eichmann threatened anti-Jewish measures and anti-Semitic pogroms. In a report by the Jewish community of Vienna in 1945 for the Nuremberg trials, Löwenherz is quoted as follows: 'Only through my repeated assurances that our desire to emigrate still existed but that, in spite of all efforts by those interested, possibilities for immigration were difficult to find and above all could not be obtained automatically, I managed to dissuade Eichmann from carrying out any of the threatened measures.'[60]

Until 1941, he was also able to point out that the international Jewish organizations would stop providing funds for emigration if the Jews were deported to Poland. But the reference to assistance from abroad no longer worked after 1940. The war closed the borders and prevented the continued expulsion of the Jews.

Apart from negotiations, appeals and requests, there were other possibilities for evading the Gestapo instructions. Within the administration, individual officials broke the Nazi laws by forging documents or helping Jews in concealment. Löwenherz knew of the illegal efforts by the Jewish welfare officer Franzi Löw but kept her anyway. The Jewish leadership also dared in rare cases to refuse to carry out certain orders.[61] When Löwenherz was ordered in November 1941 to provide Jewish employees to help the SS men with the *Aushebungen*, he initially refused to comply. Alois Brunner then recruited the *Ausheber* himself and ordered them to use particular brutality. Only in this way did he manage to persuade the Jewish administration to cooperate and appoint the *Ausheber* itself.[62]

The Jewish functionaries felt that what they were doing was the only possible course for the community. Their opinion of their role under the Nazis did not change after 1945. When they spoke, the surviving functionaries defended their actions and pointed out that they had worked to the best of their ability and conscience for the Jewish community. At the same time, they realized early on how their work would be judged should the Nazis be defeated. In 1938,

Löwenherz told his financial expert: 'Believe me, Dr Kapralik, the only appreciation we will ever have will be one of ingratitude.'[63] If the quote is correct, he did not expect indulgence later on and did not believe that the future would condone him and his actions at that time.

The Jewish leaders of the administration were the ones who had to deal with the SS functionaries. They appeared powerful compared with the other Jews but in truth they were subordinate to the lowliest SS man. Most members of the Jewish population were unaware of the constraints under which the leaders of the Jewish administration were forced to operate. If their emigration was delayed, if a hope was shattered, if others seemed to be given preference, many Jews suspected that they were the victims of corruption and nepotism within their own administration. They were often unable to appreciate that their misfortune was in no way due to a failure by the Jewish administration but solely to the Nazi terror.

Earlier analyses have regarded and judged the Jewish councils and functionaries under the Nazi regime as the 'Jewish leadership'. Hannah Arendt was able to criticize the Jewish functionaries only because she adopted this point of view. The actions of the Jewish councils were measured against expectations that a sovereign political leadership was supposed to fulfil. Arendt regarded collaboration with the enemy as betrayal.[64]

In his comparison of Jewish councils in Europe and North Africa, Dan Michman concluded by contrast that the Jewish administration under Nazi control should not be seen as an autonomous 'leadership'. He preferred the sociological concept of 'headship' used in the 1930s.[65] With a 'headship', the leader is chosen not from within the group's ranks but by external functionaries and, according to C. E. Gibb, whom Michman quotes,[66] it is a form of authority maintained by a system and not by respect or shared feelings. The leader's power comes from outside the group, which does not follow him voluntarily but obeys for fear of punishment. Like Michman, this work agrees that the Jewish functionaries were under Nazi authority and cannot therefore be regarded as genuine 'Jewish leaders'. But I also reject the term 'headship' or authority when talking of the relations within the Jewish administration in Nazi Vienna. I prefer to emphasize the schism not between the head of the Kultusgemeinde and the other Jews but between the authorities and the persecuted. For this reason, the term *Amtsleiter* (department head) used by the Sonderkommando of SD Department II-112 under Adolf Eichmann is more appropriate for Löwenherz, who was appointed by Eichmann. The Jewish functionaries had no political influence of their own but were effectively an authority without power. This authority had no political leadership but was merely administratively responsible for various charity, social or executive departments. In this regard, incidentally, the leaders of the Jewish administration did not differ from the Zionist youth functionaries, who were not appointed by the Nazis. All of them had to bow to the conditions imposed by the Nazis and to cooperate with them.

The Jewish councils were not a 'Jewish leadership' but at the same time they should not be seen as a Nazi institution that merely took orders from the perpetrators. The instructions by the authorities were discussed by the Jewish functionaries in Vienna. If they had merely been subordinate to the Nazi authorities, there would not have been any need for sham negotiations or for lies and deceptions. They acted on behalf of the Jews of Vienna, bargained for the lives of as many of them as they possibly could, refused to carry out some of the orders and ultimately carried out most of the official tasks but always in the belief that they were serving the Jewish community. The members of the councils had to be lied to because they were not recipients of orders from the Nazis, but they were easy to lie to because the crimes being committed against them must have appeared completely nonsensical. They could not be expected to believe that the basic principles of rationality had been broken with, not just in the fantasies of the anti-Semitic mob but by the state authorities themselves. It was unimaginable that Berlin would prefer destruction to exploitation and that extermination was not just a propaganda slogan but something to be pursued in reality.

The leading functionaries had different ways of reacting under these circumstances, and this will be the subject of the following section. But even if they endeavoured to oppose the SS authorities, all of the employees in the Jewish administration were still confronted by the logic of extermination. The 'Führer principle' not only characterized the Third Reich and the perpetrators' command structure but was also carried over to the victims. H. G. Adler described this situation perceptively in 1955:

> At its head was the 'Führer' and it reached down to the SS functionaries who commanded the camp. . . . This pyramid was self-affirming, setting itself as a value against the negative value of the mirror pyramid in the Jewish camp. The SS commandant, empowered by the 'Führer' to construct his pyramid, is the determining force in the camp, seldom through direct intervention – he usually calls on the mirror pyramid,

which must obey, otherwise he would break the mirror and the pyramid with its people would no longer exist, because the people trapped in it would turn to shadows and its structure, a pyramid conjured up through a mirror, would become what it is in reality – nothing. This mirror pyramid with the Elder of the Jews at its head must recognize that the other pyramid, even if it has no value and is cursed into being a mirror, is the authority and despite the curse is in fact the reality. And if the camp pyramid is to survive, the Elder of the Jews and all of his Jews must obey. Only by obeying are they entitled to live until further notice. In this reflected shadow realm, the functions that underlie the 'Führer' structure are thus reproduced, albeit inverted and strangely altered. It reflects power as authority, violence as coercion; in this way, however, the Führer principle is continued in the community of camp inmates. The 'Elder of the Jews' is the mirror image of the 'Führer', whether they want it or not, and all of the interned Jews reflect the roles of all non-Jews. The nothingness of the Jews avenged itself in the reflection of the non-Jews, because there can be no void. The nothingness of those who are regarded as non-existent becomes the something through which those who aspire to be something are themselves destroyed.[67]

Adler describes the consequences of persecutions for the persecutors and their victims. He highlights the fact that the victims were caught up in the crimes. The Jews had to become the 'agents of their own destruction'; and after the war criticism was heaped on the survivors, who in fact were nothing more than those who were left over. The crime and its logic had been victorious across the board. The verdict that the only good Jew is a dead Jew was adopted even after 1945, paradoxically by opponents of Fascism.

Questions of character – individual Jewish functionaries before and after 1945

As we have seen, the leaders of the Jewish administration had no choice; they had to cooperate with the perpetrators. But the individual leaders had the possibility of reacting in different ways. Moreover, a functionary could decide to resign. It is not my purpose here to make sweeping judgements as to whether it was more correct, honourable or courageous to continue in office or to resign. The fact nevertheless remains that total refusal was a possibility. Individuals could resign, report for deportation or commit suicide.

Those who refused to cooperate would be quickly replaced. The leading Viennese Jewish functionaries did not try to use this as a justification for refusing to accept personal responsibility: 'If I hadn't done it, someone else would have'. On the contrary, they felt responsible for the victims and hoped until the last that if they remained in office they might be able to stave off the worst, fearing that if they resigned, the SS would appoint a less scrupulous and brutal successor.

Although the range of possibilities for the Jewish functionaries was extensively limited, they nevertheless reacted differently to the constraints. Each case needs to be studied separately and the differences in personality and character analysed.

The Zionist youth leaders were not appointed by the Nazis but were answerable to the functionaries of the Jewish administration, who had been appointed from without. One of these Zionist youth leaders was Aron Menczer, born in 1917. He came from a religious family; he turned with his brothers to Zionism and belonged initially to the religious youth movement Hashomer Hadati. In 1927, two of Aron Menczer's older brothers founded the Zionist socialist youth movement Gordonia in Vienna, a more moderate spin-off of the Marxist Zionist Hashomer Hatzair. The younger Menczer brothers also joined Gordonia. After leaving school, Aron Menczer worked in various businesses and became active in the youth movement.[68] This was his main interest. In 1939, he became a leading member of the Youth Aliyah School and subsequently its director. Menczer communicated to the young Jews that in contrast to the Nazi ideology they had a right to human dignity. The charismatic youth leader fostered a will to live and a spirit of resistance in the victims. All recollections by survivors mention his strength and confidence.[69] Aron Menzcer had several opportunities to leave the German Reich. As late as December 1940, he turned down an offer to travel to Palestine.[70] He still wanted to help as many young people as possible to escape from the Third Reich. At the end of 1940, he became engaged to Lotte Kaiser, a group leader in the Berlin Zionist movement Makkabi Hatzair.[71]

On 12 May 1941, the Central Office of the Kultusgemeinde ordered the closure of the Palestine Office, the Zionist Youth Association and the Youth Aliyah within four days. The authorities had given up the policy of expulsion to Palestine; the deportation and extermination phase began. A week later, on 19 May 1941, Aron Menczer was ordered to Doppl labour camp. He handed over the leadership of the now illegal Youth Aliyah to Martin Vogel, the group leader of the

Marxist Zionist Hashomer Hatzair. Under Vogel's leadership, the remaining members of Hashomer Hatzair in Vienna met secretly in the city or the Vienna Woods. But these meetings also had to be abandoned when the Jews were ordered to wear the yellow star.[72] Menczer attempted to continue his Zionist activities in the labour camp so as to strengthen the will of the young people. He remained in contact with Josef Löwenherz, writing to him repeatedly. On 23 July 1941, he offered to reorganize the Zionist youth work in Vienna.

> From the countless letters that reach me from Vienna, I have become convinced of the urgent need for the youth to have a centre. Autumn is approaching and the youth should not waste away for want of a home. With the shortage of accommodation, the danger of that occurring is evident.
>
> I am closely attached to these youths and I realize that they rely on me. I also know that I have done everything in the last few years that I could. Of course I have made mistakes. What adult or youth doesn't? But my intentions have always been pure; I did not have any personal stake, I was only interested in one thing. Anyone who saw me working will know this. I was also proud to enjoy your trust and hope that in spite of everything I still have it. I therefore ask you to allow me to set up a centre for the young people.[73]

Menczer's mention of his mistakes was a reference to earlier disputes with Löwenherz, who had undertaken the difficult task of trying to strike a balance between the Gestapo orders and the many needs of the various Jewish groups and classes. With insufficient funds, he had to try to provide welfare, care for the aged and food for poorer Jews and to help them to emigrate. Before Menczer was sent to Doppl, he had argued with Löwenherz about financial resources for the Youth Aliyah School.[74] In his letter from the camp, he promised Löwenherz that he would erect a 'model home' within three to four weeks and that the staff of the home would work without pay. Courses would be provided in the evenings and on Sundays for youths who were forced to work. Children who were not allowed to attend school would be offered elementary and advanced education courses. Extra tuition and leisure activities were planned for older pupils. It was Menczer's intention in this way to provide the young people in Vienna with a refuge from the terror and persecution on the streets and the hardship in their parents' homes:

> And I promise and guarantee that all this will not cost the community anything. The plan could also be broken down, of course, but that would go too far. . . . Why? When I returned to Europe from Palestine

in April 1939 (where my dear parents and five brothers live) I was attracted to the young people of Vienna. Our complicity has become stronger since then. And if I have put off my Aliyah several times since war broke out, it is because I realized – and still realize – that the youth need me here. Those who know me will recognize that these are not empty words.[75]

Löwenherz did indeed speak up for Menczer with Alois Brunner[76] but could not achieve anything, as the mass deportation of the Jews to the ghettos and extermination camps began a few weeks later. On 14 September 1942, Aron Menczer returned from Doppl to Vienna. A few days later, on 22 September, he reported to the collection point and was deported two days afterwards. On the day of his arrival in Vienna, two associates sought him out by chance at his home and informed him of the situation. This meeting and the subsequent meetings in the Kultusgemeinde clarified Menczer's picture of the situation in Vienna and he decided that he could no longer continue his organizational work. The Zionist youth movement should be disbanded in a dignified manner. The same afternoon, he met with his comrades in Vienna. At his request, a meeting was to be convened that evening of the leaders of the organization. These last days of the Zionist youth movement were reconstructed by Martin Vogel with the assistance of Anny Spiere and Ernst (Brondes) Schindler in a report on the last meeting of the Youth Aliyah, which Vogel wrote at Menczer's request. Amazingly, the original document survived. Vogel, one of Menczer's closest friends and associates, buried it in the Jewish section of the Vienna Central Cemetery.[77] In the evening discussion in preparation for the last meeting, says Vogel, the main 'chaverim' or comrades managed to come together at a table without any ideological disputes.

The meeting took place on 19 September 1942 in a small room in a private home. A picture of Herzl was hung on the wall and a pennant attached underneath it. In front of the picture was a table with two candles. After the speeches, Aron Menczer called on all those present to take an oath. Those who didn't think they could keep it, said Menczer, should not take it; he would not think worse of them. The oath said: 'I solemnly swear to endeavour wherever I am to safeguard the survival of my people, to be helpful, to be loyal to Judah and to try to strengthen the faith of those around me in our Jewish home.'[78]

Then Menczer shook hands with everyone. In Vogel's 1942 report, written after Menczer's deportation, a separate chapter is devoted to Aron Menczer although, as Vogel points out, it was not usual to emphasize the achievements of individuals in the youth movement.[79]

On 24 September 1942, Menczer was deported to Theresienstadt. He continued to work for the young in the ghetto. When a transport with 1,260 children between three and fourteen years of age arrived in the ghetto on 24 August 1943, the inmates of Theresienstadt were forbidden any contact with them. They came from Bialystok and were in a desolate state. They were initially sent for delousing and, to the dismay of the assistants, they refused to enter the showers crying: 'Don't kill us. You are also Jews!'[80]

The Jews in Theresienstadt did not yet understand why the children were so afraid of the showers. It was only when they arrived in Auschwitz that they realized what 'disinfection' meant there and why the children had been so terrified. Aron Menczer volunteered to look after the children. He was put in charge of the small separate camp, possibly because he spoke Yiddish. After a few weeks, the children and their minders were boarded suddenly onto a train. In the ghetto, they had been told that the transport was going to Switzerland; later it was said that the children were already in Palestine, Eretz Israel. It is not known whether the adults who accompanied the transport knew where the train was going. The children arrived in Auschwitz on 7 November 1943 and were gassed immediately in Birkenau II, along with Aron Menczer.[81]

After 1945, Aron Menczer was regarded by the survivors as a hero. He had given them strength to bear up to the situation. In this way, he had resisted the oppression and killing. Menczer did not have the same obligations to the community as a whole, the different classes and ideological factions as the Kultusgemeinde leadership. He did not have to deal continuously with instructions and demands by the Gestapo and did not have to cooperate in the deportations. He was able to stay out of the area of the administration's work that was involved with the transports.

Whereas Menczer was admired before and after 1945 as a beacon within the Vienna community, other Jewish functionaries were despised after the war. Even before 1938, the talent and erudition of rabbi Benjamin Murmelstein had been noted, but also his violent temper.[82] Survivors are generally critical of him[83]; his arrogant manner was disliked and feared.[84] For many, he was the epitome of cooperation with the enemy. He was accused of actions that can no longer be verified. In his book *Verfolgung und Selbstbehauptung: Die Juden in Österreich 1938–1945*, for example, Herbert Rosenkranz wrote that Murmelstein had 'replied to Brunner's question as to whether 1,000 Jews could be transported by saying eagerly that he had 2,000 Jews ready.'[85] Rosenkranz bases this account on the report of a survivor Munisch (Menashe) Mautner. In his plea in Murmelstein's favour, Jonny Moser questioned this source as 'the testimony of a subordinate employee of the Kultusgemeinde who barely knew Murmelstein'.[86] In the 1956 report used by Rosenkranz, Mautner says of Murmelstein: 'In Vienna itself he was regarded as the scourge of the Jews. I will cite just one example that a colleague from the Kultusgemeinde related to me: when the Gestapo asked whether 1,000 Jews could be provided, he replied that there were 2,000. That is why he was so detested.'[87]

Murmelstein did not have any influence over whether 1,000 or 2,000 Jews were to be deported. To put it even more clearly, no Jewish functionary in Vienna, including Benjamin Murmelstein, was himself responsible for the deportation of a single Jew. Even if we believed it possible that for some abstruse reason he had wanted to do so, Murmelstein could never have provided one more single Jew than Brunner demanded of him. The context of this statement is unknown, if Murmelstein did indeed ever utter it. Brunner is not mentioned in Mautner's report. Mautner himself did not hear the utterance but was told about it by a colleague. We don't even know whether the colleague had heard Murmelstein say it. And even if this colleague had been present during the telephone call, he could only hear what Murmelstein said but not who was on the other end of the line and what he had asked. We don't know what reason or question prompted Murmelstein to make such a statement, if indeed he did so. But even if this were not the case, the fact that he in particular is accused of such things gives us some indication of what other Jews thought of him: 'In Vienna he was regarded as the scourge of the Jews'. A scholar and rabbi had been turned into a heartless bureaucrat and the organizer of emigration into an accomplice to the deportations. Murmelstein was aware of this change in his character. When Murmelstein's secretary Margarethe Mezei once addressed him as 'rabbi', Murmelstein replied: 'Don't call me that. Just say "doctor".'[88]

In an interview in 1977, Murmelstein said that he no longer went to religious services in Vienna during the deportations because he felt himself to be unworthy:

> I was so involved in the whole dirty mess, particularly during the transports, etc., that I rebelled inwardly and asked myself what was the sense of putting myself in the situation and carrying out my function. I don't know if you can understand what I mean. Someone who was in contact with Eichmann and Brunner and, even if he did so to avert the worst, even if he did so to protect Jewish interests, etc., I couldn't – you must understand that we had to work on Shabbat. I

could do nothing about it. Was there any sense in me standing up – do you understand what it means to be unworthy? Not morally disqualified but ritually. It has no meaning if someone who works Friday evening, even under coercion, then holds the Friday evening service in the temple. It's ridiculous. I had desecrated the Shabbat. Admittedly under coercion . . . On Yom Kippur, Kol Nidre [a prayer recited during Yom Kippur, the highest Jewish holy day, D. R.]. The last Kol Nidre I left and wandered the streets. This is the first time I've told anyone this, not even my wife knows. I wandered the streets. I was so distressed, that was Yom Kippur in September 1942, the complete clearout. Under those circumstances, to take part in the Kol Nidre service was more than I could bear.[89]

These words illustrate the conflict going on inside Murmelstein, but he didn't show his feelings to other people. He hadn't even told his wife about the incident on Yom Kippur. Löwenherz, by contrast, had openly cried on this holy day in the synagogue. Murmelstein did not want to show any feelings, any scruples or any sympathy. Under other circumstances, Murmelstein would probably have been a respected rabbi and scholar.

At the beginning of 1943, twelve leading Jewish functionaries from Berlin, Vienna and Prague, among them Benjamin Murmelstein, were deported to Theresienstadt. He was recruited there to the Council of Elders and was the second deputy Elder of the Jews. He was involved with hygiene and the health service and was also responsible for 'urban embellishment'. The historian H. G. Adler wrote of him:

He didn't have a good reputation in Vienna. . . . Outwardly he resembled Falstaff: he was clever, clear, superior, cynical and artful, far superior to his colleagues in intelligence but above all in shrewdness. He looked icy, cold, self-assured. The small deeply sunken eyes appeared to gaze emptily; he was impenetrable, untouched and calculating. And yet he was subject to strong emotions. No one in the camp except for his close companions ever attributed a good word or a good action to him; and yet he could even become soft on rare occasions. Unfortunately, this talented man almost never gave in to this aspect of his being; he was feared and detested. He appeared to be indifferent to the Jews for whom he was responsible. He carried out the orders of the SS meticulously and promptly and it is not much of an excuse that he might have believed that clever obedience was the only way of saving what could be saved.[90]

The historian Zdenek Lederer came to a completely different conclusion in 1953 about the Elder of the Jews, Murmelstein:

To form a judgement on this extraordinary man, it is necessary to scrutinize carefully his character and environment. Such a scrutiny must ignore such current unfounded gossip as the allegation made by some prisoners that Murmelstein had been promised that he would be enabled to Switzerland as a reward for compliance with the orders given to him. The evidence submitted in Rahm's trial proves this allegation to be utterly unfounded.

Besides being a man of scholarly attainments and great organizing abilities, he was also extremely ambitious. Though highly strung, he knew how to conceal and control his emotions. He possessed an encyclopaedic memory and his deductive powers were amazing. He feared the Germans but he knew that it was his duty to stand up to them. Hence he never contradicted them openly but, foreseeing their course of action, looked for a loophole. In doing so, he took great moral risks: had any of his clever schemes failed, he would have borne the moral responsibility and the blame. As a student of history, he found examples on which to model his conduct on becoming leader of the Jews of Theresienstadt. It is certainly more than a coincidence that his favourite characters were Herod the Idumenean and Flavius Josephus. History has hitherto failed to pass a final verdict on their careers; equally, no final verdict is possible on Dr Murmelstein's conduct as Elder of the Jews. It appears that he saw himself as another Flavius Josephus who, undeterred by the vociferous contempt of his people, worked for its salvation.[91]

Murmelstein attempted to make use of the Nazi plan of presenting Theresienstadt as a model ghetto. Even in 1989, Murmelstein said of his approach at the time that he had managed to establish good relations with the camp commandants, particularly Karl Rahm, the last commandant. He convinced Rahm of the positive effect that the embellishment of Theresienstadt as a model camp would have on the international reputation of the German Reich. He, Murmelstein, had emphatically encouraged this embellishment. It is true that he could not prevent the transports to eastern Europe, but he had not arranged them.[92] The 'embellishment' was not his doing either, but rather that of the Foreign Ministry and the German Red Cross. Murmelstein encouraged it so forcefully because he hoped that it would provide some protection. Before the first foreign delegations visited the ghetto, 7,500 additional ghetto inmates were deported in May 1944, as the mass accommodation was completely overcrowded. The idea was to deceive the world. Shops, a café, a bank, kindergartens and a school were created as a pretence and flower gardens planted. On 23 July 1944, the first international visitors arrived at Theresienstadt. Elderly and poorly clothed persons were kept out of sight. The meeting of the committee with the inmates was rehearsed down to the last detail. The Nazis were pleased with the results of this cynical presentation and they suggested that further visits be arranged. The embellishment was continued. The ghetto was filmed. The masquerade showed a picture of happiness and prosperity with cheerful Jews in their own city. The intolerable poverty, hunger, destitution and sickness were screened out. In autumn 1944 alone, over 18,000 Jews were deported to Auschwitz.[93]

On 13 December 1944, after his predecessors had been killed, Murmelstein was appointed Elder of the Jews in Theresienstadt. The Council of Elders consisted of a representative of Germany, the Protectorate of Bohemia and Moravia, Austria, the Netherlands and Denmark. The chairman and deputy Elder of the Jews was Leo Baeck.

According to an article in 1963, Murmelstein was given the commission on 3 October 1944

> to present further transport lists, this time with women and children as well. Left on my own for only a few days, this was the first time that I was confronted by this situation. I hesitated and tried to gain time; then I said that I could not carry out the task. Of course I tried somehow to dress up my refusal and became so worked up that the camp commandant erupted and yelled at me that there would be no discussion before he was able to continue. As incredible as it may sound, Hauptsturmführer Rahm described the incident in detail before the People's Court in Litoměřice in April 1947. He admitted to the court that he had threatened me with mistreatment because I had attempted in his absence to get one of his colleagues to delay the transports.
>
> For the first time in the history of the ghetto, the SS started to make their own transport lists because I was not reliable enough. More than 15,000 ghetto inmates were assembled in front of the SS building, where Eichmann's delegate Hauptsturmführer Mohs had to decide on their fate. Hannah Arendt thinks that the Elders of the Jews should have opted for non-participation. It is easy to make a demand like that in New York in 1963; it was less easy not to participate in Theresienstadt in 1944.[94]

Before October 1944, when Murmelstein was not yet Elder of the Jews but only the deputy, the transport lists were compiled by the Council of Elders. The SS commandant indicated the required number of Jews, and the Jewish administration made a list of names and a reserve list of between 10 and 25 per cent so as to provide replacements for the persons in the main list who were exempted by the SS camp commandant because of sickness or other reasons. The commandant indicated initially the groups that were to be exempt from deportation. The Jewish administration then formed committees who determined who could remain in Theresienstadt. One committee consisted of representatives of all departments and decided who was irreplaceable for the administration; national committees could postpone the deportation of persons who had been of particular service to their communities. There was resentment between the individual groups, and the SS commandant exploited the disputes between the different nationalities. Members of the Council of Elders, department heads and other prominent inmates had their own lists of protected favourites; this was a highly controversial issue. There is no doubt that it encouraged financial and sexual corruption. Another committee ensured that families were not separated.[95] After the deportations in autumn 1944, epidemics became rife in the ghetto. The streets were dirty and strewn with rubbish. Lights were left on in the empty rooms; taps continued to run; the corridors were flooded. There were over 11,000 people in the camp, of whom only a few hundred men were fit for work. Women had to do the work of men. The future of Theresienstadt hung in the balance. Hitler wanted to clear the ghetto and to march the remaining inmates to a place 200 kilometres away. Murmelstein said in 1963:

> I was unaware of Hitler's intentions in those October days; but I had heard a confidential statement by Eichmann that had been reported to us: as long as there was a columbarium with urns containing the ashes of those who had died in Theresienstadt, the ghetto had nothing to fear. On 31 October, the urns were removed and sunk in the Eger [Czech: Ohře], as we later learned. I was the only one who realized the significance because none of the other 'initiates' were still alive. It was therefore my duty to intervene. In this case the 'non-participation' demanded by Hannah Arendt would have resulted in a death march with countless victims for those who were there.[96]

Thus even in 1963, Murmelstein believed that his actions had influenced the decisions of the Nazi authorities. In 1944, he no doubt assumed that he might be able to protect the Jews of Theresienstadt from the death march. The Elder of the Jews had to attempt to second-guess the Nazis, counting at all times on a minimum portion of rationality in the hope of being able to understand and influence their plans. But even after 1945, when it had been demonstrated that the Nazis in reality had these unimaginable and inconceivable plans for the victims, Benjamin Murmelstein stood by his belief. In truth the authorities made their decisions without taking account of the actions by the Elder of the Jews. Opinion within the SS was split. Eichmann and his staff were in favour of the extermination of all the Jews in Theresienstadt. At that time, Murmelstein was horrified to notice changes in this direction. Airtight rooms with very strange ventilation devices were built. A plateau was fenced off, ideal for mass executions. Himmler, by contrast, was more conciliatory in view of the offers of money by foreign Jews. A second 'embellishment' was ordered and further inspections by the International Red Cross were announced. In the 1963 article, Murmelstein mentioned that Himmler had been willing to agree to the transport of 1,200 Theresienstadt Jews to Switzerland and to visits by international delegations. He also described his activities in Theresienstadt:

> The introduction of the seventy-hour working week, the employment of women for heavy work and the night shifts were not ordered by the SS but on *my personal initiative*. I had to transform myself into a remorseless driver of the people who were to be saved. Order and discipline had to be maintained so as to prevent the SS from intervening, which is what happened. It would have been much easier for me if I had been known for benevolence and mildness while ensuring at the same time that the streets and workplaces were patrolled occasionally by the SS. Apart from informers, who were always there, gossip, which flourished in the ghetto, was a lethal danger. I was therefore obliged to keep everything to myself. In this way a semblance of normality was quickly restored. On 5 December, the ghetto was visited by a representative of the Reich Main Security Office. I was entrusted with showing him round and overheard him say that it could stay like that.[97]

While Theresienstadt was being shown to the world and individual agreements were being made with foreign representatives, other camps and ghettos were being cleared. Murmelstein's measures served the Nazi propaganda machinery but also helped to preserve Theresienstadt. In his standard work on Theresienstadt, H. G. Adler notes that there were indeed some improvements during Murmelstein's leadership.[98] The Elder of the Jews fought against corruption and privilege. On 23 March 1945, Gestapo head Heinrich Müller told a delegate of the International Committee of the Red Cross that it would be impossible to visit a concentration camp but that a visit to Theresienstadt could be arranged in the next few days so as to put an end to the enemy's 'lying propaganda'.[99] Murmelstein stated in 1963: 'The ghetto's special status was achieved through the work carried out on the spot. It was essential that it did not appear as a dirty and run-down place.'[100] It was a cynical production; everyone present knew about the extermination of the European Jewry.

On 6 April 1945, the Nazis negotiated with the International Red Cross on the future of the Theresienstadt inmates. On 2 May 1945, representatives of the Red Cross took over responsibility for the camp, which was liberated a few days later. As late as mid-April, however, the fate of the victims had still not been decided. In the night of 17–18 April 1945, leaflets in the ghetto announced the end of the war. The inmates ran onto the streets singing and cheering, embracing one another, and began to pack their belongings. SS men came swarming out with machine guns to put down the 'uprising'. Murmelstein managed to calm Karl Rahm and to promise to restore order.[101] In the last weeks, from 20 April to 5 May 1945, a further 13,000 to 15,000 people arrived in Theresienstadt from Auschwitz and other camps. Among the emaciated, sick and dying figures were some who had been deported from Theresienstadt six months earlier. Murmelstein recalled in 1989:

> Shortly before the end of the war, typhus broke out among the emaciated and haggard people arriving in Theresienstadt from the east. I immediately arranged for them to be quarantined and for a ghetto sentry to be posted at every exit with the order to hit anyone who poked his head out. Leo Baeck described this order as inhumane. When the Russians arrived, Baeck recalled the sentries and the inmates came out of quarantine. Typhus spread in the camp and thousands died of it even after the war had ended.[102]

This description clearly indicates the way Murmelstein thought. There was no alternative to quarantine if the healthy were to be saved, but those in quarantine were practically sentenced to death. Murmelstein's undaunted determination is typical. He calculated the consequences and the result showed no scruples or mercy for individuals. The sick were not merely isolated; looking back, Murmelstein mentioned vividly and specifically that anyone who peeked out was to be 'hit over the head'.

The International Red Cross took over Theresienstadt at the beginning of May. Murmelstein met Karl Rahm as late as 5 May 1945. The memo of this meeting just a few hours before the camp was liberated reflects a daily routine, with the only difference being Rahm's refusal to recognize the judgements of the 'Jewish self-administration' courts and his order that all inmates be released.[103] Rahm fled the same day. Murmelstein resigned as Elder of the Jews; only a small group of supporters stood by him, but most people in the camp detested him. Anticipating his removal from office, he gave in to the pressure from his own Council of Elders, particularly Leo Baeck, and resigned. The first Russian tanks arrived a few days later. On 27 May 1945, Murmelstein wrote a letter to his former superior Josef Löwenherz in Vienna.

Esteemed Doctor,

[. . .] Contrary to all reasonable expectations, I have survived. I have somehow managed to come through some absolutely desperate situations. I am now a free man again for the first time in many years. At the request of the Czechoslovak leader of the Theresienstadt administration, I am writing everything about Theresienstadt that I, as the sole survivor, know about and am also helping otherwise with my experience, but on the whole I am taking a rest, which I am really in great need of.[104]

He refused the offer by the Red Cross a few days before the liberation by the Red Army to travel to Switzerland: 'It would have run counter to the principle of continuing to accept responsibility for what happened during the time in which I was responsible on my own for everything in Theresienstadt.'[105]

Murmelstein was arrested in June 1945 and detained in custody for eighteen months. He was accused of collaboration. On 6 December 1946, the public prosecutor withdrew the accusation before the People's Court in Litoměřice as there was not sufficient evidence for a conviction. Murmelstein was set free the same day after he had agreed not to claim for compensation for his detention.[106]

Karl Rahm was handed over to the Czechoslovak authorities in early January 1947. Murmelstein was a prosecution witness. The presiding judge in the People's Court in Litoměřice said in an interview: 'It should be emphasized that his [Murmelstein's; D. R.] statement in the trial against (camp commandant) Rahm was decisive. Rahm was aware of this and would certainly have spoken if he had known anything to Murmelstein's disadvantage.'[107]

Was Murmelstein completely rehabilitated? In a legal sense, yes; the People's Court in Litoměřice did not show any leniency towards those who were convicted; in less than one year, it pronounced 20 death sentences, which were also carried out, and life imprisonment in 23 cases. Altogether the sentences in Litoměřice during this period amounted to 5,334 years.[108] And yet Murmelstein was still exposed to accusations and reproaches.

After his testimony in 1947, Murmelstein went to Rome. In August 1948, he faced a tribunal of the Organization of Jewish Displaced Persons in Italy. Once again he was able to refute the accusations.[109] He nevertheless left Rome for Trieste, where he was offered a rabbinate. He was hired after a few trial sermons in Italian, but was soon obliged to resign. In an interview in 1989, he blamed Leo Baeck, who he claimed had intrigued against him.[110] In an earlier interview in 1979, he had strongly refuted this idea, saying that Baeck had merely asserted later that he was responsible for Murmelstein's departure. In fact, said Murmelstein, he had just become involved in a power struggle with a functionary in the Jewish community of Trieste:

> In reality the matter was quite simple. I was not willing be bullied by a moneybags. . . . I said to them 'it was an honour' and left. . . . That was the most natural thing to do. . . . I was used to other things and was no longer willing to be regarded as some petty official of the kille [Yiddish for community; D. R.], dependent on the whims of the chairman and the committee. Don't forget that in Vienna or Theresienstadt I had been in charge. It might have been better if it hadn't been the case, but unfortunately that's how it was. You must therefore understand, Professor, that psychologically this demotion was a little too much.[111]

The former Elder of the Jews was no longer content to be a minor spiritual official. Benjamin Murmelstein regarded the move from Elder of the Jews in Theresienstadt under the Nazis to the rabbi of the Jewish community in Trieste as a demotion of sorts. He settled in Rome with his wife and son Wolf. He attempted initially to establish his own business, then he started making money as a furniture salesman and demonstrated a talent for business.

When Adolf Eichmann was put on trial in Jerusalem, Murmelstein published a book in Italian about the Theresienstadt ghetto.[112] He was not called as a witness at the trial. In the 1963 article cited earlier, he answered the criticisms voiced in Jerusalem about the Jewish councils in general and about him in particular. He also commented on the dispute between Hannah Arendt and Gershom Sholem on this subject:

> The correspondence between Prof. Gerhard Sholem and Hannah Arendt was published in the *Neue Zürcher Zeitung* of 10 October 1963. Sholem countered the claim by the author of the book *Eichmann in Jerusalem*, which describes all of the leading characters within the Jewish communities caught up in the Nazi persecutions as traitors,

176

saying: 'In my opinion your description of the Jewish behaviour under extreme circumstances, which neither of us experienced, to be not a balanced judgement but an overstatement that often borders on the demagogic.' This emphatic refutation is followed surprisingly by a conciliatory remark: 'Certainly . . . *Murmelstein* in Theresien-stadt . . . deserved to have been hanged by the Jews.' To back up his grave charge Sholem cites hearsay ('as confirmed by all inmates of the camp I spoke to'). Hannah Arendt did not consider accepting the hand offered to her: 'Whether these people all deserved to be hanged is another matter.' In other words not *all* cases but just one case, my case, would have been sufficient to satisfy the strident demand on both sides for justice. A few well-documented facts can show how casually and untrammelled by expert knowledge Sholem and Arendt presume to make a judgement about things that should be addressed only with suitable research.[113]

Murmelstein did indeed manage to demonstrate impressively how these two major Jewish intellectuals, without knowing the motives and perspectives that had influenced his actions and without knowing the circumstances under which he was obliged to operate and what alternatives were available to him, had sentenced to death another person acting in an unprecedented predicament. It is interesting to note, however, that for all his intellectual acuity Murmelstein does not once express any retrospective regret or scruples. Even almost twenty years later, he does not doubt that his strategy saved Jews and that he had persuaded the Nazis of the utility of maintaining the ghetto. Theresienstadt was not destroyed, but thousands were deported from it to the extermination camps. Between 24 November 1941 and 20 April 1945, around 140,000 Jews were deported from their homes and transported to Theresienstadt; 33,000 died there; 88,000 were deported to extermination camps; and 19,000 survived or were among those who were allowed abroad thanks to the nego-tiations with the International Red Cross. In the extermination camps, 3,000 deportees survived.[114]

Murmelstein remained in Rome until his death. He occasionally gave interviews to historians or other interested persons. He answered some of their letters. In his last few years, he became seriously ill. He died on 27 October 1989 in a hospital in Rome.[115] The chief rabbi of Rome, Elio Toaff, ordered that he be buried at the edge of the cemetery and refused to recite the mourner's kaddish [prayer for the dead] in the synagogue. Murmelstein's son complained to the Italian rabbinate. He wrote to the Vienna-born historian Herbert Rosenkranz in Jerusalem and requested an expert opinion on his father.[116]

Rosenkranz replied, emphasizing Murmelstein's spiritual and scholarly activities before 1938 and described his contribution to the mass emigration of the Jews after the Anschluss: 'It is easy for onlookers to judge and condemn those Jews who stepped into the breach for as long as they could and fought for the community. . . . My picture of him . . . is the result of contradictory documents and testimony. . . . The overall picture of Rabb. Dr Murmelstein is positive.'[117]

Thanks, among other things, to this expert opinion, the Rabbinical Council ordered Murmelstein's body to be reburied next to his wife, but for technical reasons the chief rabbinate was unable to comply with the request.[118]

Murmelstein was not a collaborator. He cooperated with the Nazis because he believed it was the only way that he could rescue Jews. His justifications can be understood by anyone with sensitivity and they are not illogical. His actions did not differ from those of other Jewish representatives but his manner provoked hostility. In the 1963 article, Murmelstein concludes by saying:

> As the only living Elder of the Jews from the era of the Third Reich, I am, to paraphrase a well-known novel, 'the last of the unjust'. I don't wish for my words to apply solely to myself. Others whose ashes have been dispersed by the wind might possibly have been able to provide far weightier arguments. I hope at least that my comments will also give food for thought to those who don't want to be persuaded and will incite them to approach these issues with greater circumspection than has been the case in the past. With one exception, none of the former Elders of the Jews can appeal to a terrestrial court against cavalier judgements.[119]

An investigation against Murmelstein was also initiated in 1949 in Vienna. It appeared to have petered out but was taken up again in 1955, only to be finally closed in autumn of that year.[120]

This investigation was only one of many undertaken against Jews on the subject of collaboration. A warrant was issued in autumn 1946 for the arrest of the Jewish functionary Robert Prochnik, Murmelstein's right-hand man in Vienna and Theresienstadt.[121] He was listed as number 5,093 on the A list of international war criminals.[122] Prochnik worked from 1938 in the Vienna Kultusgemeinde and was involved in particular in emigration. In May 1940, he was summoned to Berlin where the consulates and travel agencies responsible for emigration were to be found. His task was to obtain transit visas, ships' passages and railway tickets for persons with immigration visas. Although he was answerable to the Central Office in Berlin, he frequently exceeded instructions so as to help those attempting to emigrate. In Berlin, he was involved not only in organizing emigration but also in preparing trains for deportation to labour camps. In 1941, he was ordered back to Vienna. Emigration had been almost completely stopped and he now worked as Murmelstein's secretary in the Kultusgemeinde. He directed the marshals employed for *Aushebung*. He was a tireless perfectionist and became a specialist in transport problems. In spring 1942, he was entrusted with the deportation transport logistics – wagon allocations and food. He was the only member of the Kultusgemeinde to witness the departure of all trains. As such, he was the last Jewish functionary to see the deportees in Vienna and was therefore a symbol for many of collaboration. After the deportations had ended, Prochnik was supposed to remain in Vienna and continue working in the Kultusgemeinde. In mid September 1942, however, he was arrested by the Gestapo and accused of sabotage. After being detained in the police cells at Rossauer Lände for some weeks, he was informed that he was to be deported to Mauthausen concentration camp. Josef Löwenherz intervened on his behalf. Whether for that reason or another, Prochnik was deported to Theresienstadt on 9 October 1942. In the following months, he was assigned to hard labour details, constructing roads, water pipelines and railways, and finally in a wainwright's workshop. When Benjamin Murmelstein was deported to Theresienstadt in February 1943, he arranged for Prochnik to become his secretary. Initially, he helped Murmelstein only after he had finished his own work.[123]

In summer 1943, he was appointed secretary to a building committee, where he was once again responsible for transport logistics. He was not involved in drawing up deportation lists but he was in charge of the Jewish assistants at the collection point. Once again he was the last Jewish functionary to be seen by the deportees. He appeared to be responsible, and the zeal with which he worked, his boots, the duelling cuts on his face, and his yelling meant that he was an object of fear for many Jews. His authority was overestimated, however; his influence on the composition of the transports was extremely limited.[124]

In February 1945, shortly before the liberation of Theresienstadt by the Red Army, the SS confiscated the transport lists and many other records. Prochnik and others managed, at considerable risk, to rescue these files from incineration and to hide them. The lists contained personal data of the dead and survivors; they were later recognized as official registers and were of great importance. Prochnik had also secured staff lists that were used to identify and arrest the SS leadership and guards after liberation.[125] In May 1945, both Murmelstein and Prochnik resigned from office. The Council of Elders under Leo Baeck accepted Prochnik's resignation 'with regret' and asked him to continue his function for a limited time. On 28 May 1945, Georg Vogel, the new head of the administration of the former ghetto, wrote to Prochnik informing him that a successor had been found but asked him to continue to support the administration; he hoped that Prochnik would comply with this respect 'in the tried and trusted manner'.[126]

Prochnik continued to work in the central secretariat until he left Theresienstadt in early August 1945. During this time, the twelve leading functionaries of the Jewish self-administration, including Benjamin Murmelstein, had been arrested by the Czechoslovak authorities and moved to Prague. Although there were negative rumours about Prochnik, he was not bothered by the Czech authorities and not even questioned. In July, he asked Georg Vogel to enquire with the responsible ministry in Prague and the government commissioner in Theresienstadt whether there was anything against him or whether there were objections to his departure. As the authorities had nothing against him and didn't want to detain him in Czechoslovakia, Prochnik left Theresienstadt three months after liberation with the knowledge of the authorities and with official papers.[127] Members of the former Council of Elders, including Leo Baeck and Heinrich Klang, and the new head of the central administration of the former Theresienstadt concentration camp, Georg Vogel, gave him positive testimonials.[128]

Robert Prochnik became a leading member of the American Jewish Joint Distribution Committee in Munich and Paris. At the same time, accusations by survivors were mounting up. Investigations opened in Vienna in 1948.[129]

Simon Wiesenthal confronted the Paris office of the Joint with the accusations against Prochnik and demanded that Murmelstein's former assistant should be dismissed. The Joint complied, perhaps for fear that these accusations would be made public. Wiesenthal did not instigate legal proceedings against Prochnik; he was merely interested in ensuring that a person who had cooperated with the SS did not continue to work in Jewish organizations.[130]

Prochnik worked as a commercial agent in Paris and Strasbourg. The case was reopened in Vienna in 1954 but he was not brought to trial. He was able to produce exonerating documents and witnesses to testify in his favour.[131]

In 1962, at which time Prochnik was living in London and working as director of a steelworks, he visited Austria and met a former friend from Vienna whom he had known in the early 1940s. Mares von Piechs's mother was Jewish and she had been persecuted as a half-Jew. She moved with her son from her first marriage to London with Prochnik and married him in 1963. He died in 1977 of multiple myeloma, a terrible bone disease with a fatal course of just a few months.[132]

Before 1941, Prochnik had helped quite a few people to escape and emigrate. He had occasionally risked his own life, for example by helping refugees in Berlin against the orders of the Nazis, or by rescuing the files in Theresienstadt. He explained why the leaders of the Vienna Kultusgemeinde and the Council of Elders in Theresienstadt had decided in desperation to cooperate, first of all to assist with emigration and then during the deportations. Those whom he helped to emigrate but also many who were deported and survived Auschwitz were able to confirm that he was a highly dependable person.

Criminal proceedings were instigated in Vienna against quite a few of the former members of the Kultusgemeinde after 1945 and various preliminary investigations were carried out. Not all of them ended in court. Any Jew who had survived in Vienna was suspect. Those who had escaped extermination found it hard to believe that members of the Jewish administration had remained in Vienna until 1945. How, the returnees would ask, had the Jewish functionaries survived? Those who survived in Vienna also accused one another. For years there had been mutual suspicions, rumours of corruption and informers. After liberation, free rein was given to these pent-up emotions. The accusations that had long been whispered could now be spoken out loud. Whether they were made openly or behind the backs of the accused, they were a feature of the power struggle within the resurrected Kultusgemeinde. And whether they were based on fact or rumour, they were long used by the various factions to compromise the earlier leaders of the community.

Dr Emil Tuchmann, the medical officer for the Jewish health service used by the Gestapo, was also prosecuted after the war. He was arrested for the first time on 15 April 1945, but then released again. Survivors from the camps sought out Tuchmann in his home in order to attack him.[133] The Vienna police brought charges against him on 13 September 1945 and Tuchmann was again held in custody. He was accused, among other things, of arranging for the deportation of employees who refused to inform him of grievances and a nurse who allowed a hospitalized Gestapo prisoner to escape.[134] Quite a few survivors whom Tuchmann had rescued spoke in favour of the Jewish doctor, however.[135] He was able to counter the legal arguments. On 19 April 1946, the case against him was dropped.[136] Tuchmann withdrew from public Jewish life. He became head physician of the Wiener Gebietskrankenkasse (statutory health insurance company), medical adviser to the Austrian social insurance, and member of the Oberster Sanitätsrat (Supreme Health Advisory Board) in Austria and Vienna.[137]

Those who survived and returned to Vienna from exile and from the camps wanted nothing to do with obsequious politicians, compromise and accommodation. They demanded a radical and unambiguous refutation of all symbols of the defeated Nazism. The opposition to the former functionaries and members of the Council of Elders was part of the reinvention of the Jewish identity after the Holocaust. It was important no longer to be seen as victims. The Jewish institutions were no longer represented by Jewish councils, and the former Jewish councillors could not therefore represent them. The resistance in the ghetto and by the partisans became the identifying model. Only in this way was it possible to expunge the perceived shame of being led like 'lambs to the slaughter' or of being exterminated like vermin. Most Jews sought pride and a new identity in the memory of resistance. Those camp survivors who found refuge after 1945 in the former capital of the Austro-Hungarian Empire, themselves for the most part coming from the former crown lands, felt only contempt for the hopes of the Jewish functionaries to rescue Jews by cooperating with the Nazi regime. Many Jews were plagued by survivors' guilt. By opposing the former functionaries of the Council of Elders, they were able to avoid conflicts within themselves and agonizing questions. Moreover, the Jewish functionaries who had survived in Vienna did indeed have a different memory of the Holocaust and the Nazi perpetrators than those who had escaped the extermination camps or who came from the east. Curious relationships and dependencies had formed between Gestapo and SS officials and the employees of the Jewish administration. In the trial of Karl Ebner, former deputy head of the Vienna police, a Jewish joiner testified in Ebner's defence. As a member of the Jewish administration, Martin Schaier had been forced to work in the home of the Nazi head of the Jewish department, who had protected him from deportation. Now the victim testified that Ebner had been 'like a father' to him. He concluded his testimony with the words: 'Herr Doktor, I should like to thank you once again for everything you did for me. If it weren't for you, I wouldn't be alive today.'[138] Then the witness bowed to the Nazi criminal and offered him his hand. Ebner's 'insurance strategy' of 'rescuing' Schaier so as to save himself had paid off.[139] Ebner had taken precautions in the event of the defeat of the Nazis. He and his assistant Johann Rixinger had been more respectful of the Jewish functionaries than their subordinate officials had been. Both made provisions in the last few months of the Third Reich for the impending collapse of the regime. When the order came from Berlin in February 1945 for the deportation of Mischlinge, Rixinger delayed and drew out its execution. The Jewish functionaries who had been attempting for years to negotiate with the Gestapo officers, for the most part without any success whatsoever, also testified in court about their rare successes with Ebner and Rixinger. After 1945, they felt obliged to mention the isolated concessions made by the perpetrators. It was as if the leaders of the Jewish administration wanted to say to the next anti-Semitic regime and its authorities: we don't forget anything, including the good things, even when they were done by our murderers. For the new Jewish leadership in Vienna after 1945, for most of the survivors of the extermination camps, for most of those returning from banishment, this behaviour merely indicated that the leaders of the Council of Elders had always betrayed them and were still doing so.[140]

This criticism came about as a result of the behaviour after 1945 of the former members of the Council of Elders. The new political climate prompted this to be said about the cooperation:

In the past we have drawn a merciful veil of silence over the role of the Council of Elders, the disgrace of these Gestapo cronies. We wanted this collaboration to vanish into oblivion. . . . We wanted to forgive and would so much like to have done so. But there was one thing we expected from these people: that as the henchmen of the most bloody persecutors in our history, they would vanish from the public eye and disappear into darkness. Instead, they are continuing their handiwork and standing in the eyes of the world on the side of Rixinger and his consorts. . . . These Jews who continue their past actions only confirm what we have always known. This festering wound must be cauterized. We want nothing to do with them; they no longer belong with us.[141]

In 1948, the *Neuer Weg* published an appeal to the Historical Commission; Jews who had cooperated with the Nazi authorities should be reported. These people should not be allowed to play a significant role in Jewish life any more. The text indicated that a member of the Council of Elders had been elected to the board of the Vienna Kultusgemeinde.[142]

183

For the prevailing Jewish identity after 1945, any conciliatory gesture towards a former Nazi criminal was a betrayal of the millions who had been killed. From this point of view, individual and institutional differences between the Nazi functionaries had to be ignored, despite the fact that the attitude of the Jewish functionaries had concentrated on those very differences between the individual state authorities and Nazi officials. The Jewish councils had been forced to identify the different interests existing among the Nazis and to exploit them. For Wilhelm Bienenfeld, the personality of every Gestapo functionary was important. If he now testified that Rixinger was more humane than other Nazi officials, it was not a betrayal but rather the result of earlier experiences and strategies, in other words, the perspective of a Jewish administration in the Third Reich.

Not all of the Jews accused of collaboration after the war were leading functionaries in the Kultusgemeinde. The trial of Wilhelm Reisz, in charge of a group of Jewish *Ausheber*, was discussed in detail in the first chapter. The court took no account of the special circumstances at the time. On the contrary, the victim, who was found guilty because he tried to save his own skin, was punished more severely than many Nazi perpetrators. The Austrian People's Court sentenced Reisz to fifteen years' imprisonment, including three months' hard labour. Reisz committed suicide by hanging in his cell.[143]

The *Ausheber* and Jupo were not answerable to the Kultusgemeinde or Council of Elders. The accusations made against individuals who were charged with working for the SS or Gestapo must be kept distinct from criticism of the members of the Jewish administration.

Anyone who worked for the Jewish administration under the Nazi regime inevitably came under suspicion. Those familiar with the history of the Jews from 1938 to 1945 will be particularly disconcerted by the accusation against Franzi Löw,[144] the Jewish social worker who helped countless children to emigrate, looked after orphans and protected them from extermination, organized forged papers, assisted prisoners of the Gestapo, obtained bread and milk illegally from non-Jewish bakers and supported those in hiding. With the aid of the non-Jewish Danneberg and Riese families, she was able to collect food stamps, clothing, money and food for children. She met the judge Dr Wilhelm Danneberg for the first time in 1938, having sought out the juvenile court in her capacity as a welfare worker. Danneberg had given her, a Jew, his hand, offered her a seat and asked how he could help. He was suspended a short time later for 'familiarity with Jews'.[145] Franzi Löw endangered not only her own life but also that of her mother, who had remained in Vienna under the protection of her daughter. She also risked the lives of those who helped her. The network created by her thwarted the enemy's plan of killing all of the Jews. It is no exaggeration to describe her illegal and legal efforts as an act of resistance against extermination. She served the IKG and the Council of Elders under Nazi control, showing through her own person that cooperation and resistance were reconcilable. The demarcation line separating the heroic struggle from the strategy of the Jewish councils did not exist in reality, in Vienna or in the other cities of Europe.

In 1945, Franzi Löw entered into the service of the city of Vienna, responsible for the welfare of handicapped persons, in the health department. She was no longer active in the Kultusgemeinde but was elected to the board. The charge against Franzi Löw was brought by Aron Moses Ehrlich, president of the Verband jüdischer Kaufleute (Association of Jewish Merchants) in autumn 1947, after he had written an open letter in June of that year to David Brill, president of the Kultusgemeinde:

I would ask you, Herr Brill, how you can justify in your dictatorial majority allowing as a member of the board this Franzi Löw, who is known to have remained in Vienna throughout the entire Hitler era and was seen to go in and out of the Gestapo headquarters. The Jewish people demand an explanation and the immediate setting up of an enquiry committee. In particular, I have heard with amazement that this Franzi Löw recently married a Nazi judge. Did you know this, Herr Brill?[146]

The so-called Nazi judge was none other than Dr Wilhelm Danneberg, who had risked his life supporting Franzi Löw's welfare work, together with his entire family.

The recently appointed board member Aron Moses Ehrlich had been approached in May 1947 by Paul Steiner, whose daughter Magdalena had died in Auschwitz. He accused Franzi Löw of being responsible for his daughter's murder and blamed the Jewish functionaries for the death of his wife and daughter. He said that Commandant Rahm in Theresienstadt had not wanted to send his child to Auschwitz but that Murmelstein had insisted and ordered that she go. It is impossible that Rahm could have intervened on Magdalena's behalf and equally impossible that Murmelstein could have insisted to the Nazi camp commandant that a Jewish child be deported. This story does not tally with the historical circumstances.

Steiner's wife went voluntarily with her daughter to Auschwitz. Steiner had not been allowed to go with them because he was a machinist in the laundry. He accused Franzi Löw of having delayed his daughter's emigration and given preference to other children. Steiner, like many Jews in Vienna, was under a misconception. He failed to realize that the Kultusgemeinde was not to blame for the restrictions on emigration. Without authorization and a visa, Franzi Löw could have done nothing for Magdalena.[147] But in 1945 it was difficult to explain to former concentration camp inmates why the Jewish welfare officer was not deported. She had risked her life to provide Gestapo prisoners with the basic needs. And now Aron Moses Ehrlich was accusing her of spending too much time at Gestapo headquarters. The charge did not come to trial but Franzi Löw drew her own conclusions and stopped working for the Kultusgemeinde, devoting her energies instead to handicapped persons in Vienna. She married Wilhelm Danneberg in 1948. In 1966, she was presented by the mayor of Vienna with the Golden Cross of Merit of the Republic of Austria.[148] Ernst Feldsberg, president of the Kultusgemeinde at the time, wrote her a letter of thanks.

Franzi Löw-Danneberg died in 1997. Her achievements were never publicly acknowledged by the Jewish community. There were only a few who realized how much she had done. One of them was Dr Ernst Feldsberg.

Ernst Feldsberg, born in Nikolsburg (Mikulov) in 1894, came to Vienna to study law. He was employed by the Kultusgemeinde from 1 November 1938 as head of the cemetery department. He managed to send his daughter Gerda to England on one of the children's transports. On 30 November 1943, he was deported with his wife Zerline to Theresienstadt. Both of them survived.[149] After 1945, he served the Vienna Chevra Kadisha, the Jewish burial society. He joined the Social Democratic Bund werktätiger Juden (Association of Working Jews). Political opponents repeatedly accused him of having had a leading role in the Nazi-controlled Jewish administration. In particular, he was charged with having been involved in the deportation of 1,600 Jews to Nisko. As mentioned earlier, when this first mass deportation took place in 1939, the Jewish administration had no idea what awaited the deportees. The Nazi Central Office promised that an autonomous Jewish settlement would be set up south of Lublin. When the Kultusgemeinde invited all of the men eligible for transport to the destroyed city temple, Ernst Feldsberg was asked, only because he had a powerful voice, to provide information about the Nisko project and to encourage volunteers.

In 1952, *Stimme*, the mouthpiece of the Allgemeine Zionisten, wrote that Feldsberg was 'a plaything in the hands of the Communists, who threatened to publish embarrassing information about him. . . . We need say only one word: Nisko! Can he not remember that he once threatened that anyone who didn't go to Nisko would be sent to a concentration camp?'[150] As the head of the cemetery department, Feldsberg could never have threatened deportation to a concentration camp as it was not in his authority. At the most, he could have warned those who had already volunteered of the possibility of punishment by the Central Office.

Simon Wiesenthal, who was one of Feldsberg's political opponents within the Jewish community, repeatedly brought up the subject of Nisko. Feldsberg's guilt might have expired by limitation under the law but not his moral responsibility for the victims of Nisko, he said, attempting in addition to recruit Nahum Goldmann, president of the World Jewish Congress, as an ally: 'We cannot get worked up that there is a Nazi in office in Austria or Germany and at the same time ignore the fact that people like Dr Feldsberg hold leading positions in Jewish institutions.'[151]

This sentence reveals Wiesenthal's motives. In a latently anti-Semitic society, a vehement anti-Nazi Jew had to be at great pains not to expose himself to attack in any way. If they were to fight against former Nazis and war criminals in Austria in the 1960s, the Jewish representatives could not be suspected of having cooperated with the perpetrators. Jews had survived in the shadow of extermination. Now the victims were accusing one another of having been in contact with the perpetrators. The suspicion voiced by one former victim against another satisfies the anti-Semites, enabling them to say that the Jews were no better than the Nazis. Simon Wiesenthal himself saw with how much relish these accusations were received. When he proved in 1975 that Friedrich Peter, head of the Freedom Party of Austria, had served in the 1st SS Infantry Brigade, a killing unit, Chancellor Bruno Kreisky felt personally attacked. Kreisky's minority government had been supported in 1970 by the Freedom Party and the chancellor wanted to keep open the possibility of a coalition with Peter. Without any proof, Kreisky, who had survived in Sweden, accused Wiesenthal of having had close contact with the Gestapo.[152] Feldsberg was not a collaborator. On the contrary, he wanted to serve the Jewish people. After Feldsberg's death, Wiesenthal admitted 'that he was basically a good Jew. I can say that with a clear conscience although he was my opponent, a major opponent.'[153]

Many of the survivors who had had to work with the SS and Gestapo during the deportations felt a sense of guilt, even if no accusations were made against them. Dr Paul Klaar was head physician at the collection point. He was in charge of the medical service and wrote opinions on who was fit to travel and who wasn't. He had to present these assessments to the commandant or Gestapo and he was subject to permanent control. He tried to rescue as many people as possible from deportation but his applications were often refused by the commandant.[154] After 1945, he received many honours on his return from Theresienstadt. He was now a real privy councillor and head physician of the Vienna police. No one accused him, and survivors only had good things to say about him. His nephew George Clare wrote about his uncle:

> Physically the big, fat, cheerful and bouncy uncle of my childhood, with his boyish love for small cameras and huge fountain pens, had shrunk to a third of his former size. His soul had withered and shrivelled to less. He functioned. He went for walks with me, took me to his office in the Police Presidium, he talked, though but little and very slowly. . . . When I sat next to him at table, as I walked next to him through the streets, I sat next to an automaton, walked next to a robot. His face was without animation, his voice monotonous, his eyes without life.[155]

Paul Klaar was haunted by what he had done earlier. Three times he tried unsuccessfully to commit suicide before being run over by a tram on the Ringstrasse. He died of his injuries two days later on 12 September 1948 at the age of sixty-two. Who knows whether he had run underneath the tram by accident or on purpose?[156]

Josef Löwenherz was already markedly affected by his work in 1938 and he continued to be haunted by his position under the Nazi regime.[157] He sympathized with the suffering of others. His compassion and his scruples plagued him after 1945, following him until his death. He had been a member of the board of the Vienna Kultusgemeinde since 1924 and later became vice-president. From being an elected vice-president, he transferred to the position of paid director in 1936. He was not a politician; he was an administrator with charisma who knew how to make appearance and attitude count and to speak in public. He was responsible and hardworking and devoted his entire energy to the community. He was a respected member of the Zionist movement. Sofie Löwenherz, his wife, was also one of the central figures in the Zionist movement and was generally respected and loved. She headed the Zionist women's charity organization Wizo. After the Anschluss, Löwenherz was not deported to Dachau but kept in Vienna. Adolf Eichmann appointed the director as head of the reopened Kultusgemeinde.

At their very first meeting, Löwenherz experienced the pressure, terror and violence at first hand when Eichmann hit him.[158] Eichmann wanted a representative who was dignified and whom the victims trusted. Charles Kapralik wrote after the war:

> Dr Löwenherz was a tall portly man and he knew how to gain respect even with the Gestapo through his composure and appearance. At his trial, Eichmann claimed that he had hit Dr Löwenherz once and had subsequently regretted it greatly. I never heard him say this, but I saw time and again that Eichmann treated Dr Löwenherz with a certain respect.[159]

Willy Stern described Löwenherz differently: '[He] was certainly a highly respectable man but he didn't know what was going on. To judge by the records, he was almost a complete fool.'[160]

Kapralik wrote his memoirs as a tribute to the work of the Kultusgemeinde during the Nazi regime. Moreover, he was already old and well established in the Nazi era and witnessed the efforts and energies that Löwenherz put into his work as director. The youthful Willy Stern by contrast saw above all how little Löwenherz's elegant appearance, his dignity and courtesy counted with the Nazis. There is also the fact that Stern did not get to know Löwenherz until later. Kapralik had been active earlier in the Kultusgemeinde. Willy Stern met Löwenherz when he was under increasing pressure from the Nazis and in despair at the mass deportations. Stern saw Löwenherz as a figure of ridicule, the head of a community that didn't exist. He knew little of the hardship under which Löwenherz operated. To some foreign Jewish functionaries, Löwenherz might have appeared to have been a Gestapo mediator. It was his job to inform the Jews of the discriminatory measures by the Nazis and to warn them not to disobey them. On Eichmann's behalf, he sought money from the Joint to enable Jews to emigrate. But whereas Eichmann wanted to banish them, Löwenherz's aim was to rescue as many of the persecuted Jews as possible by enabling them to escape. With the permission of the Nazi authorities, he travelled to Switzerland, the Netherlands, England and Hungary to meet international aid organizations and negotiate possibilities for emigration. Until 1941, his efforts to save members of the community were incredible. After the transports to Nisko in autumn 1939, he had attempted at least to delay the deportation of the community. In autumn 1941, the mass deportations to the death camps began and emigration was prohibited. Now Löwenherz attempted at least to alleviate the suffering of the victims. He saw no alternative but to cooperate. He was completely at the mercy of the SS, Gestapo, Adolf Eichmann and Alois and Anton Brunner. He always sought to achieve the least of all evils for the community. On many occasions, he dared to contradict, to make a request, to ignore an order or, in 1943, to risk asking officially what was happening to the deportees. He was in contact with foreign Jewish organizations and could easily have fled, but he felt a duty to the community. Moreover, the other functionaries, Desider Friedmann and Robert Stricker, stood as guarantees for his return. They were hostages. Löwenherz remained at his post and did not withdraw. Until summer 1941, he hoped that emigration could be stepped up and that he would eventually be able to join his children in the USA.[161]

Like many Jewish leaders in Nazi Europe, Löwenherz hoped to be able to continue saving as many Jews as possible. As we now know, the strategy of cooperation failed. He realized that he could not stop the liquidation of the community. On 4 July 1941, an article about Löwenherz appeared in the German-speaking newspaper *Yedioth Achronoth* in Israel, 'Olei Germania ve-Olei Ostria':

> According to news from Zurich, Dr Josef Löwenherz, president of the Jewish Community in Vienna, was taken to hospital with a nervous breakdown when he received the order from the Gestapo to cooperate in the deportation of all Viennese Jews to Lublin. The incident took place in February. In the meantime six transports have left but then the action was stopped. After a time, Dr Löwenherz returned to work in the offices of the Vienna Jewish Community, which he has been leading for the last three years under very difficult circumstances. The day will come when his work will be given the appreciation it is due.[162]

In other words, it had been reported publicly as early as July 1941 that Löwenherz had been ordered to cooperate with the deportations. This news did not prompt any criticisms of the head of the Kultusgemeinde. When the industrialized extermination was known after 1945, the Jewish functionaries were accused of having cooperated as far back as Nisko in 1939. The subsequent knowledge of the extermination put all earlier events in a new light.

In spite of his nervous breakdown, Löwenherz attended meetings in which it was decided which employees were indispensable to the administration and which were not.

190

Löwenherz had fought against the deportations and attempted to prevent them as long as possible. He was no coward but continually put his own life at risk, for example when he refused to carry out the order to appoint Jewish *Ausheber* or when he asked about the fate of the deportees in early 1943. He covered up some of the illegal actions carried out by his employees. In the midst of the suffering, he kept a humane face and offered many of his employees comfort and support in this way. He put up administrative resistance but his courageous manner was not in any way rebellious. He kept up formal appearances but never shirked his official responsibility and carried out his duties under all circumstances.

In May 1945, Löwenherz was arrested by the Soviet authorities.[163] Investigations against him were started in Prague.[164] On 10 August 1945, the German Jewish New York newspaper *Aufbau* carried a report about him in which the new deputy head of the Kultusgemeinde, Benzion Lazar, was quoted as having brought accusations against Löwenherz. Lazar claimed that Löwenherz and Bienenfeld had cooperated in the deportations merely to save themselves and had frequently shared the confiscated property with the Gestapo. *Aufbau* was suspicious of Lazar's statement. It noted:

> that all of these accusations appear highly dubious. We have a parallel case in Romania, where the outstanding leader of the Romanian Jews, Dr Fildermann, was arrested on the basis of similar accusations. We do not believe that we are far wrong in attributing these arrests to the very sad fact of strife among the Austrian and Romanian Jews themselves.[165]

The American Jewish Committee also disbelieved Lazar and did not take him seriously. It rejected the accusations against Löwenherz.[166] After the investigations had been concluded in Prague and the accusations rebutted, Löwenherz was able to leave with his wife. In Palestine, Alois Rothenberg, the former head of the Palestine Office, attempted to arrange for the immigration of Josef and Sofie Löwenherz, and Chaim Weizmann is said to have personally requested two certificates for them.[167] But Josef and Sofie Löwenherz wanted to rejoin their children in the United States. They travelled first to Switzerland, then to London and finally to New York.

In London, Josef Löwenherz was summoned in April 1946 before a tribunal organized by the Association of Jewish Refugees. Days before, a London periodical for German-speaking refugees had already voiced its protest.[168] The chairman of the tribunal said at the start of the session:

191

Anyone who was compelled to remain in public office in a country occupied by the Nazis or felt morally obliged to do so in the interests of those in his charge had to work with the German authorities and as such was a collaborator. He could have been the greatest hero or a scoundrel. Which he was depended on the way he performed his duties, whether bravely, disregarding death and with the constant desire to rescue what he could, or allowing himself to be used as a willing tool. After listening to Dr Löwenherz's report, you will be able to form your own opinions as to which category he belongs to.[169]

After this introduction, Löwenherz reported on his work as director. His statement was interrupted by hecklers. The *Jewish Telegraphic Agency* reported on his statement:

Dr Joseph Löwenherz, for twenty years a member of the board of the Vienna Jewish Community and its director during the seven years of Nazi occupation, reported on the tragic events during that period at a meeting arranged by the Association of Jewish Refugees.

Up to the outbreak of the war, Dr Löwenherz said, the Nazis, though treating the Jews cruelly, rather promoted emigration schemes sponsored by the Jewish Community. The policy of deporting Central European Jews to Poland was started after the occupation of that country. The Central Emigration Department of the Gestapo in Vienna alone was responsible for compiling lists of people to be deported and for arranging transports of deportees. There was no collaboration or consulting with the Jewish Community in this respect.

Thanks to the efforts of Dr Löwenherz and his colleagues, 136,000 out of a total of 206,000 Austrian Jews were able to emigrate (several thousand even during the war via Siberia or Lisbon); 15,000 died from natural causes; 47,000 were deported and of these only 1,300 have returned; and 6,000 who are married to non-Jews were able to remain in Vienna.

Dr R. Bienenfeld, who was in the chair, emphasized that Dr Löwenherz, whilst himself being in constant danger of his life, has saved the lives of tens of thousands of Jews. Of all the Jewish communities under Nazi rule, Austrian Jewry had suffered the smallest loss in proportion – about 25 per cent – in spite of the hostile attitude of the Austrian population. Amidst the applause of the audience, he thanked Dr Löwenherz on behalf of the Austrian Jewish refugees.[170]

Löwenherz was wrong about the figures. Of the Jews who left Austria, around 15,000 were rounded up by the Wehrmacht in Europe and exterminated.

At the end of the statement, the audience applauded and the chairman of the tribunal acquitted Löwenherz of all accusations. Löwenherz settled in New York but he is said not to have found peace of mind: every time he met Viennese Jews, he felt obliged to justify his behaviour.[171]

He was scheduled to testify in the trial of Eichmann in Jerusalem in 1961. He was already ill. The Israeli consul visited him in New York during the trial preparations. Löwenherz was very agitated and promised to fill out a detailed questionnaire. He never managed to do so. The memory of Eichmann was too much for him. He suffered a heart attack and died three days later.[172]

─12─

DISCUSSION OF THE JEWISH COUNCILS AND THE SITUATION IN VIENNA

For many years, historians, particularly German-speaking ones, avoided addressing the actions of the Jews themselves during the persecution and extermination of the European Jewry. An analysis of the reaction of the Jewish community and the strategies of its leaders was thought to be too sensitive an issue.

The Jews faced up to the issue early on. Tribunals were established right after the war among the surviving Jewish deportees in the displaced persons camps to punish the leaders of the Jewish administration who were thought to have been guilty and to allow those who had been falsely accused of cooperating with the Nazis to disprove the accusations and re-establish their reputations.

The discussion in Israel on Jewish involvement in the Nazi killing machinery touched on the very identity of the state. The revisionist nationalist opposition accused the Zionist leadership, particularly the left-wingers, of having betrayed existential Jewish interests and of having collaborated with the Nazis. Moreover, the political right claimed that the government parties had also collaborated with the British before independence. These two completely separate accusations were sometimes linked to discredit the policy of negotiating and agreeing compromises with the enemy. In 1954, for example, a court in Tel Aviv became the arena for this dispute. Rudolf Reszö Kasztner, a journalist and Zionist politician, had negotiated with the Nazis in 1944 to buy the freedom of Jews in Hungary. Malkiel Grünwald from Hungary accused Kasztner publicly in 1953 of being a corrupt betrayer of the Jewish people. Kasztner took him to court. Grunwald's right-wing lawyer, Shmuel Tamir, turned the case back on Kasztner. He accused not only him but also the Jewish Agency, the Zionist leadership establishment, of having negotiated with the Nazis. In 1955, Grünwald was acquitted of most charges, which was

194

equivalent to a condemnation of Kasztner. Kasztner appealed but did not survive to see his rehabilitation. In 1957, he was shot in the street in Tel Aviv by right-wing extremists. The Israeli Supreme Court overturned the first judgement in 1958, stating that most, but not all, of Kasztner's actions were justified. Public opinion in Israel did not agree with this judgement, however.

The dispute between the various Jewish factions attracted international attention in the 1961 trial of Adolf Eichmann in Jerusalem. By judging Eichmann, the Israeli court was reminding the world that the Jewish people had not forgotten and were not willing to allow surviving henchmen of the Nazis to go unpunished. The trial also had an important political message for the Jews, making it clear to them that they lived within a hostile world that had persecuted and killed them and that it was only because of the establishment of a Jewish state that they were secure and protected. Among the audience in the courtroom was Hannah Arendt, a Jewish philosopher, originally from Germany, who had fled to Paris in 1933 and then to New York in 1941. She had been commissioned by the *New Yorker* magazine to report on the trial. Her provocative series of five articles caused considerable furore. She published them in the United States of America in 1963 in book form and a German translation appeared in 1964 under the title *Eichmann in Jerusalem: Ein Bericht von der Banalität des Bösen*.

Arendt's central thesis was that Eichmann was merely a bureaucrat, an efficient implementer. He had committed his crimes against the Jews driven by no feelings except his sense of duty and sheer opportunism. Those who read the historical documents from the years after 1938 and study the testimonies of eyewitnesses, however, will arrive at a different opinion. Eichmann was not just carrying out orders but showed a good deal of initiative of his own. He was perhaps not a demon but rather a manager of the Nazi Jewish policy who nevertheless carried out his work enthusiastically and with conviction. Historically speaking, Arendt had chosen the wrong person for her tempting comments about the 'banality of evil'.

While the young Jewish state was presiding over Eichmann's trial, Arendt also levelled accusations against the Jewish leadership – including the Zionists – during the Nazi era. She claimed that the political leadership had left the Jewish people at the mercy of the Nazis: 'If the Jewish people had been really unorganized and leaderless, there would have been chaos and plenty of misery but the total number of victims would hardly have been between four and a half and six million people.'[1]

In the occupied Soviet territories the mobile killing units (Einsatzgruppen) murdered Jews without relying on the structures of the Jewish administration. There was no chaos within the killing machinery and the Jews were systematically murdered. Arendt's claim that not so many Jews would have been killed without the Jewish leadership was met with a vehement and immediate rejection from the Jewish side.[2]

Arendt referred to studies by Raul Hilberg, who had not been able to discern any strategy of Jewish self-assertion against the Nazi killing machinery. This attitude, said Hilberg, was a consequence of Jewish history: 'In exile the Jews had always been a minority, always in danger, but they had learned that they could avert or survive destruction by placating and appeasing their enemies. . . . The Jews had learned that in order to survive they had to refrain from resistance.'[3]

It is hardly surprising that Hilberg was unable to identify any resistance to the crime by the victims. To understand the mass murder of the Jews, he had studied the perpetrators' documents, according to which the Nazis did not indeed have to overcome any appreciable obstacles. But that does not mean that there were not various forms of resistance. It is not the fault of the Jews that they were unsuccessful. What could the disenfranchised and unarmed Jews, with no support from a government in exile, do against the Third Reich? It took twenty million Allied soldiers (including many Jews) to defeat Nazism.

There was resistance from the Jews nevertheless. Two questions are a constant feature of studies of Jewish resistance: what may be regarded as resistance in general and what was the nature of Jewish resistance in particular? Should the Jewish participation in the anti-Fascist resistance of the workers' movement be described as Jewish resistance? Was the organization of illegal escape to Palestine a form of resistance? It is not sufficient to confine resistance to armed struggle. Economic, cultural, social, ideological and political attitudes are also forms of resistance. For a long time, the question was considered in terms of the alternative between Jewish self-administration leading ultimately to self-sacrifice on the one hand and hopeless but defiant armed resistance on the other. In reality, there is no sharp distinction of this nature. The Jewish underground in Poland, for example, fully recognized the need for Jewish councils. It was not until the deportations started that sharp altercations occurred. There was disagreement as to whether the mass murders would be a passing phase or whether they were part of a comprehensive extermination plan. In their last hopeless struggle, the Jewish partisans and insurgents in the

Warsaw ghetto turned to posterity: if they could not defeat the Nazis, they wanted at least to ensure that the world remembered the resistance of the Jews to the genocide. They were not able to prevent it, however.[4]

A large number of survivors found refuge and a home in Israel. The Shoah became a constituting component of the Israeli identity. In the early pioneer society, Israel had been seen as a response by self-aware Jewry to the Diaspora. Israeli historiography describes the resistance as the result of Zionist awakening. The anti-Nazi struggle became a symbol of renunciation of the Diaspora. In schools and museums, the Jewish partisan organizations were portrayed as part of Israel's struggle for independence. Hannah Arendt has two points of contact with this Zionist historiography: she shared the admiration for militant Jewish resistance and she despised the Jewish councils for their unworthy and perfidious strategy.[5] The Zionist view of history blames the cooperation of the Jewish councils on their Diaspora existence. Hilberg also explains the alleged passivity of the Jews in terms of their ostensible ghetto mentality. Arendt by contrast rejects the idea of a specifically Jewish mentality, rightly pointing to the old anti-Semitic clichés that it implied. She did not blame the Jews but their Zionist functionaries.

This blanket condemnation of the Jewish councils has been gradually revised. Some researchers consider that the social and charitable bodies within the Jewish administrations should be given their due. They say that the Jewish councils attempted with their endeavours to resist extermination and to maintain Jewish life under the most terrible conditions.[6] A general condemnation of all Jewish functionaries misses the point. Every person and every situation needs to be seen in isolation. There was Adam Czerniakow in Warsaw who committed suicide rather than deliver children for extermination. In Bialystok, the Jewish council under Efraim Barasz worked together with the armed resistance. The Elder of the Jews, Weiler, in Wladzimierz refused to participate in a selection, saying: 'I am not God and will not pass judgement over who shall live and who shall die.'[7]

There was a move away from the pioneer thinking in Israel in the 1970s and the assessment of Jewish councils was also revisited in this light. But the discussion had shifted, not only in Israel, from political and ideological questions to the powerlessness of the Jewish victims in general. After the specific differences between the ghettos and Jewish councils in the various occupied countries had been distinguished and the personalities of the individual Jewish functionaries discussed, it became evident again that despite their differences the

Jewish councils throughout Europe basically faced the same problems. A comparison of the records and statements by Jewish functionaries in parts of the continent far removed from one another reveals a similarity in thoughts, hopes and feelings. The Jewish functionaries were mostly members of modern political movements and not representatives of the traditional values of a ghetto mentality. Their behaviour had little to do with Jewish history, as Hilberg suggests. Although the Nazi term 'Jewish council' referred to Jewish community structures before emancipation, the Jewish administration in the Nazi-controlled ghettos was in no way autonomous and did not have its own jurisdiction as had been granted to the Jews by their feudal masters.[8] The Jewish councils cannot be regarded as independent Jewish political leadership. The Jewish administration under Nazi control had no independent power or internally chosen leaders but merely functionaries appointed from the outside. Flight or provisions for the ghettos could be organized only through negotiation with the Nazis. The functionaries were willing to cooperate to rescue the community even after the deportations had started. Many hoped that the Jews would be deported for forced labour and not for extermination.

Jewish partisan groups were unwilling to accept children and old persons. Many people did not want to leave their families in the lurch. Jakob Gens, the Elder of the Jewish community in Vilna, argued with a group that had joined the partisans because they would reduce the number of productive workers and hence the chances of survival in the ghetto. In his eyes, the Jewish council, in contrast to the resistance, took collective responsibility for the ghetto.[9] In 1942, Gens made a speech to intellectuals and artists in the Vilna ghetto, defending his strategy:

> Many of you regard me as a traitor . . . I, Gens, am leading you to your death, and I, Gens, want to protect Jews from death. I, Gens, have hiding places forced open, and I, Gens, try to organize documents and work and obtain privileges for the ghetto. For me it is Jewish blood and not Jewish honour that counts. If they ask for 1,000 Jews – I give them up, because if we Jews don't do it, the Germans will come . . . and the entire ghetto will become chaos. By giving up 100 I rescue 1,000. With 1,000 that I give them, I rescue 10,000 people. You, people of intellect and the pen, you do not touch the dirt in the ghetto. You will leave the ghetto clean. And if you survive the ghetto, you will say: we came out with a clear conscience. But I, Jakob Gens, if I survive, I will come out dirty and will have blood on my hands. But I will give myself up for judgement. To be judged by Jews. I will say: I did everything to

rescue as many Jews as possible from the ghetto and to lead them to freedom. To enable some Jews to survive I had to lead Jews to their death. And to enable Jews to get out with a clear conscience – I had to dig in the dirt and act without a conscience.[10]

Adam Czerniakow, chairman of the Jewish council in Warsaw, by contrast, lost his faith in the strategy of cooperation when he was commanded to send children to their death. He took his own life before being forced to put together a children's transport the following day.

All of the strategies of the Jews, be it resistance or cooperation, failed and could not prevent the extermination. The attitude of the victims made no difference to their fate, which had been sealed by the Nazi policy. It is easy to say that the Jews of eastern Europe were an easy prey for the murderers because of their passive ghetto mentality, the western Jews because of assimilation, and the German Jews because of the germanophilia. If a historian claims that the Jews were not capable of resistance because of their history, he is saying that if the Jews had not been Jews, the Nazis would not have been able to kill so many of them. Such statements do nothing to shed light on the crime but blame the victims indirectly for the extent and nature of the crime. In reality, however, the Jews and those who were persecuted as Jews were not killed because they were how they were or had specific Jewish leaders whom they trusted but because the perpetrators wanted to expel, exploit and exterminate 'the Jews'. This is a distinction that must be clearly made. The Nazi rulers killed the victims, whether they had a central administration or not, whether they were Jews or Roma, prisoners of war or political enemies, homosexuals or Jehovah's Witnesses. Before the totalitarian authorities executed their victims, they set the scene. They terrorized them. They organized the community leadership according to their designs. Shouldn't Hannah Arendt of all people have emphasized this above everything? Did she not describe in *The Origins of Totalitarianism* why the victims of the systems described by her were forced to cooperate? Didn't her criticism of Jewish functionaries actually contradict her own findings?[11]

The leaders of the administration were among the victims. The Jewish councils were not a group of characterless personalities or a select band of moralists. They were composed of highly different characters. They were victims of the same hopes and illusions as those harboured by the other Jews.

At all events, the cooperation by the Jewish functionaries cannot be seen as collaboration. It is true that individual Jews, including

Jewish functionaries, betrayed other Jews. Non-Jewish collaborators in the occupied countries participated voluntarily, for opportunistic or ideological reasons, in the crimes. The Jewish councils, however, never sought to serve the aims of the Nazis but believed that they could do something about the extermination only by cooperation. They were forced to cooperate through lies, deceptions and threats of collective punishment. Most Jewish functionaries were ultimately killed. This alone demonstrates their fundamental powerlessness in spite of their temporary privileges.

Dan Diner shows that from the perspective of the Jewish councils, the Nazi killings, with extermination as their goal, simply made no rational sense.[12] The victims did not know what was being done to them. They could not understand why their life, their skills and even their labour counted for nothing. Their perception and their behaviour were not determined by Jewish history. Neither Jews nor anyone else could have acted differently in this predicament. The victims attempted to anticipate the enemy's actions so as to be able to resist them. Extermination, however, must have appeared to them simply senseless and unimaginable.

This perhaps explains what Hannah Arendt meant when she said that the knowledge of the mass murder was beyond her imagination in 1943 and that she could not believe that this crime was possible: 'It was as if the abyss had opened up. Because there was the idea that everything else could have been somehow made good, like everything can be made good again in politics. But not this. This should never have happened.'[13] The crime was beyond imagination and Arendt puts this lack of imagination at the origin of the crime. She describes Eichmann: 'He *merely*, to put the matter colloquially, *never realized what he was doing*. . . . It was sheer thoughtlessness – something by no means identical with stupidity – that predisposed him to become one of the greatest criminals of that period.'[14]

It is not a question here of whether Arendt's description of Eichmann's character is correct but rather that she describes the lack of imagination as the cause of the crime, a crime whose monstrousness was beyond all previous imagination, even that of the victims and of Arendt herself. In the light of these considerations, Arendt's angry accusation of the Jewish councils can be read as an irate lament at the failure of rationality, at the inadequacy of humanistic imagination. Those who study the Jewish functionaries under the Nazi regime find themselves at the epicentre of this disaster.

Diner stressed that paradoxically the view of the Jewish councils revealed a more radical victim perspective than that of the people in the extermination camps. The camp inmates had already been deprived of their will and ability to decide for themselves. In the ghetto, by contrast, they still had the appearance of free will and decision-making powers. They were intent on reacting to the perpetrators, to anticipating them and to agreeing on a strategy for survival.[15] It was not because the Jewish councils betrayed the Jewish community but because they attempted to act in their interests that the Jewish functionaries were condemned to see things from the perspective of the authorities. They had to think like Nazis in the interests of the Jews. They had to count on the fact that the Nazi Reich would not want to deprive itself of the economic benefits of Jewish forced labour. They followed the enemy's orders closely because they hoped that in return it would also keep to the system it had itself ordained, its law of 'work or life'. They accepted the lies and promises of the Nazis because, however they looked at it, they were the only remaining chance they had of saving lives. Because of their power, however, the Nazi authorities could change the rules at any time. The Jewish functionaries were well aware that their hopes were being dashed every day but they had no other choice than to hope that rational, economic and strategic constraints would triumph over the murderers' desire for extermination. The Jewish authorities attempted to gain time; they wanted to sacrifice a few in order to save many. Every decision for life was also one for death. To maintain the ghetto, they exposed it to destruction. All of their strategies for rescuing people were doomed to failure.

Looking at the situation in Vienna again in this light, it must first be emphasized that armed Jewish resistance there was inconceivable. In contrast to other countries occupied by the German Reich, Hitler's country of birth was incorporated into the Reich. The Jews were not a minority among a persecuted population, as was the case in Czechoslovakia or Poland, for example. Many Austrians welcomed the Anschluss or took part in anti-Semitic pogroms. Resistance by the Jewish community was impossible without the support of the non-Jewish population. But there was practically no solidarity to be found from that quarter.

In Austria in 1938, the rule of law must have been seen as the only possible chance. The Jewish administration could not act illegally on its own account but hoped rather to build on the assumption that the Nazis would also respect the law. In comparison to the anti-Semitic mob and excesses in March 1938, the Nazi authorities appeared initially to be comparatively moderate and capable of being negotiated with. Unlike Germany, all illusions of being able to remain in the country were soon shattered. The mass emigration was possible only through cooperation with the authorities; around two thirds of the persecuted managed to escape from the Third Reich.

Vienna became a model for the Nazi Jewish policy. The situation there was copied in other cities and Central Offices for Jewish Emigration were set up there as well. The Jewish organizations in Vienna were taken wholly by surprise by this new and completely unknown type of persecution.

The Kultusgemeinde under the Nazis became a prototype for the future Jewish councils. It would be wrong to describe it as the Jewish leadership. It had no power of its own. It was organized in accordance with Nazi designs; it was under Nazi control, and its representatives were not freely elected. It was not a Nazi institution but merely the recipient of orders from the perpetrators. The Jewish functionaries worked in the interests of the Jews of Vienna and believed that they were serving the Jewish community. They had to be lied to precisely because they were not part of the Nazi hierarchy, and they could be lied to all too easily because they were powerless and victims. The deportations started in Vienna while emigration was still possible. The nature of Jewish cooperation and the Jewish administration, whose attitude had already been formed through the attempts to escape, changed only gradually. The smooth transition gave an alibi for the crime and concealed the perpetrators' real intentions. The Central Office for Jewish Emigration became the deportation authority; the ration-card file was used to draw up deportation lists. The extent of the crime became clear only when the majority of the Jewish community had already been killed. The Jews in Germany were still citizens of the state by law. They hoped even after war broke out that some kind of arrangement could be arrived at for those who had not been able to leave. In other countries, in Hungary in 1944, for example, the Jewish functionaries had already been warned in advance as to when the Jews were to be deported. In Poland, the news of industrialized mass murder penetrated to the ghettos. This was not the case in Vienna. When the first mass deportations started in early 1941, it was still not clear what awaited the Jews in the east. Only after the major mass deportations in autumn 1942 did the Jewish administration in Vienna hear of the systematic extermination of European Jewry.

The Jewish functionaries saw no alternative. Cooperation with the Nazis appeared to be the lesser evil. Again and again they cherished the hope of being able to rescue some of the community. Those who study the policies of Jewish communities during the Nazi persecution will soon recognize the limits to their scope of action. The leaders of the Jewish community in Vienna were subject to the same constraints as all Jews. They had no power of their own, they were authorities without power. Even retrospectively, there appears to have been no alternative way out of the dilemma. All of this has nothing at all to do with Jewish traditions, with identification of the victim with the perpetrator or with Viennese traits. No group of victims could have reacted differently under similar circumstances; nor could they do so today either. It is not possible to draw a more comforting or comfortable conclusion.

NOTES

CHAPTER 1 PROLOGUE

1 Ruth Klüger, *Landscapes of Memory: A Holocaust Girlhood Remembered* (London, 2003), p. 70.
2 Head of the State Police at the public prosecutor's office, Vienna; 15 October 1945, criminal proceedings against Wilhelm Reisz before the Provincial Criminal Court of Vienna as People's Court; Provincial Court Archive; Vg 1b Vr 2911/45.
3 Testimony of Wilhelm Bienenfeld, criminal proceedings against Wilhelm Reisz before the Provincial Criminal Court of Vienna as People's Court; Provincial Court Archive; Vg 1b Vr 2911/45.
4 Ibid.
5 Testimony of Max F., criminal proceedings against Anton Brunner before the Provincial Criminal Court of Vienna as People's Court; Provincial Court Archive; Vr 4574/45; quoted in Hans Safrian, *Eichmann's Men* (Cambridge, 2010), p. 119; I should also like to thank Hans Safrian for referring me to this document.
6 Judgement of Wilhelm Reisz, 8 July 1946, criminal proceedings against Wilhelm Reisz before the Provincial Criminal Court of Vienna as People's Court; Provincial Court Archive; Vg 1b Vr 2911/45.
7 Testimony of Wilhelm Bienenfeld, Bruno Feyer and Alfred Neufeld; judgement of Wilhelm Reisz, 8 July 1946, criminal proceedings against Wilhelm Reisz before the Provincial Criminal Court of Vienna as People's Court; Provincial Court Archive; Vg 1b Vr 2911/45.
8 Criminal proceedings against Johann Rixinger before the Provincial Criminal Court of Vienna as People's Court; Vg 11 g Vr 4866/46/HV 1319/47.

204

9 Criminal proceedings against Bernhard Wittke before the Provincial Criminal Court of Vienna as People's Court; Vg 2b Vr 2331/45.

10 Safrian, *Eichmann's Men* (see n. 5 above), p. 219.

11 Judgement of Wilhelm Reisz, 8 July 1946, criminal proceedings against Wilhelm Reisz before the Provincial Criminal Court of Vienna as People's Court; Provincial Court Archive; Vg 1b Vr 2911/45.

12 *Gau* file of Herbert Gerbing; Austrian State Archive 337 048; I should like to thank Hans Safrian for showing me this file.

13 Gefangenenhaus II at the Provincial Court; Vienna; 11 July 1946, criminal proceedings against Wilhelm Reisz before the Provincial Criminal Court of Vienna as People's Court; Provincial Court Archive; Vg 1b Vr 2911/45.

14 Hans Safrian and Hans Witek, *Und keiner war dabei. Dokumente des alltäglichen Antisemitismus in Wien 1938* (Vienna, 1988), p. 200.

15 Record of the execution, Préfecture de Police, Direction de la Police Judiciaire, Commissariat de Police de la Circonscription de Choisy-le-Roi, Procès-Verbal, Executions capitales de Von Maltzahn, Hans Karl et Reich, Oscar; 5 July 1949. I should like to thank Hans Safrian for making copies of the relevant documents available to me.

16 Safrian, *Eichmann's Men* (see n. 5 above), p. 119.

17 Acte d'Accusation contre Oscar Reich, Joseph Weiszl, Joseph Czasny; Tribunal Militaire Permanent de Paris; 14 December 1948; I should like to thank Hans Safrian for making copies of the relevant documents available to me.

18 Procès-Verbal, Executions capitales de Von Maltzahn, Hans Karl et Reich, Oscar.

19 Safrian *Eichmann's Men* (see n. 5 above), p. 219.

20 Primo Levi, *The Drowned and the Saved* (London, 1989), p. 29.

21 Testimony of Hugo Grossmann, criminal proceedings against Wilhelm Reisz before the Provincial Criminal Court of Vienna as People's Court; Provincial Court Archive; Vg 1b Vr 2911/45.

22 Cf. Anna Freud, 'Das Ich und die Abwehrmechanismen' (1936), in Anna Freud, (1980) *Die Schriften der Anna Freud* (Munich, 1980), vol. 1, pp. 193–355; Irving Sarnoff, 'Identification with the Aggressor: Some Personality Correlates of Anti-Semitism

among Jews', dissertation, Michigan, 1951), quoted in Sander L. Gilman, *Jewish Self-Hatred: Anti-Semitism and the Hidden Language of the Jews* (Baltimore, 1993), p. 306.

23 Dan Diner (ed.), *Zivilisationsbruch. Denken nach Auschwitz* (Frankfurt am Main, 1988), p. 8.

24 Walter Otto Weyrauch, 'Gestapo Informants: Facts and Theory of Undercover Operations', *Columbia Journal of Transnational Law* 24 (1986): 591.

25 Cf. Bruno Bettelheim, *Surviving and Other Essays* (New York: Knopf, 1979); Robert J. Lifton, *Death in Life* (New York, 1967); William G. Niederland, *Folgen der Verfolgung. Das Überlebenden-Syndrom* (Frankfurt am Main, 1980).

26 Levi, *The Drowned and the Saved* (see n. 20 above), p. 63.

27 Klüger, *Landscapes of Memory: A Holocaust Girlhood Remembered* (see n. 1 above), p. 70.

28 Testimony of Friedrich, criminal proceedings against Wilhelm Reisz before the Provincial Criminal Court of Vienna as People's Court; Provincial Court Archive; Vg 1b Vr 2911/45.

29 Raul Hilberg and Alfons Söllner, 'Das Schweigen zum Sprechen bringen. Ein Gespräch über Franz Neumann und die Entwicklung der Holocaust-Forschung', in Diner (ed.), *Zivilisationsbruch. Denken nach Auschwitz* (see n. 23 above), p. 178.

30 Raul Hilberg, *The Destruction of the European Jews*, three volumes, expanded edition (London and New York, 1985).

31 Franz L. Neumann, *Behemoth. The Structure and Practice of National Socialism 1933–1945* (originally published in New York, 1944).

32 Peter Wyden, *Stella* (New York: Simon & Schuster, 1992), pp. 17 and 19.

33 Francis R. Nicosia, *The Third Reich and the Palestine Question* (London, 1985).

34 Francis R. Nicosia, *Hitler und der Zionismus* (Leoni am Starnberger See, 1989).

35 Julius H. Schoeps, 'Haben Nazis und Zionisten zusammengearbeitet? oder: Vom Mißbrauch einer wissenschaftlichen Untersuchung', *Semit. Die unabhängige jüdische Zeitschrift* 4 (1990): 21.

36 Foreword by Hans-Joachim W. Koch, in Nicosia, *Hitler und der Zionismus* (see n. 34 above).

37 *Süd-Ost-Tagespost*, Graz, 10 June 1963.

38 Alain Finkielkraut, *The Imaginary Jew* (Lincoln, Nebraska, 1994), pp. 43–4.

39 Bruno Bettelheim, 'Eichmann – das System – die Opfer and Antwort an Richter Musmanno', in F. A. Krummacher (ed.), *Die Kontroverse Hannah Arendt – Eichmann und die Juden* (Munich, 1964).

40 David Rousset, quoted in Hannah Arendt, *Eichmann in Jerusalem. A Report on the Banality of Evil* (London, 1977), p. 12.

41 Hugo Gold, *Geschichte der Juden in Wien* (Tel Aviv, 1966).

42 Jonny Moser, *Die Judenverfolgung 1938–1945* (Vienna, 1966).

43 Herbert Rosenkranz, *Verfolgung und Selbstbehauptung. Die Juden in Österreich 1938–1945* (Vienna, 1978).

44 Cf. Gerhard Botz, *Wohnungspolitik und Judendeportation in Wien 1938–1945. Zur Funktion des Antisemitismus als Ersatz nationalsozialistischer Sozialpolitik* (Vienna, Salzburg, 1975); Karl Stuhlpfarrer, 'Nationalsozialistische Verfolgungspolitik 1938 bis 1945', in Erich Zöllner (ed.), *Wellen der Verfolgung in der österreichischen Geschichte* (Vienna, 1986), p. 144–54.

45 Hannah Arendt, *The Origins of Totalitarianism* (London, 1966).

46 Michel Foucault, 'Theory of sovereignty and disciplinary power', lecture given on 14 January 1976, in Michel Foucault, *Society Must Be Defended: Lectures at the College de France, 1975–76* (London, 2004).

CHAPTER 2   THE VIENNA KULTUSGEMEINDE BEFORE 1938

1 Leopold Spira, *Feindbild 'Jud': 100 Jahre politischer Antisemitismus in Österreich* (Vienna, 1981).

2 Harriet Pass Freidenreich, *Jewish Politics in Vienna 1918–1938* (Bloomington, Indiana, 1991), p. 5.

3 Cf. *Report of the Vienna Jewish Community, Wien 1940*, Library of the Jewish Community of Vienna; and Herbert Rosenkranz, *Verfolgung* (see ch. 1, n. 43), p. 13.

4 Summary of Jewish organizations in Austria; Josef Löwenherz to Adolf Eichmann, Vienna, 4 January 1939; A/W 165,1.

5 Leo Landau, in 'Wien von 1909 bis 1939; Mitglied des Vorstandes der Israelitischen Kultusgemeinde', report noted by Dr Ball-Kaduri, 28 January 1959 and 22 February 1959; YvS-01/244; 8.

6 Summary of Jewish organizations in Austria; Josef Löwenherz to Adolf Eichmann, Vienna, 4 January 1939; A/W 165,1.

7 Ibid.

8 Freidenreich, *Jewish Politics in Vienna* (see n. 2 above), p. 219, table 6.

9 *Festschrift zur Feier des 50-jährigen Bestandes der Union österreichischer Juden* (Vienna, 1937), pp. 65 and 61.

10 Hugo Gold, *Geschichte der Juden in Wien* (see ch. 1, n. 41), p. 49.

11 Robert Weltsch, *Die deutsche Judenfrage. Ein kritischer Rückblick* (Königstein/Ts., 1981), pp. 73–7.

12 Cf. John Bunzl, *Klassenkampf in der Diaspora. Zur Geschichte der jüdischen Arbeiterbewegung* (Vienna, 1975).

13 Interview with Raul Hilberg, in *Die Presse*, 5 December 1992.

14 *Jüdische Presse*, Vienna, 5 October 1934.

15 Festschrift to commemorate the fiftieth anniversary of the Union österreichischer Juden, p. 66.

16 Willy Stern, interview, 2 May 1991.

17 Quoted in Günther Bernd Ginzel, *Jüdischer Alltag in Deutschland 1933–1945* (Dusseldorf, 1984), p. 45.

18 Leo Landau (see n. 5 above), p. 9.

19 Arno Lustiger, *Schalom Libertad! Juden im spanischen Bürgerkrieg* (Frankfurt am Main, 1989).

20 Rosenkranz, *Verfolgung* (see ch. 1, n. 43), pp. 17–18.

21 Oskar Grünbaum, Vienna, to the Zionist Executive, London, 19 February 1938. CZA; S25-9817.

22 Ibid.

CHAPTER 3   PERSECUTION

1 Quoted in *Das jüdische Echo 36* (1987), p. 194.

2 Rosenkranz, *Verfolgung* (see ch. 1, n. 43), p. 22.

3 Ibid., p. 39. G. R. Gedye, 'Nazis list 1,742 jailed in Austria' in the *New York Times*, 23 March 1938.

4 Ibid., pp. 21 and 37.

5 G. E. R. Gedye, *Fallen Bastions: The Central European Tragedy* (London, 2009), p. 308.

6 Leo Lauterbach: The Jewish Situation in Austria; report submitted to the Executive of the Zionist Organization, strictly confidential, 29 April 1938; CZA; S5-653; 6.

7 Cf. Gerhard Botz, *Wien vom "Anschluß" zum Krieg: Nationalsozialistische Machtübernahme und politisch-soziale Umgestaltung am Beispiel der Stadt Wien 1938/39* (Vienna, Munich, 1978), p. 96.

8 Rosenkranz, *Verfolgung* (see ch. 1, n. 43), p. 30.
9 Gesetze, Verordnungen und Kundmachungen aus dem Jahre 1938; A/W 12. – Gesetze und Verordnungen, Juden betreffend, sowie deren Auswirkung, 1938; A/W 11.
10 Martin Vogel, interview; 12 May 1989.
11 Jonny Moser, 'Die Katastrophe der Juden in Österreich – ihre Voraussetzungen und ihre Überwindung', in Kurt Schubert (ed.), *Der gelbe Stern in Österreich. Katalog und Einführung zu einer Dokumentation* (Eisenstadt, 1977), p. 115.
12 Raul Hilberg, *The Destruction of the European Jews* (see Ch. 1, n. 30 above), vol. 1, chs 4, 5 and 6.
13 Gesetze und Verordnungen, Juden betreffend, sowie deren Auswirkung, 1938; A/W 11.
14 Cf. Hilberg, *Destruction of the European Jews* (see n. 12 above), vol. 1, p. 176.
15 Cf. Josef Löwenherz to Gestapo headquarters, 10 January 1939; A/W 165,1.
16 Rosenkranz, *Verfolgung* (see ch. 1, n. 43), p. 28.
17 Hans Witek, 'Arisierungen in Wien', in Emmerich Tálos, Ernst Hanisch, Wolfgang Neugebauer (eds), *NS-Herrschaft in Österreich 1938–1945* (Vienna, 1988), p. 204.
18 Rosenkranz, *Verfolgung* (see ch. 1, n. 43), p. 26.
19 Quoted in Safrian and Witek, *Und keiner war dabei* (see ch. 1, n. 14), p. 96.
20 Botz, *Wohnungspolitik* (see ch. 1, n. 44).
21 Cf. Wohnungsräumungskarteizettel; Adler, Berta, Lazzenhof 2, 10, 1. Bezirk; 20. 11. 1938; A/W 438,2.
22 Josef Löwenherz: circular, Vienna, 2 October 1939; YvS-030/4.
23 Rosenkranz, *Verfolgung* (see ch. 1, n. 43), p. 500.
24 Quoted in Safrian and Witek, *Und keiner war dabei* (see ch. 1, n. 14), p. 98.
25 Ibid.

CHAPTER 4   STRUGGLE FOR SURVIVAL AND ESCAPE

1 Franzi Löw-Danneberg, interview, 19 June 1991.
2 Leo Landau (see ch. 2, n. 5), p. 11.
3 Rosa Rachel Schwarz, *Zwei Jahre Fürsorge der Kultusgemeinde Wien unter Hitler*, Tel Aviv, 14 May 1944, DÖW 2737, p. 1.
4 Rosenkranz, *Verfolgung* (see ch. 1, n. 43), p. 34.

5 Leo Landau (see ch. 2, n. 5), p. 11.

6 Safrian, *Eichmann's Men* (see ch. 1, n. 5), p. 27. In his recollections Charles J. Kapralik dates the first raid on the IKG as 15 March 1938 and says that Eichmann was already present. Cf. Charles J. Kapralik, 'Erinnerungen eines Beamten der Wiener Israelitischen Kultusgemeinde 1938–39', in *Leo Baeck Institute Year Book* 58 (1981), pp. 52–78.

7 Dan Michman, *Roschut u-manhigut. Judenrat we-ichud-jehudim be jamei-haschilton hanazi* (unpublished manuscript, August 1997), pp. 31–41.

8 Safrian, *Und keiner war dabei* (see ch. 1, n. 14), p. 41.

9 I. Klaber: Report on the IKG Vienna 1938; noted in 1944 by Dr Ball-Kaduri; YvS-01/74. Leo Landau (see ch. 2, n. 17), p. 11.

10 Arendt, *Eichmann in Jerusalem* (see ch. 1, n. 40), p. 45.

11 Jochen von Lang (ed.), *Eichmann Interrogated: Transcripts from the Archives of the Israeli Police*, New York, 1983), p. 50.

12 Safrian, *Eichmann's Men* (see ch. 1, n. 5), p. 27.

13 Wilhelm Bienenfeld, report on the IKG during the Nazi era, People's Court trial of Karl Ebner. Documentation Archive of Austrian Resistance 8919/1. The report was known as the Löwenherz report.

14 Leo Landau (see ch. 2, n. 5), p. 11.

15 Ibid.; Willy Stern, interview, 7 June 1989; Rosa Rachel Schwarz, *Zwei Jahre Fürsorge der Kultusgemeinde Wien unter Hitler* (Tel Aviv, 14 May 1944), DÖW 2737, p. 2.

16 Kapralik, *Erinnerungen* (see n. 6 above), p. 55.

17 Report; Activities of the IKG Vienna from 13 March to 31 December 1938; A/W 106; 1.

18 Schwarz, *Zwei Jahre Fürsorge* (see n. 3 above), p. 2.

19 Leo Lauterbach, 'The Jewish Situation in Austria'. Report submitted to the Executive of the Zionist Organization, strictly confidential, 29. April 1938 CZA, S5-653, 7; Samuel Graumann, *Deportiert! Ein Wiener Jude berichtet* (Vienna, 1947), p. 26.

20 Letter to Chaim Barlass, Jewish Agency, Jerusalem, unsigned; strictly confidential; Zürich, 7 May 1938; CZA; S6-4564; 2.

21 Interview with Dr Yehuda Brott by Herbert Rosenkranz, 22 March 1977. YvS-03/3912. Brott states that he met Eichmann at the 'Palestine office' on 15 March, but according to Hans Safrian's research Eichmann had not yet arrived in Vienna at that time; cf. Safrian, *Eichmann's Men* (see ch. 1, n. 5), p. 27.

22 Interview with Adolf Brunner by Herbert Rosenkranz, 13 April 1977. YvS-03/3914.
23 Kapralik, *Erinnerungen* (see n. 6 above), p. 59.
24 William R. Perl, *Operation Action: Rescue from the Holocaust* (New York, 1983), pp. 18–23.
25 Interview with Willi Ritter by Herbert Rosenkranz (in Hebrew), 5 October 1988, YvS-03/3982.
26 Safrian, *Eichmann's Men* (see ch. 1, n. 5), p. 30.
27 Letter to Chaim Barlass, Jewish Agency, Jerusalem, unsigned, marked 'strictly confidential'. Zurich, 7 May 1938, CZA; S6-4564, 2.
28 Kapralik, *Erinnerungen* (see n. 6 above), p. 55.
29 Rosenkranz, *Verfolgung* (see ch. 1, n. 43), p. 53.
30 Michman, *Roschut u-manhigut* (see n. 7 above), p. 32.
31 Israel Cohen to the Executive of the Jewish Agency for Palestine, 28 March 1938. CZA; S25-9817; Lauterbach (see ch. 3, n. 6), p. 8.
32 Rosenkranz, *Verfolgung* (see ch. 1, n. 43), p. 58.
33 Lauterbach (see ch. 3, n. 6).
34 Kapralik, *Erinnerungen* (see n. 6 above), p. 58.
35 Lauterbach (see ch. 3, n. 6), p. 10; here quoted in Rosenkranz, *Verfolgung* (see ch. 1, n. 43), p. 49.
36 *Völkischer Beobachter*, 26 April 1938.
37 Rosenkranz, *Verfolgung* (see ch. 1, n. 43), p. 55.
38 Leo Perutz, *Mainacht in Wien. Romanfragmente. Kleine Erzählprosa. Feuilletons. Aus dem Nachlaß* (Vienna, 1996), p. 69.
39 Robert Prochnik, unpublished typescript on the situation of the Jews in the Third Reich, p. 6 (written after 1945). I should like to thank Mares Prochnik for making the typescript available to me.
40 Rosenkranz, *Verfolgung* (see ch. 1, n. 43), p. 56f.

CHAPTER 5   THE VIENNA JEWISH COMMUNITY UNDER NAZI CONTROL

1 Rosenkranz, *Verfolgung* (see ch. 1, n. 43), p. 71.
2 Cf. Dan Michman, ' "Judenräte" und "Judenvereinigungen" unter nationalsozialistischer Herrschaft. Aufbau und Anwendung eines verwaltungsmäßigen Konzepts', *Zeitschrift für Geschichtswissenschaft* 4 (1998): 193–304.
3 Letter to Chaim Barlass, Jewish Agency, Jerusalem, unsigned, strictly confidential. Zurich, 7 May 1938, CZA S6-4564, p. 2.

4   Ibid. CZA S6-4564, p. 3.
5   Ibid. CZA S6-4564, p. 4.
6   Gold, *Geschichte der Juden in Wien* (see ch. 1, n. 41), p. 81; Kapralik, *Erinnerungen* (see ch. 4, n. 6), p. 56.
7   Letter to Chaim Barlass, Jewish Agency, Jerusalem, unsigned, strictly confidential. Zurich, 7 May 1938, CZA S6-4564, p. 4.
8   I. Klaber: report on the IKG Vienna 1938; noted in 1944 by Dr Ball-Kaduri; YvS-01/74.
9   Jochen von Lang (ed.), *Das Eichmann-Protokoll. Tonbandaufzeichnungen der israelischen Verhöre* (Berlin, Darmstadt, Vienna, 1985), p. 49.
10   Rosenkranz, *Verfolgung* (see ch. 1, n. 43), p. 275.
11   Landau (see ch. 2, n. 5), p. 12.
12   Rosenkranz, *Verfolgung* (see ch. 1, n. 43), p. 72.
13   Lang, *Eichmann Interrogated* (see ch. 4, n. 11), pp. 50–1.
14   Quoted in Rosenkranz, *Verfolgung*, p. 71.
15   Gold, *Geschichte der Juden in Wien*, p. 81; Kapralik, *Erinnerungen*, p. 56.
16   I. Klaber: Report on the IKG Vienna 1938; noted in 1944 by Dr Ball-Kaduri; YvS-01/74.
17   Leo Landau (see ch. 2, n. 5), p. 12.
18   Kapralik, *Erinnerungen* (see ch. 4, n. 6), p. 57.
19   Letter from Sigmund Seeligmann, Amsterdam, to Benjamin Murmelstein, 12 April 1938; Office of the Chief Rabbi, London, to Benjamin Murmelstein, 3 June 1938. P-151/7.
20   Pierre Genée (May 1989) Record of a two-hour interview with Dr Benjamin Murmelstein, Rome, unpublished. I should like to thank Pierre Genée for making this record available to me.
21   34th weekly report by the IKG Vienna of 3 January 1939, at the same time activity and situation report for the period from 2 May 1938 to 31 December 1938. A/W 165, 1, 3.
22   Kapralik, *Erinnerungen* (see ch. 4, n. 6), p. 62.
23   Letter from the Central Emigration Office C2-2994/39 R/L of 8 December 1939. Bürckel file in the Austrian State Archive, General Administrative Archive. The Reich Commissioner for the reunification of Austria with the German Reich, 1762/1.
24   Gabriele Anderl, 'Emigration und Vertreibung', in Erika Weinzierl and Otto D. Kulka (ed.), *Vertreibung und Neubeginn. Israelische Bürger österreichischer Herkunft* (Vienna, Cologne, Weimar, 1992), p. 202; Rosenkranz, *Verfolgung*, p. 74.

25 Letter to Chaim Barlass, Jewish Agency, Jerusalem, unsigned, strictly confidential. Zurich, 7 May 1938, CZA. S6-4564, p. 5; Confidential report by Georg Landauer, Trieste, to Martin Rosenblüth, London, on his experiences in Vienna, 9 May 1938. CZA, S5-439, here quoted in Rosenkranz, *Verfolgung*, p. 73.

26 Letter from Georg Landauer, Trieste, to the Central Bureau for the Settlement of German Jews in London, 7 May 1938. CZA, S25-9817.

27 Kapralik, *Erinnerungen* (see ch. 4, n. 6), p. 59.

28 Letter from Georg Landauer, Trieste, to the Central Bureau for the Settlement of German Jews in London, 7 May 1938. CZA, S25-9817.

29 Kapralik, *Erinnerungen* (see ch. 4, n. 6), p. 58.

30 Letter from Martin Rosenblüth, 11 July 1938. Quoted in Georg Landauer, letter, Jerusalem, 21 July 1938. CZA, S25-9817.

31 Cf. letters to the SD head of the SS-Oberabschnitt Österreich, 31 May, 6 June and 22 July 1938. Federal Archive Koblenz, R58 (RSHA)/982; Fiche 1,2,3. I should like to thank Erika Wantoch for making these files available to me.

32 Löwenherz report, 17 August 1938.

33 34th weekly report by the IKG Vienna of 3 January 1939, at the same time activity and situation report for the period from 2 May 1938 to 31 December 1938. A/W 165,1, 18.

34 Franzi Löw-Danneberg, interview, in Documentation Archive of Austrian Resistance (ed.), *Jüdische Schicksale. Berichte von Verfolgten* (Vienna, 1992), p. 186f.

35 Franzi Löw-Danneberg, interview, 19 June 1991.

36 Josef Löwenherz to the Liquidation Commissar, 9 January 1939. A/W 165,1; 34th weekly report by the IKG Vienna of 3 January 1939, at the same time activity and situation report for the period from 2 May 1938 to 31 December 1938. A/W 165,1, p. 28f.

37 34th weekly report by the IKG Vienna of 3 January 1939, at the same time activity and situation report for the period from 2 May 1938 to 31 December 1938. A/W 165, 1, 29.

38 Erich Stern, *Die letzten zwölf Jahre Rothschild-Spital Wien: 1931–1943* (Vienna, 1974), pp. 8–10.

39 Rosenkranz, *Verfolgung* (see ch. 1, n. 43), p. 196.

40 Report of the Vienna Jewish Community, Vienna 1940. Library of the IKG Vienna.

41 *Zionistische Rundschau*, 20 May 1938, p. 3.
42 Rosenkranz, *Verfolgung*, p. 140; 34th weekly report by the IKG Vienna of 3 January 1939, at the same time activity and situation report for the period from 2 May 1938 to 31 December 1938. A/W 165,1, 17.
43 Löwenherz report, 1 August 1938.
44 Rosa Rachel Schwarz, *Zwei Jahre Fürsorge der Kultusgemeinde Wien unter Hitler* (Tel Aviv, 14 May 1944), DÖW 2737, 7.
45 Quoted in Rosenkranz, *Verfolgung*, p. 147.
46 Kapralik, *Erinnerungen*, p. 64.
47 *Zionistische Rundschau*, 20 May 1938, 3; Kapralik, *Erinnerungen*, p. 55.
48 Löwenherz report, 20 May 1938.
49 Kapralik, *Erinnerungen* (see ch. 4, n. 6), p. 60.
50 Ibid., p. 60f.
51 Prochnik (see ch. 4, n. 39), p. 6.
52 Rosenkranz, *Verfolgung* (see ch. 1, n. 43), p. 121.
53 Kapralik, *Erinnerungen* (see ch. 4, n. 6), p. 66f.
54 Michman, *Roschut u-manhigut* (see ch. 4, n. 7), pp. 31–41.
55 Jochen von Lang (ed.), *Eichmann Interrogated* (see ch. 4, n. 11), p. 52.
56 Jonny Moser, 'Die Zentralstelle für jüdische Auswanderung in Wien', in Kurt Schmid and Robert Streibel (eds), *Der Pogrom 1938. Judenverfolgung in Österreich und Deutschland* (Vienna, 1990), p. 96f.
57 Draft action programme of a central office for the emigration of the Jews of Austria. YvS-030/94.
58 Rosenkranz, *Verfolgung* (see ch. 1, n. 43), pp. 123–5.
59 Hans Safrian and Hans Witek, *Und keiner war dabei* (see ch. 1, n. 14), p. 42.
60 Rosenkranz, *Verfolgung* (see ch. 1, n. 43), p. 99.
61 Ralph Weingarten, *Die Hilfeleistung der westlichen Welt bei der Endlösung der deutschen Judenfrage. Das 'Intergovernmental Committee on Political Refugees' 1938–1939* (Bern, Frankfurt am Main, Las Vegas, 1981), pp. 83–7; Ehud Avriel, *Open the Gates! The Dramatic Personal Story of 'Illegal' Immigration to Israel* (London, 1975), pp. 24–6.
62 Avriel, *Open the Gates*, p. 15.
63 Berit Trumpeldor, Vienna, to the Palestine office, Vienna, 12 February 1937; Rothenberg, Palestine Office, to Berit Trumpeldor, Vienna, 16 February 1937; Palestine Office, Vienna, to the Jewish Agency, Jerusalem, 16 February 1937;

Executive of the Jewish Agency in Jerusalem to the Palestine Office, Vienna, 11 March 1937. CZA, S6-3118.

64 Palestine Office, Vienna, to Werner Senator, 1 April 1937; Chaim Barlass to Rothenberg, 12 April 1937; Chaim Barlass to the Palestine Office, Vienna, 27 April 1937; Palestine Office, Vienna, to the Jewish Agency, Jerusalem, 7 May 1937; Chaim Barlass to the Palestine Office, Vienna, 20 May 1937. CZA, S6-3118.

65 Perl, *Operation Action* (see ch. 4, n. 24), p. 25 and pp. 44–58.

66 Yehuda Bauer, *Jews for Sale?* (New Haven, Connecticut, 1994), p. 48.

67 Perl, *Operation Action* (see ch. 4, n. 24), p. 71.

68 Anderl, *Emigration* (see n. 24 above), p. 260f.

CHAPTER 6   NOVEMBER POGROM – OVERTURE TO MURDER

1 Safrian, *Und keiner war dabei* (see ch. 1, n. 14), p. 159.

2 Landau (see ch. 2, n. 5), p. 19.

3 Ibid., p. 20.

4 Ibid., p. 21.

5 Rosenkranz, *Verfolgung* (see ch. 1, n. 43), p. 195.

6 Gerhard Botz, *Wohnungspolitik und Judendeportation in Wien 1938–1945. Zur Funktion des Antisemitismus als Ersatz nationalsozialistischer Sozialpolitik* (Vienna, Salzburg, 1975), p. 402; Safrian *Und keiner war dabei* (see ch. 1, n. 14), p. 160.

7 Josef Löwenherz to Adolf Eichmann, 6 January 1939. A/W 165,1.

8 Löwenherz report, 2 March 1939.

9 Safrian, *Und keiner war dabei* (see ch. 1, n. 14), p. 162.

10 Cf. Yitzhak Arad, Yisrael Gutman and Abraham Margaliot, *Documents on the Holocaust. Selected Sources on the Destruction of the Jews of Germany and Austria, Poland and the Soviet Union* (Jerusalem: Yad Vashem, 1987), p. 117.

11 Gold, *Geschichte der Juden in Wien* (see ch. 1, n. 41), p. 97; Hilberg, *The Destruction of the European Jews*, vol. 1, p. 172.

12 Erika Weinzierl, *Zu wenig Gerechte. Österreicher und Judenverfolgung 1938–1945* (Graz, Vienna: Verlag Styria, 1969), p. 36.

CHAPTER 7   THE JEWISH COMMUNITY AFTER THE POGROM

1   Löwenherz report, 29 November 1938.
2   Cf. Josef Löwenherz to Gestapo headquarters, 1 January 1939. A/W 165,1; Benjamin Murmelstein to Gestapo headquarters, 17 January 1939. A/W 165,1.
3   Josef Löwenherz to Adolf Eichmann, 16 February 1939. A/W 165,2.
4   Löwenherz reports, 16 and 28 March 1939.
5   Rosenkranz, *Verfolgung* (see ch. 1, n. 43), pp. 208–10 and 233f.
6   Josef Löwenherz to Adolf Eichmann, request for Desider Friedmann, 5 January 1939. A/W 165,1; Josef Löwenherz to Adolf Eichmann, request for Robert Stricker, 5 January 1939. A/W 165,1; Josef Löwenherz to Gestapo, request for Desider Friedmann, 5 January 1939. A/W 165,1; Josef Löwenherz to Adolf Eichmann, curriculum vitae of Desider Friedmann and Robert Stricker, 8 February 1939. A/W 165,2; Josef Löwenherz to Gestapo, 3 April 1939. A/W 165,4; Löwenherz report, 10 February 1939.
7   Rosenkranz, *Verfolgung* (see ch. 1, n. 43), p. 168f.
8   Kapralik, *Erinnerungen* (see ch. 4, n. 6), p. 72.
9   Martin Vogel, interview, 12 May 1989.
10   Rosenkranz, *Verfolgung* (see ch. 1, n. 43), p. 177.
11   Schwarz (see ch. 4, n. 3).
12   Löwenherz report, December 1938.
13   Report of the Vienna Jewish Community, Wien 1940; Bibliothek der IKG Wien; Schwarz (see ch. 4, n. 3).
14   *Auswanderung – Umschichtung – Fürsorge, Wien 1939*. Library of the IKG Vienna, Pc 147.
15   Weinzierl, *Zu wenig Gerechte* (see ch. 6, n. 12), p. 52.
16   Rosenkranz, *Verfolgung* (see ch. 1, n. 43), p. 71.
17   *Zionistische Rundschau, Wochenschrift*, Vienna, 20 May–4 November 1938.
18   The postcard is enclosed with the Vienna university library's 1938 volume of the *Zionistische Rundschau*.
19   Herbert Freeden, *Die jüdische Presse im Dritten Reich* (Frankfurt am Main, 1987), p. 172.
20   YvS-01/133. Quoted in Freeden, *Presse* (see n. 19 above), p. 173.
21   Löwenherz report, 4 January 1939.
22   Freeden *Presse* (see n. 19 above), p. 178f.

23 Ibid., p. 179.
24 Weekly reports of the IKG Vienna; A/W 112.
25 M. Mitzmann *A Visit to Germany, Austria and Poland in 1939*. YvS-02-151, 12a.
26 Memo of a telephone call from SS-Hauptsturmführer Adolf Eichmann, 21 December 1938, A/W 3022.
27 Löwenherz report, 31 July 1939.
28 Ibid., 3, 7 and 11 August 1939.
29 Heinrich Stahl to the IKG and Palestine Office, 1 March 1939. YvS-Tr3-1120.
30 Josef Löwenherz and Alois Rothenberg: memo of the meeting with SS-Hauptsturmführer Eichmann, 9 March 1939. YvS-Tr3-1120.
31 Michman (see ch. 5, n. 2), p. 198.
32 Benno Cohn, Summons of Representatives of German Jewry in March 1939; report n.d. by Dr Ball-Kaduri, p. 2 April 1958; YvS-01/215.
33 Ibid.
34 Ephraim [Erich] Frank: Summons of the representatives of the Jewish umbrella organizations in Berlin, Vienna and Prague to the Gestapo in Berlin in March 1940. Tel Aviv, 2 April 1958, reported noted by Dr Ball-Kaduri, YvS-01/227.
35 Letter to Josef Löwenherz, 27 November 1939, A/W 181.
36 Charlotte Ambrus to Sofie Löwenherz, 26 July 1940, A/W 180,1.
37 Charlotte Ambrus to the Gestapo, July 1940. A/W 180,1; cf. Rosenkranz *Verfolgung*, pp. 110–14.
38 Josef Löwenherz to Prof. Dr M. Ehrenpreis, 10 February 1941, A/W 180,1.
39 Benjamin Murmelstein, *Adam. Ein Beitrag zur Messiaslehre*, dissertation (Vienna, 1927).
40 Cf. Rosenkranz, *Verfolgung* (see ch. 1, n. 43), p. 37f.
41 Pierre Genée (May 1989) record of two long interviews with Dr Benjamin Murmelstein, Rome, unpublished. I should like to thank Pierre Genée for making this memo available to me.
42 Benjamin Murmelstein, *Einige Fragen an Prof. Dr P. Severin Grill O. Cist. Verfasser der theologischen Studie 'Der Talmud und Schulchan Aruch'* (Vienna, 1935).
43 Benjamin Murmelstein, *Geschichte der Juden* (Vienna, 1938), p. 406.
44 Pierre Genée (see n. 41 above).

45 Cf. Sigmund Seeligmann to Benjamin Murmelstein, Amsterdam, 12 April 1938; Office of the Chief Rabbi to Benjamin Murmelstein, London, 3 June 1938, P-151/7.

46 Pierre Genée (see n. 41 above).

47 Josef Löwenherz to Bernhard Altmann, 1 December 1938, A/W 180,1; Josef Löwenherz, testimonial for Murmelstein, 1 December 1939, A/W 180,1; Josef Löwenherz to Morris C. Tropper, 25 September 1940, A/W 180,1; Josef Löwenherz to M. Ehrenpreis, 23 January 1941, A/W 180,1; Josef Löwenherz to M. Ehrenpreis, 10 February 1941, A/W 180,1; Josef Löwenherz to M. Ehrenpreis, 14 February 1940, A/W 180,1; Desider Friedmann to M. Ehrenpreis, 11 March 1941, A/W 180,1.

48 Josef Löwenherz to Emil Engel, 10 October 1940, A/W 180,1.

49 Pierre Genée (see n. 41 above).

50 Lang, *Eichmann Interrogated* (see ch. 4, n. 11), p. 55f.

51 Hans Günther Adler, *Theresienstadt. 1941–1945. Das Antlitz einer Zwangsgemeinschaft. Geschichte, Soziologie, Psychologie* (Tübingen, 1955), p. 117.

52 Willy Stern, interview, 2 May 1991.

53 Order of services for 30 September to 6 October 1938, A/W 136.

54 Willy Stern, interview, 2 May 1991.

55 Franzi Löw-Danneberg, interview, 19 June 1991.

56 Schwarz (see ch. 4, n. 3).

57 Ibid.

58 Cf. Benjamin Murmelstein, 'Das Ende von Theresienstadt. Stellungnahme eines Beteiligten', *Neue Zürcher Zeitung* (17 December 1963), p. 3; Benjamin Murmelstein, 'Das Ende des Ghettos Theresienstadt. Die Stellungnahme eines Beteiligten. Eine Antwort an diejenigen, die nicht dabeigewesen sind', *Die Welt* (14 January 1964), p. 6.

59 Cf. Interim report of the Vienna police headquarters, 13 May 1946, criminal proceedings against Robert Prochnik, Provincial Court Archive, Vienna, Vg 8c Vr 3532/48, continued under Vg 8c Vr 41/542; Statement by Dr Heinrich Klang, criminal proceedings against Robert Prochnik, Provincial Court Archive Vienna Vg 8c Vr 3532/48, continuation under Vg 8c Vr 41/542; testimony of Robert Prochnik, 24 June 1954, criminal proceedings against Robert Prochnik, Provincial Court Archive, Vienna, Vg 8c Vr 3532/48, continued under Vg 8c Vr 41/542.

60 Willy Stern, interview, 2 May 1991.

61 Benjamin Murmelstein (ed.), *Flavius Josephus* (Vienna, 1938), p. 5; Pierre Genée also ended his report with this quote, cf. Genée (see n. 41 above).

62 List of employees, 13 March 1938, A/W 558.

63 Handwritten list and recapitulation of employees in autumn 1938, A/W 559.

64 Meeting of Löwenherz, Engel, Stössel, Murmelstein, 16 October 1938, A/W 3022.

65 Cf. Max Goldschmidt to Josef Löwenherz, 7 May 1939, A/W 180,2; Dr Theodor Blau to the board, 7 May 1939, A/W 180,2.

66 Official permission for Rosa Schwarz to be on the streets after 4 p.m., A/W 2699,2.

67 Josef Löwenherz to the head of municipal council group I for the attention of senior senate councillor Dr Otto Schaufler, 10 March 1939, A/W 165,3; Emil Engel to the NSDAP housing department, 16 January 1939, A/W 165,1.

68 Löwenherz report, 3 August 1939.

69 Emil Tuchmann, report of my activities in the Vienna IKG during the Nazi regime from 1938 to 1945, criminal proceedings against Dr Emil Tuchmann, Provincial Court Archive, Vienna, Vg 3c 1955/45; 12.

70 Josef Löwenherz, monthly salaries over RM 200, 2. June 1940, A/W 165,6.

71 List of average salaries, A/W 165,6.

72 Emil Engel, personnel expenses, 4 June 1940, A/W 165,6.

73 Josef Löwenherz, redundancies, 18 June 1940, A/W 165,6.

74 Record of the recruitment of Ignatz Marlé, 21 October 1938, A/W 624,13.

75 Cf. Ignatz Marlé file, A/W 624,13.

76 Leopold Ferster to Ignatz Marlé, 1 July 1940, A/W 624,13.

77 Ignatz Marlé to Josef Löwenherz, 1 July 1940, A/W 624,13.

78 Ibid.

79 Josef Löwenherz to all IKG employees, 1 May 1940, A/W 134,3; Josef Löwenherz to all IKG employees, 27 October 1940, A/W 134,3.

80 Josef Löwenherz to the Employment Office, 17 May 1940, A/W 165,5.

81 Willy Stern, interview, in Dokumentationsarchiv des österreichischen Widerstands (ed.), *Jüdische Schicksale*, p. 289.

82 Willy Stern, interview, 15 April 1998.

83 Franzi Löw-Danneberg, interview, 19 June 1991.

84 Wilhelm Bienenfeld to the Gestapo headquarters, 21 July 1940, A/W 3022.

85 Ibid.

86 Database query in the project 'Register of names of Austrian Holocaust victims', DÖW.

87 Avriel *Open the Gates!* (see ch. 5, n. 61), pp. 6f., 16f. and 26.

88 Elisabeth Klamper, *'We'll Meet Again in Palestine': Aron Menczer's Fight to Save Jewish Children in Nazi Vienna* (Vienna, 1996).

89 Rosenkranz, *Verfolgung* (see ch. 1, n. 43), p. 246.

90 Klamper, *Aron Menczer* (see n. 88 above), pp. 30 and 36.

91 Rosenkranz, *Verfolgung* (see ch. 1, n. 43), pp. 55 and 83–5.

92 Interview with Rudolf Hönigsfeld recorded by Herbert Rosenkranz, 29 July 1975, YvS-03/3908.

93 Rosenkranz, *Verfolgung* (see ch. 1, n. 43), pp. 193 and 239f.

94 Curriculum vitae of Berthold Storfer, 27 May 1940, A/W 165,5.

95 Rosenkranz, *Verfolgung* (see ch. 1, n. 43), pp. 34 and 98.

96 Heinrich Neumann and Berthold Storfer, *Bericht über die Evianer Konferenz für das Wanderungsamt*, 23 July 1938, quoted in Anderl, *Storfer*, p. 23.

97 File memo, 5 August 1938, quoted in Anderl, *Storfer*, p. 24.

98 Anderl, *Storfer*, p. 24.

99 Löwenherz reports, 27 March and 30 March 1940.

100 Avriel, *Open the Gates!* (see ch. 5, n. 61), p. 75.

101 Quoted in Anderl, *Storfer*, p. 26.

102 Avriel, *Open the Gates!* (see ch. 5, n. 61), p. 73.

103 Erich Frank, 26 January 1941, CZA; S7-966. Here quoted in Anderl, *Storfer*, p. 27.

104 Ephraim (Erich) Frank, report, Tel Aviv, 2 May 1958. Recorded by Dr Ball-Kaduri, YvS-01/227. Quoted in Anderl, *Storfer*, p. 27.

105 Jewish Emigration Aid Prague to Berthold Storfer, 21 November 1940, A/W 2515. Here quoted in Anderl, *Storfer*, p. 27.

106 Josef Löwenherz to Emil Engel, 10 October 1940, A/W 180,1.

107 Cf. Anderl, *Storfer*, p. 26.

108 Pierre Genée (May 1989), record of two long interviews with Dr Benjamin Murmelstein, Rome, unpublished.

109 Criminal proceedings against Johann Rixinger, Provincial Court Archive, Vienna, Vg 11g Vr 1866/46.

110 Arendt, *Eichmann in Jerusalem* (see ch. 1, n. 40), p. 51.

111 Ibid.

CHAPTER 8 BEGINNING OF THE END

1 Wilhelm Bienenfeld, report on the IKG during the Nazi era, 10 September 1939. People's Court proceedings against Karl Ebner, DÖW 8919/1. The report is known as the 'Löwenherz report'.
2 Ibid.
3 Jonny Moser Nisko, 'Ein geplantes Judenreservat in Polen', *Das jüdische Echo* 38 (1989): 119.
4 Weinzierl, *Zu wenig Gerechte* (see ch. 6, n. 12), p. 70.
5 Josef Löwenherz, file memo on meeting with Obersturmführer Günther at the Central Office for Jewish Emigration on 10 October 1939. YvS-Tr 3-1135; ibid. A/W465, p. 23f.
6 Ibid.
7 Ibid.
8 Moser, *Nisko* (see n. 3 above), p. 120.
9 Josef Löwenherz, file memo on a meeting with Obersturmführer Günther on 17 October 1939. A/W 465, 26.
10 Willy Stern, interview, 7 June 1989.
11 Moser, *Nisko* (see n. 3 above), p. 120.
12 Rosenkranz, *Verfolgung* (see ch. 1, n. 43), p. 217.
13 Moser, *Nisko* (see n. 3 above), p. 121.
14 Josef Löwenherz to the Central Office for Jewish Emigration, Vienna; request to desist from sending Dr Benjamin Murmelstein to Mähr.-Ostrau, 11 October 1939. YvS-030/25.
15 Löwenherz report, 27 September 1940.
16 Note by order of SS-Hauptsturmführer Eichmann. Subject: Withdrawal of Jewish functionaries, 13 October 1939. YvS-030/25; Moser *Nisko* (see n. 3 above), p. 12; Prochnik (see ch. 4, n. 39), p. 23.
17 Löwenherz report, 20 and 27 October 1939.
18 Gold, *Geschichte der Juden in Wien* (see ch. 1, n. 41), p. 100.
19 Benjamin Murmelstein, *Terezin. Il Ghetto-Modello di Eichmann* (Bologna: Capelli Editori, 1961), p. 5.
20 Gold, *Geschichte der Juden in Wien* (see ch. 1, n. 41), p. 100.
21 Prochnik, *Die Situation der Juden im Dritten Reich* (see n. 16 above), p. 23.
22 Julius Boschan, Nisko, to Josef Löwenherz, Vienna, 31 October 1939. A/W 271,2.
23 Murmelstein, *Terezin* (see n. 19 above), pp. 5–8; cf. Ruth Bondy, *'Elder of the Jews'. Jakob Edelstein of Theresienstadt* (New York, 1989), p. 159–65.

24 Central Office for Jewish Emigration in Nisko, 6 November 1939, P-151,12; Rosenkranz *Verfolgung*, p. 344.

25 Julius Boschan, Nisko, to Josef Löwenherz, Vienna, 31 October 1939. A/W 271,2.

26 Report by a member of the second Nisko transport, 10 January 1940. A/W 2794. Quoted in Florian Freund and Hans Safrian (1993) *Vertreibung und Ermordung. Zum Schicksal der österreichischen Juden 1938–1945. Das Projekt 'Namentliche Erfassung der österreichischen Holocaustopfer'*. DÖW, Vienna, p. 14f.

27 Telegramme, 10 January 1940, A/W 180,1; Telegramme from Richard Weich in Lemberg to Emil Engel, 13 January 1940, A/W 180,1.

28 Weinzierl, *Zu wenig Gerechte* (see ch. 6, n. 12), p. 72; Moser, *Nisko* (see n. 3 above), p. 121f.

29 Rosenkranz, *Verfolgung* (see ch. 1, n. 43), p. 218.

30 Löwenherz reports, 13 and 19 December 1939.

31 Löwenherz report, 26 January 1940.

32 Michael R. Marrus and Robert E. Paxton, *Vichy et les Juifs* (Paris, 1983), p. 158.

33 Weinzierl, *Zu wenig Gerechte* (see ch. 6, n. 12), pp. 45 and 50.

34 Elisabeth Klamper, 'Die Situation der jüdischen Bevölkerung in Wien vom Ausbruch bis zum Ende des Krieges', in Dokumentationsarchiv des österreichischen Widerstands (ed.), *Jüdische Schicksale. Berichte von Verfolgten* (Vienna, 1992), p. 164.

35 Emil Engel, endorsement for Josef Löwenherz, 13 February 1940, YvS-030/4.

36 Josef Löwenherz to police headquarters, 17 May 1940, A/W 165,5.

37 Josef Löwenherz to the Gestapo, 22 June 1940, A/W 165,5.

38 Löwenherz reports, 10 March and 25 November 1940; cf. memo on meeting by Löwenherz with Eichmann of the same date, YvS-Tr3-1139.

39 Julius Rosenfeld, report, April 1956. YvS-01/177; 2f.

40 'Räumungsauftrag ohne Zuweisung', A/W 165,6; Ignaz Karniol, 24 May 1940, A/W165,6.

41 Jakob Padawer, undated, A/W 165,6; Valérie Grünwald, 31 May 1940, A/W 165,6.

42 Cf. criminal proceedings against Bernhard Wittke before the Provincial Court for Criminal Matters, Vienna. Provincial Court Archive, Vg 2b Vr 2331/45.

43 Botz, *Wohnungspolitik* (see ch. 1, n. 44), p. 102.
44 Gerhard Botz, *Wien vom Anschluß zum Krieg. Nationalsozialistische Machtübernahme und politisch-soziale Umgestaltung am Beispiel der Stadt Wien 1938/39* (Vienna, Munich, 1978), p. 463.
45 Löwenherz report, 16 June 1940.
46 Julius Rosenfeld, report, April 1956. YvS-01/177; 2; Löwenherz report, 1 November 1940.

CHAPTER 9 DEPORTATION AND EXTERMINATION

1 Else Rosenfeld and Gertrud Luckner, *Lebenszeichen aus Piaski. Briefe Deportierter aus dem Distrikt Lublin 1940–1943* (Munich, 1968), p. 168. Also quoted in Rosenkranz *Verfolgung* (see ch. 1, n. 43), p. 262.
2 Wilhelm Bienenfeld, Report on the IKG during the Nazi era, 4 July 1940. People's Court proceedings against, DÖW 8919/1. The report is known as the Löwenherz report.
3 Memo by Bormann on a discussion in Hitler's residence on 2 October 1940 about the Generalgouvernement. Quoted in Safrian *Eichmann's Men* (see ch. 1, n. 5), p. 68.
4 Ibid.
5 Copy of a letter by Reich Minister and head of the Reich Chancellery, Berlin, 3 December 1940, to the Reichsstatthalter in Vienna, Gauleiter v. Schirach. YvS-018/213. Quoted in Safrian *Eichmann's Men* (see ch. 1, n. 5), p. 68.
6 Löwenherz report, 23 January 1941.
7 Josef Löwenherz, memo of the meeting in the Gestapo with Reg. Rat Dr Ebner in the presence of SS-Obersturmführer Brunner on 1 February 1941. YvS-Tr-1147.
8 Ibid.
9 Ibid.
10 Ibid.
11 Löwenherz report, 1 February 1941.
12 Ibid.
13 Josef Löwenherz, fifth weekly report and first monthly report by the IKG Vienna, 4 February 1941. A/W 114, 6.
14 Josef Löwenherz, sixth weekly report of the IKG Vienna, 11 February 1941. A/W 114, 4.
15 Cf. testimony of Wilhelm Bienenfeld, criminal proceedings against Johann Rixinger before the Provincial Court for

223

Criminal Matters, Vienna, as People's Court. Archive of the Provincial Court. Vg 11 g Vr 4866/46/HV 1319/47; 49; conflict prevention. also the following chapter.

16 Rosenkranz, *Verfolgung* (see ch. 1, n. 43), p. 261.
17 Löwenherz report, 17.6.1941.
18 Freund and Safrian, *Vertreibung* (see ch. 8, n. 26), pp. 19–21.
19 Löwenherz reports, 1 June and 8 September 1941.
20 Ibid.
21 Florian Freund, Bertram Perz and Karl Stuhlpfarrer, 'Das Getto in Litzmannstadt (Lodz)', in Hanno Loewy and Gerhard Schoenberner (eds), *'Unser einziger Weg ist Arbeit'. Das Getto in Lodz. 1940–1944* (Vienna, 1990), p. 17.
22 Josef Löwenherz, memo on a meeting at Gestapo headquarters with SS-Obersturmführer Brunner on 30 September 1941, 2 October 1941. YvS-Tr-1151.
23 Prochnik (see ch. 4, n. 39), p. 59.
24 Freund and Safrian, *Vertreibung* (see ch. 8, n. 26), p. 22f.; Moser, *Die Judenverfolgung 1938–1945* (see ch. 1, n. 42), pp. 28–30; Rosenkranz, *Verfolgung* (see ch. 1, n. 43), p. 285.
25 Löwenherz reports, 27 October, 5 and 13 November 1941.
26 Ibid., 13 November 1941.
27 Freund and Safrian, *Vertreibung* (see ch. 8, n. 26), p. 22f.; Moser, *Judenverfolgung* (see ch. 1, n. 42), pp. 28–30; Rosenkranz, *Verfolgung* (see ch. 1, n. 43), pp. 23–5.
28 Moser, *Judenverfolgung* (see ch. 1, n. 42), p. 28.
29 Freund and Safrian, *Vertreibung* (see ch. 8, n. 26), pp. 25–8.
30 Report of a deportee from Vienna to Minsk on 6 May 1942, DÖW 854. Quoted in Freund und Safrian, *Vertreibung* (see ch. 8, n. 26), p. 28.
31 Freund and Safrian, *Vertreibung* (see ch. 8, n. 26), pp. 28–31.
32 Löwenherz report, 19 February 1942.
33 152nd Police Station: incident report, Vienna, 20 June 1942 regarding transport unit for transport of Jews from Vienna Aspangbahnhof to Sobibor on 14 June 1942; YvS-051/63.
34 Ibid.
35 Ibid.
36 Moser, *Judenverfolgung* (see ch. 1, n. 42), p. 46.
37 Jonny Moser, 'Die Katastrophe der Juden in Österreich – ihre Voraussetzungen und ihre Überwindung', in *Der gelbe Stern in Österreich* (Eisenstadt, 1977), p. 130.
38 Willy Stern, interview, 7 June 1989; Franzi Löw-Danneberg, interview, 19 June 1991.

224

39 Report on the activity of the Council of Elders of the Jews in Vienna in 1943. A/W 117.
40 Freund and Safrian, *Vertreibung* (see ch. 8, n. 26), p. 37.
41 Brigitte Ungar-Klein, 'Leben im Verborgenen – Schicksale der "U-Boote"', in Dokumentationsarchiv des österreichischen Widerstands (ed.), *Jüdische Schicksale. Berichte von Verfolgten* (Vienna, 1992), p. 604.
42 Quoted in Rosenkranz, *Verfolgung* (see ch. 1, n. 43), p. 302.

CHAPTER 10   THE ADMINISTRATION OF EXTERMINATION

1 Munisch (Menashe) Mautner, *Erinnerungen an Wien 1938–1942* (Tel Aviv, 1956), YvS-01/163, 8f.
2 Paul Eppstein and Josef Löwenherz, memo of summons to the Reich Security Main Office by Sturmbannführer Günther and Sturmbannführer Regierungsrat Suhr, 6 September 1941, YvS-Tr-1150.
3 Police order on the identification of Jews, issued in Berlin on 5 September 1941, A/W 466,1.
4 Paul Eppstein and Josef Löwenherz, memo of summons to the Reich Security Main Office by Sturmbannführer Günther and Sturmbannführer Regierungsrat Suhr, 6 September 1941, YvS-Tr-1150.
5 Ibid.; police order on the identification of Jews, issued in Berlin on 5 September 1941, A/W 466,1.
6 Paul Eppstein and Arthur Lilienthal, Reichsvereinigung der Juden in Deutschland, circular, 9 September 1941, A/W 466,1.
7 Benjamin Murmelstein, Guidelines on implementation of the police order on the identification of Jews, 10 September 1941, A/W 466,1.
8 Benjamin Murmelstein, memo regarding identification of Jews, 10 September 1941, A/W 466,1.
9 Willy Stern, interview, 25 March 1998.
10 IKG Vienna: Communication in connection with the distribution of the Jewish identification marking in accordance with the police order of 1 September 1941, 17 September 1941, A/W 137.
11 Oberbahnrat Schön to Amtsdirektion, 18 September 1941, A/W 466,1; search of electronic database in the project 'Registration by name: Austrian victims of the Holocaust', DÖW.

12 Instructions regarding the police order on the identification of Jews, A/W 466,1.

13 Ibid.

14 Order forms for Jewish stars, A/W 466,2.

15 IKG Vienna: communication regarding an official order of 1 April 1942, A/W 137; issue of identification of Jewish dwellings, 1942, A/W 431.

16 IKG Vienna: communication, 4 April 1942; A/W 137.

17 Report on the activities of the IKG Vienna and the Council of Elders of the Jews in Vienna in 1942; A/W 116.

18 Fritz Rubin-Bittmann, 'Leben in Wien, Illusion ohne Ende, Ende einer Illusion', in Wolfgang Plat (ed.), *Voll Leben und voll Tod ist diese Erde. Bilder aus der Geschichte der jüdischen Österreicher (1190 bis 1945)* (Vienna, 1988), p. 313.

19 Josef Löwenherz: memo of a meeting in the Reich Ministry of the Interior, Reich Security Main Office Berlin, department IV B 4, on Friday, 29 May 1942, 10.30 a.m., and with SS Obersturmbannführer Eichmann on Saturday, 30 May 1942 at 12.30 p.m. in the same office; 1 June 1942; YvS-Tr-1156.

20 Bruno Blau, *Das Ausnahmerecht für die Juden in Deutschland 1933–1945* (Düsseldorf, 1965), p. 94.

21 11th Regulation on the Reich Citizenship Act of 25 November 1941, quoted in Blau, *Ausnahmerecht* (see n. 20 above), p. 99.

22 Josef Löwenherz: circular to the Jews in the Ostmark, 1 December 1941; A/W 137. Cf. also: Order by the supervisory authorities on restrictions on movable assets of Jews of 1 December 1941, quoted in Blau, *Ausnahmerecht* (see n. 20 above), p. 102. See also Schreiben zur Beachtung (betrifft Verfügung über bewegliches Vermögen der Juden); A/W 137.

23 Löwenherz reports, 21 May 1941, 29 May 1941, 1 June 1941, 2 July 1941. Management board: memo concerning old people's homes, 22 May 1942; A/W 274; also: A/W 1884.

24 Walter Brumlik-Fantl, interview, 2 September 1998; Herbert Schrott, interview, 2 September 1998.

25 Löwenherz report, 16 December 1941.

26 Criminal proceedings against Johann Rixinger before the Provincial Criminal Court of Vienna as People's; Vg 11g Vr 4866/46 / HV 1319/47; 54 and 59.

27 See also evacuation, 16 March 1942; A/W 434.

28 Management board, room 8, regarding evacuations; report 1–31 July 1942; A/W 434.

29 Official order concerning the handing over of fur and wool items, 10 January 1942, quoted in Blau, *Ausnahmerecht* (see n. 20 above), p. 103; see also Order for the handling over of clothing items, *Jüdisches Nachrichtenblatt*, 9 June 1942, quoted in Blau, *Ausnahmerecht*, p. 108.

30 Order concerning the handing over of optical appliances, etc., *Jüdisches Nachrichtenblatt*, 19 June 1942, quoted in Blau, *Ausnahmerecht* (see n. 20 above), p. 109.

31 Report on the activity of the IKG and Council of Elders in 1942; A/W 116; 13.

32 Löwenherz report, 10 October 1942.

33 See Josef Löwenherz, head of the Council of Elders, to police department for the 2nd district, accounts department, regarding property tax, 29 January 1943; A/W 3022.

34 Löwenherz reports, 10 and 31 October 1942.

35 13th regulation on the Reich Citizenship Act, 1 July 1943, quoted in: Blau, *Ausnahmerecht* (see n. 20 above), p. 115.

36 See Raul Hilberg, *The Destruction of the European Jews* (Ch. 1, n. 30), vol. 2, pp. 417–30.

37 Prochnik (see ch. 4, n. 39), p. 59.

38 Ibid.

39 Löwenherz report, 1 February 1941.

40 Jewish blind self-help group to Josef Löwenherz, 25 February 1941; A/W 273; 1587.

41 In this regard I do not agree with those researchers who believe that the Jewish administration chose the replacements itself. See Rosenkranz, *Verfolgung* (see ch. 1, n. 43), p. 285. The reference in the files to the fact that the 'Kultusgemeinde had to provide replacements' is merely bureaucratic language stating unclearly that other members of the Jewish community were designated – by the Nazi authorities – instead of those with deferrals. I base this on the statements by Wilhelm Bienenfeld and by the Nazi perpetrators Johann Rixinger and Anton Brunner.

42 Testimony of Wilhelm Bienenfeld, criminal proceedings against Johann Rixinger before the Provincial Criminal Court of Vienna as People's Court, Provincial Court Archive; Vg 11g Vr 4866/46/HV 1319/47; 49.

43 Testimony of Emil Gottesmann, criminal proceedings against Johann Rixinger before the Provincial Criminal Court of Vienna as People's Court, Provincial Court Archive; Vg 11g Vr 4866/46/HV 1319/47; 63.

44 Ibid.; Vg 11g Vr 4866/46/HV 1319/47; 63 und 65.

45 Statement by Robert Prochnik, 24 June 1954, criminal proceedings against Robert Prochnik before the Provincial Criminal Court of Vienna as People's Court, Provincial Court Archive; Vg 8c Vr 3532/48, continuation: Vg 8c Vr 41/542; 63f.

46 Testimony of Wilhelm Bienenfeld, criminal proceedings against Johann Rixinger before the Provincial Criminal Court of Vienna as People's Court, Provincial Court Archive; Vg 11g Vr 4866/46 / HV 1319/47; 55.

47 Hermann Altmann to Josef Löwenherz, October 1941; A/W 180,2.

48 Database query, 'Registration by name: Austrian victims of the Holocaust'; DÖW.

49 Kurt Mezei: Tagebuch 13.8.1941–30.11.1941; Jüdisches Museum Wien; Inventarnr. 4465/3.

50 Transcript of statement by Siegfried Kolisch, 30 August 1945, criminal proceedings against Dr Emil Tuchmann before the Provincial Criminal Court of Vienna as People's Court, Provincial Court Archive, Vg 3c 1955/45; 24; statement by Robert Prochnik (see n. 45 above), Vg 8c Vr 3532/48, continuation: Vg 8c Vr 41/542; 66 and 10.

51 Ibid.

52 Ibid.

53 Minutes of war victims' conference chaired by Kolisch, 30 September 1941; YIVO; 0cc E 6a-18. Copy courtesy of YIVO Hans Safrian.

54 Memo by Siegfried Kolisch, 13 and 14 October 1941, YIVO; occ E 6a-18.

55 Hilberg, *Destruction of the European Jews* (see Ch. 1, n. 30), vol. 2, p. 433.

56 Kolisch (see n. 54 above).

57 Fürth, memo, 15 October 1941, YIVO; 0cc E 6a-18.

58 Kolisch (see n. 54 above).

59 Minutes of war victims' conference (see n. 53 above).

60 Ibid.

61 Ibid.

62 Ibid.

63 Ibid.

64 Siegfried Kolisch, list of war invalids and front soldiers employed by the Kultusgemeinde and members of the association, 14 August 1942, YIVO; occ E 6a-18.

65 Löwenherz report, 4 September 1942.

66 Transcript of statement by Wilhelm Bienenfeld, 3 September 1945, criminal proceedings against Dr Emil Tuchmann before the Provincial Criminal Court of Vienna as People's Court, Provincial Court Archive; Vg 3c 1955/45; 30. Questioning of the defendant Emil Tuchmann, 15 September 1945, ibid., Vg 3c 1955/45; 67.

67 Criminal proceedings against Dr Emil Tuchmann before the Provincial Criminal Court of Vienna as People's Court, Provincial Court Archive, Vg 3c 1955/45.

68 Franz Hahn, interview, 3 September 1998.

69 Transcript of statement by Max Birnstein, 22 October 1945, criminal proceedings against Dr Emil Tuchmann before the Provincial Criminal Court of Vienna as People's Court, Provincial Court Archive; Vg 3c 1955/45; 91. Franz Hahn, interview, 3 September 1998.

70 Former Gestapo prisoners: letter, 20 April 1945, criminal proceedings against Dr Emil Tuchmann before the Provincial Criminal Court of Vienna as People's Court, Provincial Court Archive; Vg 3c 1955/45; 117/a.

71 Final report, criminal proceedings against Dr Emil Tuchmann before the Provincial Criminal Court of Vienna as People's Court, Provincial Court Archive; Vg 3c 1955/45.

72 Council of Elders of the Jews in Vienna (ed.), Report of activities in 1944; A/W 118; 47–9.

73 Rosenkranz, *Verfolgung* (see ch. 1, n. 43), p. 302.

74 IKG Vienna: To all members of the community; YvS-030/4.

75 IKG Vienna: Directive; A/W 137. Transcript of statement by Bruno Feyer, 1 September 1945, criminal proceedings against Leopold Balaban before the Provincial Criminal Court of Vienna as People's Court, Provincial Court Archive; Vg 2 f Vr 2943/45; 29.

76 Testimony of Anton Brunner, criminal proceedings against Anton Brunner before the Provincial Criminal Court of Vienna as People's Court, Provincial Court Archive; Vg 2d VR 4574/45; 16.

77 Transcript of statements by Wilhelm Bienenfeld and Leo Balaban, criminal proceedings against Dr Emil Tuchmann before the Provincial Criminal Court of Vienna as People's Court, Provincial Court Archive; Vg 3c 1955/45. Allocation to transport selection unit, 28 June 1942; A/W 574. Deportation transports, 25 April–2 May 1942; A/W 2756. The description

of Murmelstein by Fritz Rubin-Bittmann in his otherwise interesting document is not consistent with my research. The relationship between Murmelstein and Eichmann is described by Rubin-Bittmann as 'excellent' without account being taken of the different interests characterizing a relationship between perpetrator and victim. Murmelstein never allocated more people for transport than Eichmann instructed. See Rubin-Bittmann, *Leben in Wien, Illusion ohne Ende, Ende einer Illusion*, pp. 303 and 309. The rumour that Murmelstein allocated more people for transport than demanded is probably based on a false interpretation of an interview with Menasche Munisch in Rosenkranz, *Verfolgung* (see ch. 1, n. 43), p. 285.

78 IKG Vienna: To the researchers; A/W 2750.
79 Walter Lindenbaum, 'Das Couplet von den Rechercheuren', in Kurt Mezei, *Liederheft; handschriftlich; Wien um 1941/42*, pp. 18–21, Jewish Museum Vienna, inv. no. 4465/3.
80 Walter Lindenbaum, in Herbert Exenberger and Eckart Früh (eds), *Von Sehnsucht wird man hier nicht fett. Texte aus einem jüdischen Leben* (Vienna, 1998), pp. 19–23. Database query 'Registration by name: Austrian victims of the Holocaust'; DÖW.
81 Communication by researcher Kollmann to Kolisch; YIVO; occ E 6a-10.
82 Löwenherz report, 4 September 1942.
83 Testimony of Wilhelm Bienenfeld, criminal proceedings against Wilhelm Reisz before the Provincial Criminal Court of Vienna as People's Court, Provincial Court Archive; Vg 1b Vr 2911/45. Prochnik (see ch. 4, n. 39), p. 59. Statement by Robert Prochnik, 24 June 1954; criminal proceedings against Robert Prochnik before the Provincial Criminal Court of Vienna as People's Court, Provincial Court Archive; Vg 8c Vr 3532/48, continuation: Vg 8c Vr 41/542; 63f. Questioning of Oskar Münzer, 3 November 1945; criminal proceedings against Oskar Münzer before the Provincial Criminal Court of Vienna as People's Court, Provincial Court Archive; Vg 4 Vr 2916/45.
84 Transcript of statement by Wilhelm Reisz, 1 September 1945, criminal proceedings against Wilhelm Reisz before the Provincial Court of Vienna as People's Court, Provincial Court Archive; Vg 1b Vr 2911/45; 6.
85 Joe Singer, *Erlebnisse in Wien und Theresienstadt* (London, 1955); Wiener Library 02/1025; 6.

86 Testimony of Wilhelm Reisz, criminal proceedings against Wilhelm Reisz before the Provincial Criminal Court of Vienna as People's Court, Provincial Court Archive; Vg 1b Vr 2911/45; 131.

87 Lindenbaum was a Gruppenführer. Contrary to Reisz, survivors said nothing negative about him and he was remembered as a writer and friendly person.

88 Transcript of statement by Wilhelm Reisz, 1 September 1945, criminal proceedings against Wilhelm Reisz before the Provincial Criminal Court of Vienna as People's Court, Provincial Court Archive; Vg 1b Vr 2911/45; 142.

89 Singer, *Erlebnisse* (see n. 85 above), p. 3. Herbert Rosenkranz: memo of testimony of Rudolf Hönigsfeld, 29 July 1975; YvS-03/3908; 4.

90 Testimony of Bruno Feyer, 20 November, criminal proceedings against Oskar Münzer before the Provincial Criminal Court of Vienna as People's Court, Provincial Court Archive; Vg 4 Vr 2916/45; 86.

91 Benjamin Murmelstein to Herbert Rosenkranz, Rome, 27 April 1980; I am grateful to Herbert Rosenkranz for providing me with a copy of the letter.

92 Rosenkranz, *Verfolgung* (see ch. 1, n. 43), p. 305. Documentation Archive of Austrian Resistance (ed.), *Jüdische Schicksale*, p. 634. Testimony of Johann Rixinger, 6 October 1945, criminal proceedings against Johann Rixinger before the Provincial Criminal Court of Vienna as People's Court, Provincial Court Archive; Vg 11g Vr 4866/46/HV 1319/47. Testimony of Anton Brunner, criminal proceedings against Anton Brunner before the Provincial Criminal Court of Vienna as People's Court, Provincial Court Archive; Vg 2d VR 4574/45; 80.

93 Singer, *Erlebnisse* (see n. 85 above), 3.

94 DÖW (ed.), *Jüdische Schicksale*, p. 503.

95 Benjamin Murmelstein to the hospital management, 3 September 1942; A/W 2752.

96 Benjamin Murmelstein to the management of the children's hospital, 4 September 1942; A/W 2752. Database query, 'Registration by name: Austrian victims of the Holocaust'; DÖW.

97 DÖW (ed.), *Jüdische Schicksale*, p. 508.

98 Testimony of Anton Brunner, criminal proceedings against Anton Brunner before the Provincial Criminal Court of Vienna as People's Court, Provincial Court Archive; Vg 2d VR 4574/45;

16. See Bestand zur Verpflegung der Sammellager; DÖW E 21677.

99 Franzi Löw, interview, in DÖW (ed.), *Jüdische Schicksale*, p. 193.

100 Löwenherz report, 13 November 1941.

101 Otto Kalwo, *Evakuiert* (Deggendorf, 23 August 1945); YvS-033 E/1408. Testimony of Ernst Weiss, 13 August 1945, criminal proceedings against Anton Brunner before the Provincial Criminal Court of Vienna as People's Court, Provincial Court Archive; Vg 2d VR 4574/45; 9.

102 Testimony of Wilhelm Bienenfeld, criminal proceedings against Johann Rixinger before the Provincial Criminal Court of Vienna as People's Court, Provincial Court Archive, Vg 11g Vr 4866/46 / HV 1319/47; 47.

103 Testimony of Anton Brunner, criminal proceedings against Anton Brunner before the Provincial Criminal Court of Vienna as People's Court, Provincial Court Archive; Vg 2d VR 4574/45; 17

104 Testimony of Ernst Weiss, 13 August 1945, criminal proceedings against Anton Brunner before the Provincial Criminal Court of Vienna as People's Court, Provincial Court Archive; Vg 2d VR 4574/45; 9. Testimony of Walter Lackenbacher, 14 August 1945, criminal proceedings against Anton Brunner before the Provincial Criminal Court of Vienna as People's Court, Provincial Court Archive; Vg 2d VR 4574/45; 10.

105 Memo by Josef Löwenherz, 21 December 1941; YvS-Tr-1152; see also Hilberg, *Destruction of the European Jews* (see Ch. 1, n. 30), vol. 2, p. 459.

106 Singer, *Erlebnisse* (see n. 85 above), p. 5. Kalwo, *Evakuiert* (see n. 101 above), p. 1f. Franzi Löw, interview (see n. 99 above), p. 193.

107 Testimony of Ernst Weiss, 13 August 1945, criminal proceedings against Anton Brunner before the Provincial Criminal Court of Vienna as People's Court, Provincial Court Archive; Vg 2d VR 4574/45; 9.

108 Interrogation of Anton Brunner, 12 October 1945; criminal proceedings against Anton Brunner before the Provincial Criminal Court of Vienna as People's Court, Provincial Court Archive; Vg 2d VR 4574/45; 83.

109 IKG: Instructions for organization of evacuation transports; A/W 2750.

110 IKG: Leaflet on forthcoming transports to Poland; YvS-030/4.

111 IKG, activity report, 1 January–30 June 1941; A/W 115.

112 Prochnik (see ch. 4, n. 39), pp. 53–7.
113 Löwenherz report, 27 October 1941.
114 Ibid., 10 November 1941.
115 Ibid., January 1942.
116 Mizzi Felber to IKG Vienna, Lodz, 17 May 1944. IKG to Mizzi Felber; A/W 2099.
117 Franzi Löw, interview (see n. 99 above), p. 192.
118 See A/W 2098, A/W 2100 and A/W 2102.
119 See also Chaim Rumkowski, Jewish Elder in Lodz ghetto to Kultusgemeinde Vienna, 10 December1941; A/W 2099.
120 Löwenherz report, January 1942.
121 See: A/W 2101.
122 Franzi Löw, interview (see n. 99 above), p. 188.
123 Ibid., pp. 188–90.
124 Ibid., p. 191.
125 Ibid., pp. 192–4 and 196.
126 Arnold Raschke to management board, 26 December 1941; A/W 1884. See also List of patients; A/W 1884. List of out-patients with address and diagnosis; A/W 424.
127 Emil Tuchmann, Annual report for 1941, 31 December 1941; A/W 1827.
128 Löwenherz report, 6–24 August, 4 September 1942.
129 Ilse Mezei, diary 19 April–October 1941. Jewish Museum Vienna, inv. no. 4465.
130 Report on the activity of the IKG Vienna and the Council of Elders of the Jews in Vienna in 1942; A/W 116; 20.
131 Gestapo to Josef Löwenherz, 1 January 1943; YvS-030/4. Database query, 'Registration by name: Austrian victims of the Holocaust'; DÖW.
132 Report (see n. 130), pp. 20–4.
133 Ibid., p. 27. Council of Elders of the Jews in Vienna (ed.), Report of activities in 1943; A/W 117; 20 and 31. See also tables at the end of the report.
134 Rosenkranz, *Verfolgung* (see ch. 1, n. 43), p. 308f.
135 Franzi Löw interview (see n. 99 above), p. 195.
136 Ibid., p. 196.

CHAPTER 11   THE KULTUSGEMEINDE – AUTHORITIES WITHOUT POWER

1 Theodor W. Adorno, *Negative Dialectics* (New York, 1973), pp. 362 and 371.

2 Michaela Ronzoni, 'Lebensverhältnisse der jüdischen Bevölkerung in Österreich zwischen Herbst 1938 und Frühling 1939. Unbearbeitete Gesuche von jüdischen Österreichern', dissertation (Vienna, 1985).

3 Moser, 'Die Katastrophe der Juden in Österreich – ihre Voraussetzungen und ihre Überwindung', in *Der gelbe Stern in Österreich* (Eisenstadt, 1977), p. 202.

4 Leo Goldhammer, *Die Juden Wiens. Eine statistische Studie* (Vienna, 1927), p. 15f.

5 Claudia Koonz, 'Courage and Choice among German-Jewish Women and Men', in Arnold Paucker (ed.), *Die Juden im nationalsozialistischen Deutschland 1933–1943* (Tübingen, 1986), pp. 283–93.

6 Rosenkranz, *Verfolgung* (see ch. 1, n. 43), p. 103.

7 Konrad Kwiet and Helmut Eschwege, *Selbstbehauptung und Widerstand. Deutsche Juden im Kampf um Existenz und Menschenwürde 1933–1945* (Hamburg, 1984), pp. 141–50.

8 Dokumentationsarchiv des österreichischen Widerstandes (ed.), *Widerstand und Verfolgung in Wien 1934–1945*, (Vienna, 1974), vol. 3, pp. 314–25. Erich Stern, *Die letzten zwölf Jahre Rothschild-Spital Wien: 1931–1943* (Vienna, 1974), p. 14.

9 Brigitte Ungar-Klein 'Bei Freunden untergetaucht. U-Boote in Wien', in Kurt Schmid and Wolfgang Streibel (eds), *Der Pogrom 1938. Judenverfolgung in Österreich und Deutschland* (Vienna, 1990).

10 Rosenkranz, *Verfolgung* (see ch. 1, n. 43), p. 43.

11 DÖW (ed.), *Widerstand*, vol. 3 (see n. 8 above), p. 311.

12 Kwiet and Eschwege, *Selbstbehauptung* (see n. 7 above), p. 113.

13 Ibid., p. 129.

14 DÖW (ed.), *Widerstand*, vol. 3 (see n. 8 above), pp. 349–51.

15 Julius H. Schoeps, *Leiden an Deutschland: Vom antisemitischen Wahn und der Last der Erinnerung* (Munich, 1990), p. 80.

16 Arnold Paucker, 'Jüdischer Widerstand in Deutschland', in Arno Lustiger (ed.), *Zum Kampf auf Leben und Tod! Vom Widerstand der Juden 1933–1945* (Frankfurt am Main, 1997), p. 53.

17 Rosenkranz, *Verfolgung* (see ch. 1, n. 43), p. 40f.

18 Moser, 'Österreichs Juden unter der NS-Herrschaft', in Emmerich Tálos, Ernst Hanisch und Wolfgang Neugebauer (eds), *NS-Herrschaft in Österreich 19381945* (Vienna, 1988), p. 189.

19   G. E. R. Gedye, *Als die Bastionen fielen* (see ch. 3, n. 5), p. 305.
20   Kwiet und Eschwege, *Selbstbehauptung* (see n. 7 above), p. 199.
21   Ibid., p. 214f.
22   Herbert Schrott, interview, 2 September 1998.
23   Primo Levi, *The Drowned and the Saved* (London, 1989), p. 1; Simon Wiesenthal, *The Murderers Among Us* (London, 1967), pp. 292–3.
24   Max Domarus (ed.), *Hitlers Reden und Proklamationen. 1932–1945* (Würzburg, 1963), vol. 2, pp. 1946–73.
25   Rosenkranz, *Verfolgung* (see ch. 1, n. 43), p. 344.
26   Ibid., p. 217f.
27   Wilhelm Bienenfeld, *Bericht über die IKG in der NS-Zeit* (13 November 1939); the report is referred to as the Löwenherz report.
28   Josef Löwenherz, memo of meetings at Gestapo headquarters with Reg. Rat Dr Ebner in the presence of SS-Obersturmführers Brunner on 1 February 1941. YvS-Tr-1147.
29   Quoted in Klamper, *'We'll Meet Again in Palestine'* (see ch. 7, n. 88), p. 43.
30   Martin Vogel, interview, 10 June 1999.
31   IKG legal office to board, 3 September 1941. A/W 173.
32   Josef Löwenherz, memo of a meeting at Gestapo headquarters with SS-Obersturmführer Brunner on 30 September 1941. 2 October 1941. YvS-Tr-1151.
33   Prochnik (see ch. 4, n. 39), p. 59.
34   Jossele to Munisch (Menasche) Mautner in Vienna (Yiddish); Lanczyn, 15 April 1942. In: Munisch Mautner, Report on Vienna 1938, noted in 1956 by Dr Ball-Kaduri. YvS-01/1631.
35   Munisch (Menasche) Mautner, Vienna, to Karl Seidner, Tel Aviv (Yiddish); 19 April 1942. Ibid. YvS-01/1631.
36   Ibid.
37   Martha Weissweiler to Sofie Löwenherz, 14 September 1942. YvS-030/4.
38   Ibid.
39   See letters from F. Ullmann, Geneva, to Dr L. Lauterbach, Jerusalem. CZA; S6-4559.
40   Israel Gutman, Eberhard Jäckel, Peter Longerich and Julius H. Schoeps (eds), *Enzyklopädie des Holocaust. Die Verfolgung und Ermordung der europäischen Juden*, 3 vols (Munich, Zurich, 1998), vol. 2, pp. 1226–8.

41 Explanation by Karl Ebner, 20 September 1961. Quoted in Raul Hilberg, *The Destruction of the European Jews – Student Edition* (see Ch. 1, n. 30), vol. 2, p. 459.

42 Hannah Arendt, 'Was bleibt? Es bleibt die Muttersprache: Ein Gespräch mit Günter Gaus', in A. Reif (ed.), *Gespräche mit Hannah Arendt* (Munich, 1976), p. 24.

43 Richard Breitman, *Staatsgeheimnisse: Die Verbrechen der Nazis – von den Alliierten toleriert* (Munich, 1999).

44 Testimony of Samuel Storfer, criminal proceedings against Johann Rixinger before the Provincial Criminal Court of Vienna as People's Court, Provincial Court Archive; Vg 11g Vr 4866/46/HV 1319/47. Testimony of Samuel Storfer; proceedings against Karl Ebner before the Provincial Criminal Court of Vienna as People's Court, Provincial Court Archive; Vg 2 f 2911/4.5, Vg 12g Vr 1223/4.

45 Vogel (see n. 30 above).

46 Cf. Personalaufstellung; Recherchegruppe bei der Auswanderung; 1940; A/W 586,1. Personalaufstellung; Recherchegruppe; January 1941, A/W 586,2. Personalaufstellung; Recherchegruppe; end of 1941, A/W 586,4.

47 Josef Löwenherz to all Kultusgemeinde employees, undated, A/W 134,8.

48 Josef Löwenherz to all departments, sections and employees regarding resettlement transports, undated; A/W 134,8. Board to all departments, sections and institutions, undated; A/W 134,8.

49 Administrative director, order, 20 May 1941; A/W 271.

50 Josef Löwenherz to all departments and sections of the IKG Vienna, 15 December 1941; A/W 134,4.

51 Ibid.

52 Cf. Edith Neumann to Josef Löwenherz, 28 September 1941; A/W 180,2.

53 Josef Löwenherz to Vienna Employment Office, Jewish section, 27 July 1942; A/W 274.

54 Josef Löwenherz to the Gestapo and the Central Office. List of employees, 17 January 1943; A/W 571.

55 Josef Löwenherz, 5 September 1944; A/W 134,7.

56 Josef Löwenherz: Merkblatt. Zweite Anordnung des Generalbevollmächtigten für den Arbeitseinsatz zur Sicherung der Ordnung in den Betrieben, 23 September 1944. Extract; A/W 134,7.

57 Transcript of testimony of Siegfried Kolisch, 30 August 1945, criminal proceedings against Dr Emil Tuchmann before the

Provincial Criminal Court of Vienna as People's Court, Provincial Court Archive; Vg 3c 1955/45; 24.

58 Josef Löwenherz, Alois Rothenberg and Emil Engel to Gestapo headquarters Vienna, 4 January 1939; A/W 165,1.

59 Josef Löwenherz to foreign exchange office Vienna, 17 March 1939; YvS-030/4.

60 Quoted in Gideon Hausner, *Die Vernichtung der Juden. Das größte Verbrechen der Geschichte* (Munich, 1979), p. 48.

61 Cf. Löwenherz report, 27 September 1940.

62 Testimony of Wilhelm Bienenfeld, criminal proceedings against Wilhelm Reisz before the Provincial Criminal Court of Vienna as People's Court, Provincial Court Archive; Vg 1b Vr 2911/45. Prochnik (see ch. 4, n. 39), p. 59. Testimony of Robert Prochnik, 24 June 1954; proceedings against Robert Prochnik before the Provincial Criminal Court of Vienna as People's Court, Provincial Court Archive; Vg 8c Vr 3532/48, continuation Vg 8c Vr 41/542; 63f. Interrogation of Oskar Münzer, 3 November 1945; proceedings against Oskar Münzer, Provincial Court Archive; Vg 4 Vr 2916/45.

63 Charles J. Kapralik, 'Erinnerungen eines Beamten der Wiener Israelitischen Kultusgemeinde 1938–39', in *Bulletin des Leo Baeck Institutes* 58 (1981): 77.

64 Hannah Arendt, *Eichmann in Jerusalem* (see ch. 1, n. 40).

65 Dan Michman (see ch. 5, n. 2), p. 194f.

66 E. Gibb, 'Leadership', in G. Lindezey und E. Aronson (eds), *The Handbook of Social Psychology*, vol. 4 (New York, 1985). Quoted in Michman (see ch. 5, n. 2), p. 195.

67 Adler, *Theresienstadt* (see ch. 7, n. 51), p. 242f.

68 Arieh Menczer and Mordechai Menczer, interview recorded by Herbert Rosenkranz, Haifa, 6 June 1976; YvS-03/3913; 2.

69 Angelika (Shoshanna) Jensen, *Sei stark und mutig! Chasak we'emaz! 40 Jahre jüdische Jugend in Österreich am Beispiel der Bewegung "Haschomer Hazair" 1903 bis 1943* (Vienna, 1995); Klamper, Menczer, Israelitische Kultusgemeinde Wien (ed.), *Trotz allem... Aron Menczer 1917–1943* (Vienna, Cologne, Weimar, 1993).

70 Ibid., p. 36.

71 Ibid., p. 41.

72 Ibid., p. 45.

73 Aron Menczer to Josef Löwenstein, Doppl, 23 July 1941; A/W 180,1.

74 Vogel (see n. 30 above).

75 Aron Menczer to Josef Löwenstein (see n. 73 above).

76 Josef Löwenherz, memo of a meeting with SS-Obersturmführer Brunner on 30 September 1941; YvS-Tr-1151.

77 Martin Vogel, Report on the moatzah on 19 and 20 September 1942 during the liquidation of the Youth Aliyah, Histadruth noar, Vienna, Vienna, 28 November 1942; YvS-030/9.6.

78 Ibid.

79 Ibid.

80 Heinz Berger, *Dem Gedenken an Aron Menczer* (15 April 1949); YvS-4203; 3.

81 Klamper, Menczer (see n. 69 above), p. 48.

82 Arieh Menczer and Mordechai Menczer (see n. 68 above).

83 A sister-in-law of Aron Menczer, the wife of Arieh Menczer, who had studied with Murmelstein, recalled in 1976 that she had told Murmelstein in 1939 that she and her husband would be emigrating to Palestine. He is said to have asked her if it was so bad in Vienna and whether she was going to break stones in Zion. Cf. Arieh Menczer and Mordechai Menczer (see n. 69 above). In a letter to the historian Herbert Rosenkranz in 1980, Murmelstein claimed that he had been quoted out of context. The sentence referred to the fact that in January 1939 he had addressed the British chief rabbi Dr Joseph Herman Hertz in an attempt to get permits for IKG functionaries 'although the natural emigration destination for a practising Jew is Palestine, but what were they to do there? Break stones?' Murmelstein claimed that as Arieh Menzcer spoke modern Hebrew, the comment was not directed at him and he did not in any way want to prevent Menczer from emigrating. Cf. Benjamin Murmelstein to Herbert Rosenkranz, Rome, 27 April 1980. I am grateful to Herbert Rosenkranz for providing me with a copy of this letter.

84 Transcript of testimony of Leo Balaban, criminal proceedings against Dr Emil Tuchmann before the Provincial Criminal Court of Vienna as People's Court, Provincial Court Archive, Vg 3c 1955/45. Willy Stern, interview, 2 May 1991.

85 Rosenkranz, *Verfolgung* (see ch. 1, n. 43), p. 285.

86 Jonny Moser, *Dr Benjamin Murmelstein, ein ewig Beschuldigter? Theresienstadt in der Geschichte der nazistischen 'Endlösung der Judenfrage'*, typescript; DÖW 24931.

87 Munisch Mautner (see n. 34 above).

88 Margarethe Mezei, communicated orally to Pierre Genée, 1987. Quoted in Gabi Anderl und Pierre Genée, 'Wer war Dr

Benjamin Murmelstein. Biographische Streiflichter', in *David. Jüdische Kulturzeitschrift* 10 (1998): 19.

89 Benjamin Murmelstein, several interviews recorded by Leonhard Ehrlich, Rome, 1977. I am grateful to Professor Leonhard Ehrlich for providing me with copies of these interviews and to Dr Pierre Genée, who transmitted them to me.

90 Adler, *Theresienstadt* (see ch. 7, n. 51), p. 117.

91 Zdenek Lederer, *Ghetto Theresienstadt* (London, 1953), p. 166f.

92 Genée (see ch. 5, n. 20).

93 Anderl and Genée (see n. 88 above), 16; *Enzyklopädie des Holocaust*, vol. 3, p. 1406.

94 Benjamin Murmelstein, 'Das Ende von Theresienstadt. Die Stellungnahme eines Beteiligten', *Neue Zürcher Zeitung*, (17 December 1963), 3.

95 Prochnik (see n. 62 above); Vg 8c Vr 3532/48, continuation Vg 8c Vr 41/542.

96 Murmelstein (see n. 94 above).

97 Ibid.

98 Adler, *Theresienstadt* (see ch. 7, n. 51), p. 195.

99 Ibid. p. 203. Murmelstein (see n. 94 above).

100 Murmelstein (see n. 94 above).

101 Anderl und Genée (see n. 88 above), p. 17.

102 Genée (see ch. 5, n. 20).

103 Benjamin Murmelstein, memo of a meeting with SS-Obersturmführer Rahm on 5 May 1945; YvS-064/107.

104 Benjamin Murmelstein to Josef Löwenherz, Theresienstadt, 27 May 1945; YvS-030/4; 21.

105 Ibid.

106 Murmelstein (see n. 94 above).

107 Murmelstein (see n. 94 above). Anderl and Genée (see n. 88 above), p. 17f.

108 Murmelstein *Terezin* (see ch. 8, n. 19), pp. 233–324.

109 Philip Friedman, 'Aspects of the Jewish Communal Crisis in the Period of the Nazi Regime in Germany, Austria and Czechoslovakia', in Joseph Blau, Arthur Herzberg, Philip Friedman und Isaac Mendelsohn (eds), *Essays on Jewish Life and Thought* (New York, 1959), p. 230.

110 Genée (see ch. 5, n. 20).

111 Benjamin Murmelstein, several interviews recorded by Leonhard Ehrlich, Rome, 1977.

112 Murmelstein, *Terezin* (see ch. 8, n. 19).

113 Murmelstein (see n. 94 above).

114 *Enzyklopädie des Holocaust*, vol. 3, p. 1406.
115 Anderl and Genée (see n. 88 above), p. 18.
116 Wolf Murmelstein to Herbert Rosenkranz in Jerusalem, Rome, 9 December 1990. I am grateful to Herbert Rosenkranz for providing me with copies of this correspondence.
117 Herbert Rosenkranz to Consulata Rabbinica, 27 December 1990.
118 Wolf Murmelstein to Herbert Rosenkranz. Enclosure: Ruling by the Rabbinical Council concerning the appeal on behalf of Dr Wolf Murmelstein, 16 May 1991.
119 Murmelstein (see n. 94 above).
120 Criminal proceedings against Dr Benjamin Murmelstein before the Provincial Criminal Court of Vienna as People's Court, Provincial Court Archive; Vg 7a Vr 895/49; continuation Vg 8e Vr 698/55. Gauakte Murmelstein; Archiv der Republik; Zl.26 271-2/56.
121 Memo, police department, Vienna, 5 November 1946, criminal proceedings against Robert Prochnik, Provincial Court Archive; Vg 8c Vr 3532/48, continuation: Vg 8c Vr 41/542.
122 Council of the Jewish communities in Bohemia and Moravia to the Jüdische Historische Dokumentation in Linz (at the time Simon Wiesenthal's office), Prague, 28 April 1948; Dokumentationszentrum des Bundes jüdischer Verfolger des Naziregimes; 1301 M9/110.
123 Prochnik (see n. 62 above).
124 Ibid.
125 Ibid. and testimony of Georg Nushbaum, 4 November 1954, criminal proceedings against Robert Prochnik; Vg 8c Vr 3532/48, continuation Vg 8c Vr 41/542.
126 Leo Baeck to Robert Prochnik, 3 May 1945; Robert Prochnik to Georg Vogel, 12 May 1945; Georg Vogel to Robert Prochnik, 28 May 1945; annexes to Prochnik (see n. 62 above); Robert Prochnik to Josef Löwenherz, Theresienstadt, 27 May 1945; YvS-030/4.
127 Prochnik (see n. 62 above).
128 Leo Baeck, Heinrich Klang et al., testimony 12 June 1945; Georg Vogel: confirmation, 26 July 1945; annexes to Prochnik (see n. 62 above).
129 Police department Vienna, section 1 to public prosecutor's office Vienna, 29 April 1948, criminal proceedings against Robert Prochnik; Provincial Court Archive; Vg 8c Vr 3532/48, continuation Vg 8c Vr 41/542.

130 Ibid.; Mares Prochnik, interview, 3 September 1998.
131 Ibid.
132 Mares Prochnik (see n. 130 above).
133 Criminal proceedings against Emil Tuchmann, Provincial Court Archive; Vg 3c 1955/45; Walter Brumlik-Fantl, interview, 2 September 1998; Herbert Schrott, interview, 2 September 1998.
134 Police department to Provincial Court, 13 September 1945; criminal proceedings against Emil Tuchmann, Provincial Court Archive; Vg 3c 1955/45.
135 Ibid.
136 Provincial Court of Appeal to Provincial Court, 19 April 1946, criminal proceedings against Emil Tuchmann; Provincial Court Archive; Vg 3c 1955/45.
137 Bestand Gauakten: Tuchmann; Archiv der Republik; 04/Inneres 26013-2A/61.
138 Testimony of Martin Schaier, 7 August 1948, criminal proceedings against Karl Ebner, Provincial Court Archive; Vg 4c Vr 1223/47.
139 Thomas Mang (1998) Retter, um sich selbst zu retten. Die Strategie der Rückversicherung. Dr Karl Ebner. Leiter-Stellvertreter der Staatspolizeistelle Wien 1942–1945. Dissertation, Vienna, p. 95.
140 *Der neue Weg. Jüdisches Organ mit amtlichen Mitteilungen der Israelitischen Kultusgemeinde Wien*, no. 19, October 1947, p. 1f.
141 Ibid., p. 2.
142 Transcript of testimony of Leo Balaban, criminal proceedings against Leopold Balaban; Provincial Court Archive; Vg 2 f Vr 2943/45.
143 Prison II to Provincial Court, Vienna, 11 July 1946, criminal proceedings against Wilhelm Reisz ; Provincial Court Archive; Vg 1b Vr 2911/45.
144 File on Franziska Löw, Provincial Court Archive; Vg 5c Vr 6078/47, 2/1.
145 Franzi Löw-Danneberg, interview, 19 June 1991; Franzi Löw, interview. In Dokumentationsarchiv des österreichischen Widerstands (ed.), *Jüdische Schicksale. Berichte von Verfolgten* (Vienna, 1992), p. 187.
146 Aron Moses Ehrlich, Nachtrag zu meinem offenen Briefe, June 1947; file on Franziska Löw (see n. 144 above).

147 Charge against Aron Moses Ehrlich, 9 September 1947; file on Franziska Löw (see n. 144 above).
148 Memo by Paul Steiner, 28 June 1947; file on Franziska Löw (see n. 144 above).
149 Employee list, 1940; A/W 165,6; Database query, 'Registration by name: Austrian victims of the Holocaust'; DÖW.
150 *Die Stimme* 45 (1951): 1.
151 Simon Wiesenthal to Nahum Goldmann, 28 June 1966, CZA; Z6/1175.
152 Martin von Ameringen, *Kreisky und seine unbewältigte Vergangenheit* (Graz, 1977).
153 *Heruth* (March 1989): 4.
154 See Paul Klaar to IKG board, 4 September 1942; IKG board to hospital, 4 September 1942; Robert Prochnik to investigation group, 19 September 1942; A/W 2752.
155 George Clare, *Last Waltz in Vienna. The Destruction of a Family 1842–1942* (London, 1982), p. 222.
156 Ibid., p. 276.
157 See Arieh Menczer and Mordechai Menczer, interview recorded by Herbert Rosenkranz, Haifa, 6 June 1976; YvS-03/3913.
158 Jochen von Lang (ed.), *Eichmann Interrogated: Transcripts from the Archives of the Israeli Police* (New York, 1983), p. 50.
159 Kapralik, 'Erinnerungen' (see n. 63 above), p. 77.
160 Willy Stern, interview, 2 May 1991.
161 Josef Löwenherz to Arthur Albers, 19 June 1941; A/W 180,1.
162 Jedioth Achronoth, *Olei Germania we-Olei Ostria*. 4 July 1941, p. 2. I am grateful to Evelyn Adunka for providing me with a copy of this document.
163 Testimony of Wilhelm Bienenfeld, 5 April 1946, criminal proceedings against Karl Ebner, Provincial Court Archive; Vg 2 f 2911/45; Vg 12g Vr 1223/47.
164 Wilhelm Bienenfeld to Josef Löwenherz, 11 September 1945; YvS-030/4.
165 *Aufbau*, 10 August 1945; transcript of article in: YvS-030/4.
166 Eugene Hevesi, The American Jewish Committee, to Dr Slawson, 8 August 1945; YvS-030/4.
167 Arno Erteschik to Josef Löwenherz, 26 October 1945; YvS-030/4.
168 *Zeitspiegel*, 13 April 1946. I am grateful to Evelyn Adunka for providing me with a copy of this document.

169 *Zeitspiegel*, 20 April 1946.
170 Jewish Telegraphic Agency, 15 April 1946; YIVO; DP Camps in Austria, reel 1; 0283. I am grateful to Evelyn Adunka for providing me with a copy of this document.
171 George E. Berkley, *Vienna and its Jews. The Tragedy of Success* (Cambridge, 1988), p. 343.
172 Gideon Hausner, *Die Vernichtung der Juden. Das größte Verbrechen der Geschichte* (Munich, 1979), p. 38f.

CHAPTER 12   DISCUSSION OF THE JEWISH COUNCILS AND
THE SITUATION IN VIENNA

1 Arendt, *Eichmann in Jerusalem* (see ch. 1, n. 40), p. 125.
2 See F. A. Krummacher (ed.), *Die Kontroverse Hannah Arendt, Eichmann und die Juden* (Munich, 1964); here also the essay by Norman Podhoretz, and Jacob Robinson *And The Crooked Shall Be Made Straight. The Eichmann Trial, the Jewish Catastrophe and Hannah Arendt's Narrative* (Philadelphia, 1965).
3 Raul Hilberg, *The Destruction of the European Jews* (see ch. 11, n. 41), p. 300.
4 See Israel Gutman, 'Jüdischer Widerstand. Eine historische Bewertung', in Arno Lustiger (ed.), *Zum Kampf auf Leben und Tod! Vom Widerstand der Juden in Europa 1933–1945* (Ergstadt, 2004).
5 Arendt, *Eichmann in Jerusalem* (see ch. 1, n. 40), pp. 158–60.
6 See Isaiah Trunk, *Judenrat. The Jewish Councils in Eastern Europe under Nazi Occupation* (New York, 1972); Leonard Tushnet, *The Pavement of Hell [Three Leaders of the 'Judenrat']* (New York, 1972); Aharon Weiß, 'The Relations between the Judenrat and the Jewish Police' in *Patterns of Jewish Leadership in Nazi Europe 1933–1945* (Jerusalem, 1977), pp. 201–17.
7 Quoted in Dan Diner, *Beyond the Conceivable: Studies on Germany, Nazism, and the Holocaust* (Berkeley, Los Angeles, London, 2000), p. 122.
8 Dan Michman, 'Understanding the Jewish Dimension of the Holocaust', in Jonathan Frankel (ed.), *The Fate of the European Jews 1939–1945. Continuity or Contingency?* (New York, Oxford, 1997), pp. 225–49.
9 Diner, *Beyond the Conceivable* (see n. 7 above), pp. 122–3.

10 Quoted in Ran Leyzer (ed.), *Jerusalem of Lithuania* (New York, 1974), vol. 2, p. 439.

11 Hannah Arendt, *Elemente und Ursprünge totaler Herrschaft* (Frankfurt am Main, 1955), pp. 713 and 738.

12 Dan Diner, 'Die Perspektive des "Judenrats". Zur universellen Bedeutung einer partikularen Erfahrung', in '*Wer zum Leben, wer zum Tod. . . .*' *Strategien jüdischen Überlebens im Ghetto*, p. 25.

13 Hannah Arendt, 'Was bleibt? Es bleibt die Muttersprache. Ein Gespräch mit Günter Gaus', in A. Reif (ed.), *Gespräche mit Hannah Arendt* (Munich, 1976), p. 24.

14 Arendt, *Eichmann in Jerusalem* (see ch. 1, n. 40), p. 287.

15 Diner, 'Perspektive des "Judenrats"', p. 27f.

GLOSSARY

Altreich	Territories that were part of Nazi Germany before 1938 (excluding Austria, the Sudetenland and other territories annexed after 1937)
Anschluss	Occupation and annexation of Austria by Nazi Germany in 1938
Aryanization	Forced transfer of Jewish businesses to German 'Aryan' ownership
Ausheber	Literally 'lifter out', Jews used by the Nazis to help with the removal of Jews from their apartments
Aushebung	'Lifting out' (see *Ausheber*)
Einsatzgruppe	Mobile killing unit in the occupied territories of eastern Europe
Gauleiter	Nazi party official, head of a 'Gau' or region
Generalgouvernement	Occupied Polish territories
German army ranks and British army equivalents	Oberst: Colonel Rittmeister: Captain Hauptmann: Captain
Gestapo	Nazi secret police
Gruppenführer	Here: Jew subordinate to an SS member and head of a team of *Ausheber* (not to be confused with SS-Gruppenführer!)

IKG	Israelitische Kultusgemeinde ('Israelite Religious Community'), Viennese Jewish community authorities
Kapo	Privileged inmate of a concentration camp acting as a supervisor
Kultusgemeinde	See 'IKG' above
Mischling	Under the Nuremberg Race Laws, a person with one ('second degree') or two ('first degree') Jewish grandparents who did not belong to the Jewish religion or was married to a Jew
Obersekretär	Senior secretary
Ordner	Jewish marshal, *Ausheber*
Ostjuden	Jews from eastern Europe
Ostmark	Austria's name as part of Nazi Germany
Protectorate	Protectorate of Bohemia and Moravia, German-occupied ethnic Czech regions of Czechoslovakia
Regierungsrat	Administrative official
Reichskommissariat Ostland	Civilian regime of the Ostland, German-occupied territories including the Baltic states, Belarus and parts of eastern Poland
Reichsstatthalter	Head of a region, state official representing the central government (often but not always also Gauleiter)
SA	Storm troopers ('brown shirts'), paramilitary organization of the Nazi Party, effectively superseded by the SS in 1934
SD	Nazi intelligence and security service, branch of the SS
SS	Elite Nazi force with fighting units (Waffen-SS) and other branches that provided concentration camp guards and was mainly responsible for implementing the anti-Jewish policy and extermination of the Jews and other groups

SS ranks and British
army equivalents

SS-Gruppenführer: Major-General
SS-Standartenführer: Colonel
SS-Obersturmführer: Lieutenant-Colonel
SS-Sturmbannführer: Major
SS-Hauptsturmführer: Captain
SS-Obersturmführer: Lieutenant
SS-Untersturmführer: Second Lieutenant
SS-Scharführer: Sergeant
SS-Unterscharführer: Corporal
SS-Rottenführer: Lance Corporal

INDEX